The Couch Potato's Guide to Growing Green

Cultivating Wealth Without Breaking a Sweat

Volodymyr Rybaiev

TABLE OF CONTENTS

Introduction: From Spuds to Studs - Your Financial Glow-Up Begins Here 2

Chapter 1: Couch Change - Finding Money in Your Cushions (and Other Surprising Places) 4

Chapter 2: Netflix and Bill - Streaming Your Way to Savings 15

Chapter 3: Lazy Budgeting - Because Math is Hard, But Being Broke is Harder 36

Chapter 4: Couch Investing - Making Money While Horizontal 73

Chapter 6: Credit Score Hacking: Boost Your Numbers Without Lifting a Finger 129

Chapter 7: Taxes for Dummies (and Proud of It) 159

Chapter 8: Retirement Planning for Those Who'd Rather Not Think About It 192

Chapter 9: Homeownership: The Ultimate Adulting Move (With Minimal Effort) 218

Chapter 10: Travel on a Shoestring (While Wearing Slippers) 246

Conclusion: From Couch Potato to Financial Hot Potato - Your Lazy Success Story 283

Bonus Chapter: The Emergency Fund - Because Life Happens, Even to Lazy People 294

Appendix A: Glossary of Financial Terms for the Perpetually Confused 332

Appendix B: Resources for the Marginally Motivated 338

Appendix C: Worksheets (That You'll Probably Never Fill Out, But Hey, They're Here) 345

INTRODUCTION: FROM SPUDS TO STUDS - YOUR FINANCIAL GLOW-UP BEGINS HERE

Welcome, fellow couch potatoes! If you've picked up this book, you're probably wondering how you can turn your financial situation from "mashed" to "loaded" without actually having to, you know, do stuff. Well, my horizontally-inclined friend, you've come to the right place. This is "The Couch Potato's Guide to Growing Green: Cultivating Wealth Without Breaking a Sweat," where we'll explore the art of making money while maintaining your commitment to minimal movement.

Now, I know what you're thinking: "But I can barely motivate myself to change the TV channel, let alone change my financial future!" Fear not, for this book is designed with your dedication to inertia in mind. We're going to take you on a journey from financial spud to financial stud, and the best part? You won't even have to leave your sacred sofa.

In the pages that follow, we'll uncover the secrets of lazy wealth-building, from finding money in your couch cushions (literally and figuratively) to investing in your sleep. We'll explore the wonders of automation, the magic of apps that do the work for you, and the surprisingly lucrative world of opinion-sharing (turns out, your thoughts on that new Netflix series could be worth cold, hard cash).

But before we dive in, let's address the elephant in the room – or should I say, the potato on the couch. Yes, managing your money does require some effort. But here's the thing: a little bit of strategic laziness now can lead to a whole lot of relaxation later. Imagine a future where you can binge-watch to your heart's content without worrying about your bank balance. That's the dream we're chasing here, folks.

Throughout this book, we'll be operating on a few key principles:

Introduction: From Spuds to Studs - Your Financial Glow-Up Begins Here

1. If there's an app for it, use it.
2. Automation is your new best friend.
3. Small, consistent efforts beat grand, exhausting gestures.
4. Your time is valuable (especially your nap time).
5. Money should work harder than you do.

So, prop up those feet, grab your favorite snack, and get ready for a financial makeover that won't require you to break a sweat or, heaven forbid, put on real pants. We're about to embark on a journey that will transform you from a couch potato into a money magnet – all while maintaining your commitment to comfort.

Remember, in the world of lazy finance, slow and steady wins the race. And by "slow and steady," we mean "mostly stationary with occasional bursts of minimal effort." Ready to get started? Great! Now, reach for that remote and... oh wait, wrong kind of guide. Let's turn the page instead and begin your journey to effortless wealth. Your future self (still on the couch, but with a much fatter wallet) will thank you.

CHAPTER 1: COUCH CHANGE - FINDING MONEY IN YOUR CUSHIONS (AND OTHER SURPRISING PLACES)

Welcome to the first chapter of your journey from financial flab to fiscal fab, all without leaving the comfort of your beloved couch. In this chapter, we're going to explore the hidden treasures lurking in your everyday life – yes, including those mysterious depths between your couch cushions. So, get ready to embark on a treasure hunt that doesn't require a map, a shovel, or even standing up.

1. The Loose Change Challenge: Turn Those Pennies into Dollars

Let's start with the most literal interpretation of finding money in your cushions. It's time for the Loose Change Challenge!

Step 1: The Great Couch Excavation

- Arm yourself with a flashlight (or your phone's flashlight app – we're not monsters expecting you to get up).
- Reach into the crevices of your couch. Don't be afraid to go deep – that's where the real treasure lies.
- Collect all the coins you find. Yes, even the pennies. Every cent counts in this lazy person's financial revolution.

Step 2: Expand Your Search

- Once you've conquered the couch, expand your territory (but not too much – we don't want to overexert ourselves).
- Check under cushions in other chairs.
- Look in coat pockets, especially those winter coats you haven't worn since last year.

Chapter 1: Couch Change - Finding Money in Your Cushions (and Other Surprising Places)

- Scour the bottom of your gym bag (assuming you have one and it's within arm's reach).
- Don't forget the car! The area between the seats is a goldmine.

Step 3: Count Your Loot

- Gather all your found treasure in one place.
- Sort the coins by denomination (if you're feeling extra motivated).
- Count it up and prepare to be amazed (or at least mildly surprised) by how much you've accumulated.

Step 4: The Bank Heist (Kind of)

- Now comes the tricky part – you might actually have to leave the house for this one. But fear not, it's for a good cause!
- Take your coin collection to your local bank or a coin-counting machine.
- Pro tip: Many banks offer free coin counting for account holders. If yours doesn't, consider switching to one that does. It's all about maximizing laziness, after all.

Step 5: Celebrate Your Windfall

- Marvel at the amount of money you've found just by reaching between cushions.
- Resist the urge to immediately spend it on pizza delivery (we'll talk about smart spending later).

The Power of Pocket Change

Chapter 1: Couch Change - Finding Money in Your Cushions (and Other Surprising Places)

Now, you might be thinking, "Great, I found $7.53. How is this going to change my financial life?" Well, my couch-bound comrade, let's do some lazy math:

- Let's say you do this challenge once a month and find an average of $5 each time.
- That's $60 a year – enough for a nice dinner out or a couple of months of your favorite streaming service.
- But wait, there's more! If you invest that $60 each year (we'll get to painless investing later), over 10 years at a modest 7% return, you'd have about $835.
- Over 20 years? You're looking at nearly $2,500.

All from coins you found while barely moving. Not too shabby for a couch potato, eh?

2. Subscription Detox: Canceling Services You Forgot You Had

Now that we've tackled the physical realm of hidden money, let's dive into the digital world. It's time for a subscription detox!

The Subscription Creep

In today's world of convenient digital services, it's incredibly easy to sign up for subscriptions. A streaming service here, a meal kit delivery there, a meditation app to help you relax (because managing all these subscriptions is stressful). Before you know it, you're hemorrhaging money on services you barely use or completely forgot about.

Let's put an end to this subscription creep with some lazy-friendly steps:

Step 1: The Great Subscription Audit

Chapter 1: Couch Change - Finding Money in Your Cushions (and Other Surprising Places)

- Grab your laptop or phone (they're probably within reach anyway).
- Log into your bank account and credit card portals.
- Look at your last three months of statements.
- Make a list of all recurring charges. Yes, ALL of them.

Step 2: The Brutal Truth Session For each subscription, ask yourself these questions:

- Do I actually use this service?
- If yes, how often?
- Does the value I get justify the cost?
- Is there a free alternative that's just as good?
- Did I even know I was still subscribed to this?

Be honest with yourself. Remember, we're not here to judge your past subscription choices. We're here to free up some cash for future lazy endeavors.

Step 3: The Great Purge

- For any subscription that didn't pass the brutal truth test, it's time to say goodbye.
- Most services make it surprisingly easy to cancel online. No phone calls required – perfect for us couch potatoes.
- If you do need to call, steel yourself for the retention specialist who will try to keep you subscribed. Stay strong! Your laziness is more powerful than their sales pitch.

Step 4: Reap the Rewards

Chapter 1: Couch Change - Finding Money in Your Cushions (and Other Surprising Places)

- Add up how much you'll be saving each month from canceling these subscriptions.
- Give yourself a pat on the back (or don't, if that seems like too much effort).
- Consider redirecting some of these savings into your "found money" fund or towards a subscription you actually use and enjoy.

Subscription Optimization Tips

For the subscriptions you decide to keep, let's make sure you're getting the most bang for your buck:

1. *Share the wealth (and the cost):* Many streaming services offer family plans. Team up with friends or family to split the cost.
2. *Annual vs. Monthly:* Some services offer discounts if you pay annually instead of monthly. If you're sure you'll use it for a year, this can lead to significant savings.
3. *Student and senior discounts:* If you qualify, many services offer discounted rates for students and seniors. It never hurts to ask!
4. *Free trials:* Before committing to a new subscription, always check if there's a free trial. Just remember to set a reminder to cancel if you don't want to continue (we'll talk about easy reminder systems later).
5. *Rotate subscriptions:* Do you really need five different streaming services at once? Consider rotating them. Subscribe to one for a month, binge what you want, then switch to another the next month.

The Subscription Detox Challenge

Chapter 1: Couch Change - Finding Money in Your Cushions (and Other Surprising Places)

Here's a challenge for the slightly more ambitious couch potato:

1. Cancel all your subscriptions for one month.
2. Only resubscribe to services you genuinely miss.
3. See how much money you save and how little your life is actually impacted.

You might be surprised at how many subscriptions you can live without. Plus, think of all the new shows you'll have to binge when you resubscribe!

3. The Art of Saying "Nah": Mastering the Polite Decline

Now that we've found some extra cash and cut unnecessary expenses, it's time to tackle one of the biggest threats to your lazy financial goals: the pressure to spend money on things you don't really want or need. Welcome to the fine art of saying "Nah."

Why Saying "Nah" is Important

As couch potatoes, we're naturally inclined to go with the flow. It's easier to say yes than to argue or come up with an excuse. But this passive approach can be disastrous for our wallets. Learning to say "Nah" (politely, of course) is a crucial skill in your lazy money-saving arsenal.

The "Nah" Toolkit

Here are some strategies to help you say "Nah" without burning bridges or exerting too much energy:

1. *The Vague Schedule Conflict*
    - "Ah, I'd love to, but I've got a thing that day."
    - What's the "thing"? A date with your couch and Netflix. But they don't need to know that.

Chapter 1: Couch Change - Finding Money in Your Cushions (and Other Surprising Places)

2. *The Budgeting Boss*
   - "That sounds fun, but it's not in my budget this month."
   - This has the added benefit of making you sound financially responsible.

3. *The Gracious Gratitude*
   - "Thanks so much for thinking of me! I'll have to pass this time."
   - Kill them with kindness, and they might just stop asking.

4. *The Honest Approach*
   - "You know, I'm really trying to save money right now."
   - Sometimes, honesty is the best policy. Plus, it might inspire others to join your thrifty crusade.

5. *The Procrastinator's Dodge*
   - "Let me check my schedule and get back to you."
   - Then conveniently forget to get back to them. (Warning: Use sparingly with close friends and family.)

Common "Nah" Scenarios

Let's practice our "Nah" skills in some real-world situations:

1. *The Group Gift* Scenario: Your coworker is collecting money for a gift for the boss. Response: "I prefer to give personal gifts. But thanks for organizing this!"

2. *The Expensive Night Out* Scenario: Friends invite you to a pricey new restaurant. Response: "That place looks

Chapter 1: Couch Change - Finding Money in Your Cushions (and Other Surprising Places)

amazing, but it's a bit out of my price range. How about we do a potluck at my place instead?"

3. *The Donation Request* Scenario: A friend asks you to sponsor them for a charity run. Response: "Wow, that's a great cause! I can't contribute financially right now, but I'd be happy to share your fundraising page on social media."

4. *The Subscription Pressure* Scenario: A salesperson is pushing you to sign up for a service. Response: "I appreciate the offer, but I'm not interested in adding any new subscriptions right now. I'll keep it in mind for the future, though!"

5. *The Impulse Purchase Temptation* Scenario: You're browsing online and see a "limited time offer" for something you kind of want. Response to yourself: "Nah, if I still want it in a week, I can reconsider."

The Power of the Pause

One of the most effective "Nah" techniques is simply to pause before responding. This works especially well for impulse purchases or spontaneous invitations. Give yourself 24 hours to think about it. Often, the urge to say yes (and spend money) will pass, and you'll find it easier to decline.

Saying "Nah" to Yourself

Sometimes, the hardest person to say "Nah" to is yourself. Here are some strategies:

1. *The 30-Day Rule:* For non-essential purchases, wait 30 days. If you still want it after a month, it might be worth buying.

2. *The "Hours Worked" Calculation:* Before buying something, calculate how many hours you'd have to work to pay for it. Is it worth it?

3. *The One In, One Out Rule:* For every new item you bring into your home, one has to go. This makes you think twice about new purchases.

4. *The "But I'm Lazy" Excuse:* Remember, new purchases often come with maintenance, cleaning, or setup. Is it worth the effort?

The "Nah" Mindset

Saying "Nah" isn't about depriving yourself. It's about being intentional with your time and money. Every "Nah" to an unnecessary expense is a "Yes" to your financial goals and your chosen lifestyle of comfortable leisure.

Putting It All Together: Your Couch Change Action Plan

Congratulations! You've made it through the first chapter of your lazy financial journey. Let's recap what we've learned and set up an action plan that even the most dedicated couch potato can follow:

1. *Loose Change Challenge*
    - Set a reminder on your phone for a monthly couch excavation.
    - Designate a jar or container for your found money.
    - Plan a quarterly trip to the bank to deposit your findings.

2. *Subscription Detox*
    - Schedule a quarterly subscription audit.
    - Set calendar reminders for when free trials end.
    - Keep a running list of subscriptions you've canceled and how much you're saving.

3. Mastering the "Nah"
    - Practice your "Nah" responses in the mirror (or don't, if that seems like too much effort).
    - Set a monthly savings goal from declined invitations or purchases.
    - Reward yourself for successful "Nah" moments (in budget-friendly ways, of course).

The Lazy Money Tracker

To keep yourself motivated (without too much work), create a simple "Lazy Money Tracker." This can be a note on your phone or a sheet of paper stuck to your fridge. Each time you save money through one of these methods, jot it down:

- Found Chango: $XX.XX
- Canceled Subscriptions: $XX.XX/month
- Successful "Nah" Moments: $XX.XX

Watch as these small amounts add up over time. Remember, every dollar saved is a dollar you don't have to earn – which means more time for your couch-based activities.

Final Thoughts

As we wrap up this chapter, remember that the journey to financial freedom doesn't have to be a grueling uphill battle. Sometimes, the laziest path can lead to the greatest rewards. By making these small, low-effort changes, you're setting yourself up for a future where your money works hard so you don't have to.

In the next chapter, we'll explore how to turn your love for binge-watching into a money-saving superpower. Get ready to Netflix and bill your way to savings!

Chapter 1: Couch Change - Finding Money in Your Cushions (and Other Surprising Places)

Until then, keep calm and couch on. Your financial future is looking brighter already, and you barely had to lift a finger.

CHAPTER 2: NETFLIX AND BILL - STREAMING YOUR WAY TO SAVINGS

Welcome back, savvy couch potatoes! In our last chapter, we unearthed hidden treasure from your couch cushions and mastered the art of saying "nah" to unnecessary expenses. Now, it's time to tackle one of the most beloved pastimes of the modern lazy person: streaming. That's right, we're about to turn your binge-watching habit into a money-saving superpower. Grab your remote, settle into your favorite spot, and let's dive into the world of "Netflix and Bill."

1. Cutting the Cord Without Cutting the Fun

Remember the days when cable TV was the only option for vegging out in front of the screen? Those days are long gone, my friend. Welcome to the era of cord-cutting, where you can watch what you want, when you want, and often for a fraction of the cost of traditional cable.

The Great Cable Escape

If you haven't already cut the cord, here's why you should consider it:

- *Cost Savings:* The average cable bill in the U.S. is over $100 per month. Most streaming services are a fraction of that cost.
- *Flexibility:* Watch on your schedule, not the network's.
- *No Contracts:* Most streaming services are month-to-month, so you can cancel anytime.
- *Targeted Content:* Choose services that align with your interests, rather than paying for 200 channels you never watch.

Steps to Cutting the Cord

1. *Assess Your Viewing Habits:*

Chapter 2: Netflix and Bill - Streaming Your Way to Savings

- What shows do you actually watch?
- Are they available on streaming platforms?
- Do you need live TV (for sports or news)?

2. *Check Your Internet:*
   - Streaming requires a decent internet connection.
   - Aim for at least 25 Mbps for HD streaming, more if multiple people will be streaming at once.

3. *Choose Your Streaming Services:*
   - Start with 1-2 services that cover most of your favorite shows.
   - Remember, you can always add or switch later.

4. *Consider a Streaming Device:*
   - Smart TVs often have built-in streaming apps.
   - If not, devices like Roku, Amazon Fire Stick, or Chromecast are affordable options.

5. *Cut the Cord:*
   - Call your cable company and cancel.
   - Be prepared for their retention offers – stay strong!

6. *Enjoy Your Savings:*
   - Calculate how much you're saving each month.
   - Consider putting some of those savings towards your financial goals (or maybe a comfier couch).

Chapter 2: Netflix and Bill - Streaming Your Way to Savings

The Lazy Person's Guide to Live TV

But wait, you say. What about live TV? Fear not, fellow couch dweller. There are options for those who still want their live sports or breaking news:

- *Antenna:* For local channels, a good old-fashioned antenna can work wonders. And they're much sleeker now than the rabbit ears of yore.
- *Live TV Streaming Services:* Options like YouTube TV, Hulu + Live TV, or Sling offer live channels without the cable commitment.
- *Sports-Specific Services:* Many leagues offer their own streaming services for die-hard fans.

Remember, the key to lazy finances is to pay only for what you'll actually use. If you find yourself never watching live TV, don't pay for it!

2. Sharing is Caring (and Saving): Maximizing Family Plans

Now that you've cut the cord, let's talk about how to squeeze every penny out of your streaming subscriptions. Enter the world of family plans and account sharing.

The Family Plan Advantage

Many streaming services offer family plans that allow multiple users to share one account. Here's why they're great:

- *Cost Savings:* Often cheaper than individual accounts.
- *Separate Profiles:* Keep your viewing history and recommendations separate.
- *Multiple Streams:* Watch different shows simultaneously.

Popular Family Plan Options

Let's break down some popular services and their family offerings:

1. *Netflix:*
    - Standard Plan (2 screens): $15.49/month
    - Premium Plan (4 screens): $19.99/month
    - Potential Savings: Up to 50% per person on a maxed-out Premium plan

2. *Spotify:*
    - Individual Plan: $9.99/month
    - Family Plan (up to 6 accounts): $15.99/month
    - Potential Savings: Up to 73% per person

3. *Disney+:*
    - Individual Plan: $7.99/month
    - Bundle with Hulu and ESPN+ (6 profiles): $13.99/month
    - Potential Savings: Varies, but significant if you use all three services

4. *Apple One:*
    - Individual Plan: $16.95/month
    - Family Plan (up to 5 people): $22.95/month
    - Potential Savings: Up to 73% per person

The Art of Account Sharing

Now, let's address the elephant in the room: sharing accounts with friends or extended family. While terms of service vary, many services turn a blind eye to password sharing. Here's how to do it responsibly:

1. *Choose Your Sharing Circle Wisely:*
   - Stick with people you trust.
   - Ensure everyone understands the sharing arrangement.
2. *Set Clear Guidelines:*
   - Decide who pays for what.
   - Agree on how to handle changes (like if someone wants to leave the sharing group).
3. *Use Separate Profiles:*
   - Keep your recommendations pure and your viewing history private.
4. *Be Mindful of Simultaneous Streaming Limits:*
   - Know how many screens your plan allows.
   - Consider upgrading if you're constantly bumping into limits.
5. *Stay Informed About Policy Changes:*
   - Some services are cracking down on password sharing.
   - Be prepared to adjust your strategy if needed.

The Ethical Consideration

While account sharing can save money, it's important to consider the ethical implications. If you love a service and use it frequently, supporting it financially ensures it can continue producing content you enjoy. Balance your frugality with supporting the services you value.

3. Free Trial Surfing: Ride the Wave of Entertainment Deals

Chapter 2: Netflix and Bill - Streaming Your Way to Savings

Ah, the free trial. It's like a all-you-can-watch buffet with no upfront cost. For the savvy couch potato, free trials can be a goldmine of entertainment. But beware – they can also be a trap for the unwary. Let's learn how to ride the wave of free trials without wiping out your wallet.

The Free Trial Strategy

1. *Keep a Calendar:*
    - Note when each free trial starts and ends.
    - Set reminders a few days before the trial ends.
2. *Use Different Email Addresses:*
    - Some services allow multiple free trials if you use different emails.
    - Consider setting up a dedicated "free trial" email account.
3. *Capitalize on Special Offers:*
    - Many services offer extended free trials during holidays or special events.
    - Keep an eye out for these promotions.
4. *Binge Strategically:*
    - Plan what you want to watch before starting the trial.
    - Maximize your viewing during the free period.
5. *Cancel Immediately:*
    - After signing up, immediately schedule the cancellation.
    - Most services will still let you use the full trial period.

Chapter 2: Netflix and Bill - Streaming Your Way to Savings

6. *Use Virtual Credit Cards:*
    - Some banks offer virtual credit card numbers for online use.
    - These can be cancelled easily, preventing unexpected charges.

Popular Free Trial Options

Let's look at some services with generous free trials:

1. *Amazon Prime Video:* 30-day free trial
2. *HBO Max:* 7-day free trial
3. *YouTube TV:* 14-day free trial
4. *Hulu:* 30-day free trial
5. *Apple TV+:* 7-day free trial (or 3 months free with new Apple device purchase)

The Free Trial Rotation Strategy

For the truly dedicated free trial surfer, consider the rotation strategy:

1. Start with Service A's free trial.
2. Binge watch your chosen content.
3. Cancel before the trial ends.
4. Move to Service B's free trial.
5. Repeat with Services C, D, E, etc.
6. By the time you've gone through all services, new content might be available on Service A, allowing you to start the cycle again.

Caution: The Free Trial Trap

While free trials can be great, they're designed to convert you into a paying customer. Here are some pitfalls to avoid:

1. *Forgetting to Cancel:* This is how they get you. Always set reminders.
2. *Getting Hooked:* Be prepared to walk away, even from a show you're enjoying.
3. *Overcommitting:* Don't sign up for more trials than you can manage.
4. *Impulse Subscribing:* Stick to your plan, don't let FOMO drive your decisions.

The Freebie Frontier: No-Cost Streaming Options

For the ultimate penny-pinching couch potato, there are completely free streaming options available. While they often come with ads, the price is right. Some options include:

1. *Pluto TV:* Live TV and on-demand content, all for free.
2. *Tubi:* A large library of movies and TV shows.
3. *Crackle:* Sony's free streaming service with a rotating selection of content.
4. *Peacock (Free Tier):* NBC's streaming service offers a free tier with limited content.
5. *Kanopy:* Free streaming through many public libraries and universities.

Remember, these free services often have older or less popular content, but for the discerning (and thrifty) viewer, there are often hidden gems to be found.

4. The Streaming Budget: Balancing Entertainment and Economy

Now that we've explored the various ways to save on streaming, it's time to create a streaming budget that balances your entertainment needs with your financial goals. Because even couch potatoes need to keep an eye on their spending!

Assessing Your Streaming Needs

Before we dive into numbers, let's consider what you really need from your streaming services:

1. *Content Preferences:*
    - What genres do you watch most?
    - Are there specific shows or franchises you can't live without?
2. *Viewing Habits:*
    - How many hours per week do you typically stream?
    - Do you binge-watch series or prefer to watch movies?
3. *Live TV Requirements:*
    - Do you need access to live sports or news?
    - How important are local channels to you?
4. *Family Considerations:*
    - Are there children in the household with specific viewing needs?
    - Do different family members have vastly different tastes?

Creating Your Streaming Budget

Now, let's put some numbers to these needs:

1. *Set a Monthly Limit:*

Chapter 2: Netflix and Bill - Streaming Your Way to Savings

- Decide how much you're willing to spend on streaming each month.
- A good rule of thumb: Aim for less than half of what you were paying for cable.

2. *Prioritize Services:*
   - List out all the services you're interested in.
   - Rank them based on how well they meet your needs.

3. *Mix and Match:*
   - Start with your top-ranked service.
   - See how many services you can add before hitting your monthly limit.

4. *Consider Rotating Services:*
   - Instead of subscribing to everything at once, rotate services monthly.
   - This allows you to access more content while staying within budget.

Sample Streaming Budget

Let's create a sample budget for our fictional couch potato, Lazy Larry:

Lazy Larry's Monthly Streaming Budget: $50

1. Netflix Standard: $15.49
2. Hulu (ad-supported): $7.99
3. Disney+ (annual plan, averaged monthly): $6.99
4. HBO Max (50% split with a friend): $7.50

Total: $37.97

Chapter 2: Netflix and Bill - Streaming Your Way to Savings

Remaining Budget: $12.03 (saved for occasional rentals or rotating in other services)

Optimizing Your Streaming Spend

Here are some additional tips to get the most bang for your streaming buck:

1. *Annual Plans:* Many services offer discounts for paying annually. If you're sure you'll use a service all year, this can lead to significant savings.
2. *Bundle Deals:* Look for bundles like the Disney+/Hulu/ESPN+ package or deals through your cell phone provider.
3. *Student and Senior Discounts:* If you qualify, many services offer reduced rates for students and seniors.
4. *Ad-Supported Tiers:* If you don't mind commercials, choosing ad-supported plans can significantly reduce costs.
5. *Use Reward Points:* Some credit cards allow you to use reward points to pay for streaming services.
6. *Periodically Reassess:* Every few months, review your subscriptions. Are you using them all? Could you downgrade any plans?

The "One In, One Out" Rule

To keep your streaming budget in check, consider implementing the "One In, One Out" rule:

- If you want to add a new streaming service, you must cancel an existing one.
- This keeps your number of subscriptions (and total cost) constant.
- It also encourages you to regularly evaluate which services you're actually using.

Chapter 2: Netflix and Bill - Streaming Your Way to Savings

Tracking Your Streaming ROI

For the data-loving couch potato, consider tracking your "Streaming Return on Investment" (ROI):

1. Keep a log of what you watch each month.
2. At the end of the month, count how many hours of content you watched on each service.
3. Divide the cost of each service by the hours watched.
4. This gives you a "cost per hour" for each service.

For example:

- If you pay $15.49 for Netflix and watch 20 hours in a month, your cost per hour is $0.77.
- If you pay $7.99 for Hulu and only watch 2 hours, your cost per hour is $3.99.

This can help you identify which services are giving you the most value for your money.

5. Maximizing Your Streaming Experience

Now that we've optimized our streaming budget, let's look at ways to enhance your viewing experience without spending extra cash. After all, a true couch potato deserves the best!

Optimize Your Streaming Setup

1. *Internet Speed:*
    - Run a speed test to ensure you're getting what you're paying for.
    - If speeds are consistently low, contact your provider or consider switching.
2. *Wi-Fi Optimization:*
    - Place your router in a central location.

- Consider a Wi-Fi extender for large homes.
- Use the 5GHz band for faster speeds if your router supports it.

3. *Device Selection:*
   - Choose the right streaming device for your needs (Roku, Fire Stick, Apple TV, etc.).
   - Consider factors like 4K support, voice control, and app availability.

4. *TV Settings:*
   - Calibrate your TV for optimal picture quality.
   - Many streaming services offer test patterns to help with this.

Maximize Content Discovery

1. *Use Multiple Profiles:*
   - Create separate profiles for different moods or genres.
   - This keeps your recommendations more accurate.

2. *Explore Categories:*
   - Many services have hidden categories accessible through special codes.
   - For Netflix, for example, you can access these by adding a code to the URL.

3. *Use Third-Party Sites:*
   - Websites like JustWatch or Reelgood can help you find where a specific show or movie is streaming.

4. *Rate What You Watch:*
    - o Take the time to rate shows and movies.
    - o This improves the accuracy of recommendations.

Streaming Hacks for the Savvy Couch Potato

1. *Keyboard Shortcuts:*
    - o Learn keyboard shortcuts for your favorite services.
    - o For example, on Netflix:
        - F for full screen
        - M for mute
        - Spacebar for play/pause
2. *Download for Offline Viewing:*
    - o Many services allow you to download content for offline viewing.
    - o Great for travel or areas with spotty internet.
3. *Use Extensions:*
    - o Browser extensions like Netflix Party allow you to watch with friends remotely.
    - o Language learning extensions can display subtitles in two languages simultaneously.
4. *Clear Your Viewing History:*
    - o If you share an account and want to hide your guilty pleasure binge-watching, learn how to clear your viewing history.
5. *Customize Subtitles:*

- Most services allow you to customize the appearance of subtitles.
- Adjust size, color, and background for optimal readability.

The Art of the Binge

For those marathon viewing sessions, here are some tips to enhance your binge-watching experience:

1. *Prepare Your Space:*
   - Gather snacks, drinks, and blankets before you start.
   - Ensure your viewing area is comfortable for long periods.
2. *Use "Continue Watching" Features:*
- Most services keep track of where you left off.
- Use this to easily pick up where you stopped, even across devices.
3. *Avoid Spoilers:*
   - Consider browser extensions that block spoilers on social media.
   - Be cautious when reading episode descriptions.
4. *Take Breaks:*
   - Use natural break points in the show to stretch or rest your eyes.
   - Some services have built-in "are you still watching?" prompts – use these as reminders to move around.
5. *Engage with the Community:*

- Join online discussions about your favorite shows.
- This can enhance your viewing experience without costing a dime.

6. Cutting Costs Without Cutting Content

While we've covered many ways to save on streaming, let's dive deeper into some advanced techniques for the truly frugal couch potato.

The Art of Account Hopping

Some services offer promotions for new subscribers. Here's how to take advantage:

1. *Create a new email address:* Use this for your new account.
2. *Use a different payment method:* If possible, use a different credit card or payment option.
3. *Clear cookies and use a VPN:* This can help you appear as a new user.
4. *Take advantage of the new subscriber offer:* Sign up and enjoy the discounted rate.
5. *Set a reminder:* When the promotional period ends, cancel and repeat the process.

Note: Always check the terms of service. Some companies are cracking down on this practice.

Seasonal Subscriptions

Not all content is released year-round. Consider subscribing seasonally:

1. *Sports Fans:* Subscribe to sports-specific services only during the season you watch.

2. *Show-Specific:* Subscribe to a service when your favorite show releases a new season, then cancel.

3. *Holiday Content:* Some services have great holiday content. Subscribe in December, then cancel in January.

Credit Card Perks

Some credit cards offer streaming perks:

1. *Cash back:* Some cards offer higher cash back rates for streaming services.

2. *Free subscriptions:* Certain cards come with free subscriptions to services like Disney+ or Netflix.

3. *Statement credits:* Some premium cards offer statement credits for streaming purchases.

Utilize Free Offerings

Many streaming services offer some content for free:

1. *Peacock:* Offers a free tier with limited content.

2. *Pluto TV:* Completely free, ad-supported live TV and on-demand content.

3. *YouTube:* While not a traditional streaming service, it offers a vast amount of free content.

The Library Connection

Don't forget about your local library:

1. *Kanopy and Hoopla:* Many libraries offer free access to these streaming services.

2. *Physical media:* Libraries still loan out DVDs and Blu-rays. Perfect for those hard-to-find titles.

7. The Future of Streaming: Staying Ahead of the Curve

Chapter 2: Netflix and Bill - Streaming Your Way to Savings

As a savvy couch potato, it's important to keep an eye on the horizon. The streaming landscape is constantly evolving, and staying informed can help you make smart decisions about your entertainment budget.

Emerging Trends

1. *Consolidation:* Streaming services are merging and bundling. This could lead to better deals but fewer choices.

2. *Original Content:* Services are investing heavily in original shows and movies. This could make it harder to choose which services to keep.

3. *Interactive Content:* Some platforms are experimenting with choose-your-own-adventure style shows.

4. *Virtual Reality:* VR streaming could become more common, offering immersive experiences.

5. *AI-Driven Recommendations:* Expect more personalized content suggestions as AI improves.

Potential Challenges

1. *Password Sharing Crackdowns:* Some services are implementing stricter policies on account sharing.

2. *Price Increases:* As production costs rise, subscription fees may follow.

3. *Content Fragmentation:* Popular shows may be split across multiple services, potentially increasing costs for viewers.

4. *Advertising:* More services may introduce ad-supported tiers to offset costs.

Staying Ahead

1. *Stay Informed:* Keep up with streaming news to anticipate changes.
2. *Be Flexible:* Be prepared to adjust your streaming strategy as the landscape changes.
3. *Embrace New Technologies:* Early adopters often get the best deals on new services or features.
4. *Voice Your Opinion:* Participate in surveys and feedback sessions. Your input could shape future offerings.

8. The Couch Potato's Guide to Streaming Etiquette

Even as we lounge on our couches, it's important to be good digital citizens. Here's how to stream responsibly:

1. *Respect Content Creators:* While we're all about saving money, remember that your subscriptions support the creation of the content you enjoy.
2. *Be Mindful of Shared Accounts:* If you're sharing an account, be considerate of others' viewing habits and preferences.
3. *Avoid Piracy:* It's tempting, but illegal streaming sites can be risky and don't support content creators.
4. *Manage Your Data:* Be aware of your data usage, especially if you have a limited internet plan.
5. *Practice Good Password Hygiene:* Use strong, unique passwords for each service to protect your accounts.

Conclusion: Your Streaming Strategy Action Plan

Congratulations, couch potato! You've made it through our deep dive into the world of savvy streaming. Let's recap with an action plan to optimize your streaming experience:

1. *Assess Your Current Situation:*

- List all your current subscriptions and their costs.
- Track your viewing habits for a month.

2. *Set Your Streaming Budget:*
    - Decide on a monthly amount you're comfortable spending.
    - Remember, aim for less than half of what you were paying for cable.

3. *Optimize Your Subscriptions:*
    - Cut unnecessary services.
    - Look for bundle deals or annual plans that save money.
    - Consider rotating services monthly.

4. *Maximize Free Trials and Offers:*
    - Create a calendar for free trials.
    - Set reminders to cancel before trials end.

5. *Improve Your Viewing Experience:*
    - Check and optimize your internet speed.
    - Consider upgrading your streaming device if necessary.

6. *Stay Informed:*
    - Keep an eye on streaming news and trends.
    - Be prepared to adjust your strategy as the landscape changes.

7. *Practice Good Streaming Etiquette:*
    - Be a responsible account sharer.

- - Support the content you love (within your budget).

Remember, the goal is to maximize your entertainment while minimizing your costs. With these strategies, you'll be well on your way to becoming a streaming savant, all from the comfort of your beloved couch.

In our next chapter, we'll explore how to turn your everyday laziness into a budgeting superpower. Get ready to learn about "Lazy Budgeting - Because Math is Hard, But Being Broke is Harder." Until then, happy streaming, and may your couch always be comfy and your Wi-Fi always be strong!

CHAPTER 3: LAZY BUDGETING - BECAUSE MATH IS HARD, BUT BEING BROKE IS HARDER

Welcome back, financial fledglings! You've made it to the chapter that might just change your life – or at least your bank account. We're about to dive into the world of lazy budgeting, where we'll turn your natural inclination towards inertia into a superpower for saving. Buckle up (or don't, we know moving is hard) as we explore how to make your money work harder than you do.

1. The 50/30/20 Rule for People Who Can't Count Past 10

Let's start with a budgeting method so simple, you could do it in your sleep (which, let's face it, is when you're most productive anyway).

The Basics of 50/30/20

This rule suggests dividing your after-tax income into three categories:

- 50% for Needs
- 30% for Wants
- 20% for Savings and Debt Repayment

Sounds easy, right? Let's break it down further for the mathematically challenged among us.

Needs (50%) This category includes:

- Rent/Mortgage
- Utilities
- Groceries
- Transportation
- Insurance

Chapter 3: Lazy Budgeting - Because Math is Hard, But Being Broke is Harder

- Minimum debt payments

Wants (30%) Here's where the fun stuff goes:

- Streaming services (you knew we'd mention this)
- Dining out
- Shopping
- Hobbies
- Entertainment

Savings and Debt Repayment (20%) This is for:

- Emergency fund contributions
- Retirement savings
- Extra debt payments

Making It Work for the Lazy

1. *Use Round Numbers:* If math isn't your strong suit, round your income to the nearest hundred or thousand. It's not perfect, but it's better than giving up entirely.

2. *The Envelope System for the Digital Age:* Create separate bank accounts for each category. Have your paycheck automatically divided between them.

3. *The "Close Enough" Approach:* Don't stress if you're not hitting exactly 50/30/20. Aim for "in the ballpark" and adjust as needed.

4. *The Lazy Person's 50/30/20:* If three categories seem like too much work, simplify:
   - 80% for Spending (Needs + Wants)
   - 20% for Saving

Chapter 3: Lazy Budgeting - Because Math is Hard, But Being Broke is Harder

Remember, any budgeting is better than no budgeting!

2. Apps That Do the Work While You Nap

In this digital age, there's an app for everything – including managing your money while you catch some Z's. Let's explore some of the best budgeting apps for the productivity-challenged.

1. Mint

- *Why It's Great for Lazy Budgeters:* It automatically categorizes your spending.
- *Key Features:*
    - Links to all your financial accounts
    - Creates budgets based on your spending habits
    - Sends alerts when you're approaching budget limits
- *Laziness Level:* High. It does most of the work for you.

2. YNAB (You Need A Budget)

- *Why It's Great for Lazy Budgeters:* It enforces the "give every dollar a job" principle, making you think less about day-to-day spending.
- *Key Features:*
    - Encourages you to budget for future months
    - Provides real-time updates on your budget status
    - Offers educational resources to improve your financial habits

Chapter 3: Lazy Budgeting - Because Math is Hard, But Being Broke is Harder

- *Laziness Level:* Medium. It requires some initial setup, but then it's smooth sailing.

3. PocketGuard

- *Why It's Great for Lazy Budgeters:* It tells you how much you have left to spend after accounting for bills and savings goals.
- *Key Features:*
    - Identifies bills you're overpaying for
    - Shows a simple "In My Pocket" amount for guilt-free spending
    - Tracks recurring subscriptions
- *Laziness Level:* High. It simplifies your finances to one number.

4. Goodbudget

- *Why It's Great for Lazy Budgeters:* It's based on the envelope system, but digital.
- *Key Features:*
    - Syncs across devices for shared budgeting
    - Allows you to plan for big, irregular expenses
    - Provides spending reports
- *Laziness Level:* Medium. You need to fill your envelopes, but then it's easy to stick to.

5. Personal Capital

- *Why It's Great for Lazy Budgeters:* It focuses on investment tracking and retirement planning alongside basic budgeting.
- *Key Features:*

Chapter 3: Lazy Budgeting - Because Math is Hard, But Being Broke is Harder

- o Provides a holistic view of your finances
- o Offers investment checkup tools
- o Tracks your net worth
- *Laziness Level:* High for budgeting, Medium for investing.

Choosing the Right App for Your Level of Laziness

Consider these factors:

1. *Automation:* How much does the app do for you?
2. *User Interface:* Is it easy to understand at a glance?
3. *Customization:* Can you adjust it to your specific brand of laziness?
4. *Cost:* Some apps are free, others have subscription fees. Weigh the cost against the energy you'll save.

Making the Most of Your Chosen App

1. *Set It and Forget It:* Take the time to set up your app properly, then let it do its thing.
2. *Enable Notifications:* Let the app tell you when you need to pay attention.
3. *Regular Check-Ins:* Schedule a monthly "money date" with your app to review your progress.
4. *Use the Insights:* Many apps offer tips based on your spending habits. It's like having a financial advisor who doesn't judge your latte habit.

Remember, the best budgeting app is the one you'll actually use. Don't be afraid to try a few before settling on your perfect lazy budgeting companion.

3. Automation Nation: Set It and Forget It Finances

Chapter 3: Lazy Budgeting - Because Math is Hard, But Being Broke is Harder

Welcome to the pinnacle of lazy money management: automation. This is where we set up our finances to run themselves, leaving us free to focus on important things like perfecting our couch groove.

The Beauty of Automation

Automation is the lazy person's best friend when it comes to finances. Here's why:

- It removes the need for willpower
- It ensures bills are paid on time
- It makes saving effortless
- It reduces decision fatigue

Let's dive into how to automate every aspect of your financial life.

1. Automate Your Income

- *Direct Deposit:* If you haven't already, set up direct deposit for your paychecks.
- *Split Your Deposit:* Many employers allow you to split your direct deposit between accounts. Use this to automatically divvy up your money as soon as it comes in.

2. Automate Your Bills

- *Set Up Auto-Pay:* For all fixed bills (rent, utilities, subscriptions), set up automatic payments.
- *Choose the Right Date:* Schedule these payments for shortly after your payday to ensure funds are available.
- *Use Credit Cards:* For variable bills, consider putting them on a credit card with auto-pay. This consolidates

multiple payments into one and can earn you rewards.

3. *Automate Your Savings*

- *Emergency Fund:* Set up an automatic transfer to your emergency fund each payday.
- *Retirement Savings:* Contribute to your 401(k) through payroll deductions.
- *Other Savings Goals:* Create separate savings accounts for different goals (vacation, new gadget, etc.) and set up automatic transfers.

4. *Automate Your Investments*

- *Regular Investments:* Set up automatic investments into your brokerage account.
- *Robo-Advisors:* Consider using a robo-advisor for hands-off investing.
- *Dividend Reinvestment:* Enable automatic dividend reinvestment in your investment accounts.

5. *Automate Your Debt Repayment*

- *Minimum Payments:* Set up auto-pay for at least the minimum on all debts.
- *Extra Payments:* If you're targeting a specific debt, set up an additional automatic payment.

6. *Automate Your Financial Maintenance*

- *Credit Score Monitoring:* Sign up for a free credit monitoring service.
- *Account Alerts:* Set up notifications for large transactions, low balances, or unusual activity.

Chapter 3: Lazy Budgeting - Because Math is Hard, But Being Broke is Harder

- *Annual Financial Review:* Set a yearly calendar reminder to review your overall financial picture.

The Lazy Person's Guide to Setting Up Automation

1. *Gather Your Info:* Collect all your account numbers, websites, and passwords.
2. *Block Out Time:* Set aside a few hours to set everything up at once.
3. *Start with Income:* Begin by automating your paycheck distribution.
4. *Move to Fixed Expenses:* Set up auto-pay for all your regular bills.
5. *Automate Savings:* Set up transfers to your various savings accounts.
6. *Tackle Investments:* Set up automatic investments or contributions.
7. *Don't Forget Debt:* Ensure all debt payments are automated.
8. *Set It and Forget It:* Once everything is set up, sit back and relax!

Potential Pitfalls and How to Avoid Them

1. *Overdraft Risk:* Keep a buffer in your checking account to avoid overdrafts.
2. *Complacency:* While automation is great, don't completely ignore your finances. Do a quick check-in monthly.
3. *Forgotten Subscriptions:* Regularly review your automated payments to catch any subscriptions you no longer use.

Chapter 3: Lazy Budgeting - Because Math is Hard, But Being Broke is Harder

4. *Missed Opportunities:* Revisit your automation setup annually to ensure it still aligns with your goals.

Remember, the goal of automation is to make your financial life easier, not to set it up and never think about money again. A little attention goes a long way in keeping your lazy financial system running smoothly.

4. The Lazy Person's Guide to Cutting Expenses

Now that we've set up our automatic money management system, let's look at ways to trim our expenses without expending too much energy. After all, every dollar saved is a dollar you don't have to earn (and earning money sounds like work).

The Low-Hanging Fruit

Let's start with the easiest cuts:

1. *Subscriptions Audit:*
   - Use a service like Truebill or Trim to identify and cancel unused subscriptions.
   - For subscriptions you want to keep, see if there's a cheaper plan or an annual option that saves money.

2. *Food Waste Reduction:*
   - Plan meals around what's already in your fridge/pantry.
   - Freeze leftovers for lazy day meals.
   - Use apps like Supercook that suggest recipes based on ingredients you already have.

3. *Energy Vampires:*

Chapter 3: Lazy Budgeting - Because Math is Hard, But Being Broke is Harder

- Unplug devices when not in use (or use a smart power strip).
- Switch to LED bulbs (they last longer, so you change them less often).
- Use a programmable thermostat to optimize heating/cooling.

4. *Automate Savings on Purchases:*
    - Use browser extensions like Honey or Capital One Shopping to automatically apply coupons.
    - Set up price drop alerts for items you're planning to buy.

Negotiate Without the Hassle

Negotiating sounds like work, but these methods make it easier:

1. *Bill Negotiation Services:*
    - Services like BillShark or BillCutterz will negotiate your bills for you.
    - They only charge if they save you money.
2. *Annual Call Strategy:*
    - Set a yearly reminder to call your cable, internet, and phone providers.
    - Simply asking, "What's the best deal you can offer me?" can lead to savings.
3. *Insurance Bundling:*
    - Check if bundling your various insurance policies (auto, home, etc.) could save you money.

Chapter 3: Lazy Budgeting - Because Math is Hard, But Being Broke is Harder

4. *Credit Card Interest Rates:*
   - If you carry a balance, a simple call to ask for a lower interest rate can save you significantly.

The "Set It and Forget It" Approach to Saving

1. *Round-Up Apps:*
   - Apps like Acorns or Chime round up your purchases and save the difference.
2. *Cashback Credit Cards:*
   - Choose a card that aligns with your spending habits and set up automatic redemption of rewards.
3. *Bank Account Bonuses:*
   - Many banks offer bonuses for opening new accounts. Set a yearly reminder to check for these offers.
4. *Automatic Rate Shopping:*
   - Services like Gabi automatically shop for better insurance rates for you.

The Lazy Person's Home Economics

1. *Bulk Buying:*
   - For items you use regularly, buying in bulk can save money and reduce shopping trips.
2. *Generic Brands:*
   - Switching to generic for staple items can lead to significant savings over time.
3. *Meal Prepping:*

Chapter 3: Lazy Budgeting - Because Math is Hard, But Being Broke is Harder

- Dedicate one lazy Sunday to meal prep for the week. It saves money and daily decision-making.

4. The "$5 Meal" Challenge:
    - See how many meals you can make for $5 or less. Turn it into a game!

Mindset Shifts for Effortless Saving

1. The 24-Hour Rule:
    - For non-essential purchases, wait 24 hours before buying. Often, the urge will pass.
2. The "Hours of Life" Calculation:
    - Before a purchase, calculate how many hours you'd need to work to pay for it. Is it worth it?
3. The One In, One Out Rule:
    - For every new item you bring into your home, one has to go. It reduces clutter and impulse buys.
4. The "Do I Already Have This?" Check:
    - Before buying something, ask if you already own something that could serve the same purpose.

Remember, the key to lazy expense cutting is to make small, sustainable changes that add up over time. You don't need to become an extreme couponer or start making your own laundry detergent (unless that sounds fun to you). The goal is to find ways to save that align with your lazy lifestyle.

5. Lazy Investing: Making Your Money Work Harder Than You Do

Chapter 3: Lazy Budgeting - Because Math is Hard, But Being Broke is Harder

Investing might sound like it requires effort, but fear not! There are plenty of ways to grow your wealth while maintaining your commitment to minimal exertion. Let's explore how to invest the lazy way.

The Magic of Index Funds

Index funds are the lazy investor's best friend. Here's why:

- They provide broad market exposure
- They have low fees
- They require minimal research or management

How to Get Started with Index Funds:

1. Choose a broad market index fund (like one that tracks the S&P 500)
2. Set up automatic investments
3. Ignore it for the next few decades

It's that simple!

Robo-Advisors: Your AI Investment Buddy

Robo-advisors take the laziness of index fund investing to the next level. They:

- Automatically create a diversified portfolio based on your risk tolerance
- Rebalance your investments for you
- Often offer tax-loss harvesting to optimize your returns

Popular Robo-Advisors:

- Betterment
- Wealthfront
- Vanguard Digital Advisor

Chapter 3: Lazy Budgeting - Because Math is Hard, But Being Broke is Harder

To get started:

1. Choose a robo-advisor
2. Answer some questions about your financial goals and risk tolerance
3. Link your bank account
4. Set up automatic contributions
5. Let the robot do its thing

The Ultimate Lazy Investment: Target Date Funds

If even choosing an index fund sounds like too much work, consider a target date fund. These funds:

- Automatically adjust your asset allocation as you approach retirement
- Provide a diversified portfolio in a single fund
- Require zero maintenance

To use a target date fund:

1. Choose a fund with a date close to when you plan to retire
2. Invest regularly
3. Do absolutely nothing else

Dividend Investing for Passive Income

For those who like the idea of getting paid for doing nothing, dividend investing might be appealing. Here's how to do it the lazy way:

1. Choose a dividend ETF or mutual fund
2. Set up automatic investments and dividend reinvestment

Chapter 3: Lazy Budgeting - Because Math is Hard, But Being Broke is Harder

3. Watch your income stream grow over time

The Lazy Person's Guide to Retirement Accounts

Maximizing your retirement accounts is crucial, but it doesn't have to be complicated:

1. 401(k):
    - Contribute at least enough to get your full employer match
    - Choose a target date fund or a simple mix of index funds
    - Increase your contribution whenever you get a raise
2. IRA:
    - Set up automatic monthly contributions
    - Choose a robo-advisor or a simple index fund strategy
    - Max it out if you can ($6,000 per year, or $7,000 if you're 50 or older)
3. HSA (Health Savings Account):
    - If eligible, max out your HSA
    - Invest the funds in low-cost index funds
    - Don't use it for current medical expenses if you can avoid it (let it grow tax-free)

The Lazy Investor's Checklist

To make sure you're on track without exerting too much effort, go through this checklist once a year:

1. Am I maxing out my tax-advantaged accounts (401(k), IRA, HSA)?

Chapter 3: Lazy Budgeting - Because Math is Hard, But Being Broke is Harder

2. Is my asset allocation still appropriate for my age and risk tolerance?
3. Are my investments still low-cost?
4. Have I rebalanced my portfolio in the last year?
5. Am I reinvesting my dividends?

If you can answer "yes" to most of these, you're doing great! If not, make the necessary adjustments and then get back to your regularly scheduled lounging.

Avoiding Common Lazy Investor Mistakes

Even lazy investors can fall into traps. Here's what to watch out for:

1. *Overcomplicating Things:* Stick to simple, broad-market index funds or target date funds.
2. *Checking Too Often:* Resist the urge to constantly check your investments. Once a year is plenty.
3. *Reacting to Market News:* The lazy investor's mantra: "This too shall pass." Ignore the noise and stick to your plan.
4. *Forgetting to Increase Contributions:* Set a yearly reminder to bump up your investment contributions.
5. *Neglecting Tax Efficiency:* Use tax-advantaged accounts and consider tax-loss harvesting (or let your robo-advisor handle it).

Remember, the beauty of lazy investing is that less is often more. By keeping things simple and automated, you're more likely to stick to your plan and achieve long-term success.

6. The Art of Lazy Side Hustles

Chapter 3: Lazy Budgeting - Because Math is Hard, But Being Broke is Harder

While the idea of a "side hustle" might sound like it involves, well, hustling, there are plenty of ways to earn extra cash with minimal effort. Let's explore some side gigs that won't interrupt your lounging schedule.

1. Rent Out Your Stuff

You've already got stuff, why not make it work for you?

- *Rent out your parking space:* Use apps like JustPark or Neighbor to rent out your driveway or garage.
- *Rent out storage space:* Got an empty closet or attic? Rent it out on Neighbor or StoreAtMyHouse.
- *Rent out your car:* When you're not using it, rent your car on Turo or Getaround.
- *Rent out your gear:* Have camping equipment, camera gear, or tools? Rent them out on Friendwitha or Fat Llama.

2. Passive Income Through Cash Back and Rewards

Earn money on things you're already doing:

- *Cash back credit cards:* Choose a card that aligns with your spending habits and set up automatic redemption.
- *Receipt scanning apps:* Use apps like Ibotta or Fetch Rewards to earn cash back on your purchases.
- *Cashback websites:* Shop through sites like Rakuten or TopCashback to earn cash back on online purchases.
- *Get paid to walk:* Apps like Sweatcoin or Achievement pay you for the steps you're already taking.

3. Low-Effort Online Gigs

Chapter 3: Lazy Budgeting - Because Math is Hard, But Being Broke is Harder

Earn money from your couch:

- *Online surveys:* While not highly lucrative, sites like Survey Junkie or Swagbucks can earn you some pocket money.
- *Microtasks:* Platforms like Amazon Mechanical Turk offer small, quick tasks you can do in your downtime.
- *Transcription:* If you're a fast typist, consider transcription work through sites like Rev or TranscribeMe.
- *Website testing:* Test websites and apps for usability on platforms like UserTesting or TestingTime.

4. Automated Investments

Let your money do the work:

- *Real estate crowdfunding:* Platforms like Fundrise or RealtyMogul let you invest in real estate with as little as $500.
- *Peer-to-peer lending:* Lend money to others and earn interest through platforms like Prosper or LendingClub.
- *Dividend stocks:* Invest in dividend-paying stocks or ETFs for regular passive income.

5. Sell Your Creations (Once)

Create once, sell infinitely:

- *Digital products:* Create and sell digital products like ebooks, templates, or printables on Etsy or your own website.
- *Print-on-demand:* Design t-shirts, mugs, or other items and sell them through sites like Redbubble or Society6.

Chapter 3: Lazy Budgeting - Because Math is Hard, But Being Broke is Harder

- *Stock photography:* Upload your photos to stock photography sites like Shutterstock or iStockphoto.
- *Online courses:* Create a course on a topic you're knowledgeable about and sell it on platforms like Udemy or Teachable.

6. Monetize Your Hobbies

Turn your leisure activities into cash:

- *Gaming:* Stream your gaming sessions on Twitch or create gaming content for YouTube.
- *Writing:* Start a blog and monetize it with ads or affiliate marketing.
- *Pet sitting:* If you love animals, sign up for Rover or Wag to pet sit or dog walk.
- *Crafting:* Sell your handmade items on Etsy or at local craft fairs.

The Lazy Person's Guide to Starting a Side Hustle

1. *Choose wisely:* Pick a side hustle that aligns with your interests and lifestyle.
2. *Start small:* Don't overwhelm yourself. Start with one side hustle and see how it goes.
3. *Automate where possible:* Use tools and apps to streamline your side hustle.
4. *Set realistic expectations:* Remember, the goal is to earn extra money without adding stress.
5. *Know when to quit:* If a side hustle is taking up too much time or energy, it's okay to let it go.

Chapter 3: Lazy Budgeting - Because Math is Hard, But Being Broke is Harder

Remember, the best side hustle is one that you can maintain consistently without disrupting your lazy lifestyle. It's about working smarter, not harder!

7. Emergency Fund: Because Life Happens, Even to Lazy People

Even the most dedicated couch potato can't avoid life's unexpected curveballs. That's where an emergency fund comes in. Let's explore how to build and maintain one with minimal effort.

Why You Need an Emergency Fund

An emergency fund is your financial safety net. It's there to catch you when life throws unexpected expenses your way, like:

- Car repairs
- Medical bills
- Job loss
- Unexpected travel
- Home repairs

Having an emergency fund means you don't have to resort to high-interest credit cards or loans when these situations arise.

How Much Should You Save?

Financial experts typically recommend having 3-6 months of living expenses saved. But for the lazy budgeter, even a small emergency fund is better than none. Here's a lazy person's guide to building an emergency fund:

1. *Start Small:* Aim for $1,000 as your initial goal.

Chapter 3: Lazy Budgeting - Because Math is Hard, But Being Broke is Harder

2. *Build Gradually:* Once you hit $1,000, work towards one month of expenses, then two, and so on.

3. *Adjust Based on Your Situation:* If you have a stable job and low expenses, you might need less. If you're self-employed or have a family to support, you might want more.

The Lazy Way to Build Your Emergency Fund

1. *Automate It:* Set up automatic transfers from your checking to your emergency savings account.

2. *Use Round-Up Apps:* Apps like Acorns or Chime round up your purchases and save the difference.

3. *Save Your Windfalls:* Any unexpected money (tax refunds, work bonuses, birthday cash) goes straight to your emergency fund.

4. *The 52-Week Challenge, Lazy Edition:* Save $1 the first week, $2 the second week, and so on. By the end of the year, you'll have $1,378. Too much math? Just save $26.50 each week for a year.

5. *The "Keep the Change" Method:* Every time you break a bill, put the change in a jar. Once a month, deposit it into your emergency fund.

6. *The "Forget About It" Account:* Open a high-yield savings account at a different bank than your main account. Out of sight, out of mind, but earning interest.

Where to Keep Your Emergency Fund

Your emergency fund should be:

- Easily accessible
- Separate from your regular spending money

- Earning some interest (but that's a bonus, not the main goal)

Good options include:

- High-yield savings accounts
- Money market accounts
- No-penalty CDs

Using Your Emergency Fund

Now that you've built your emergency fund (good job, by the way!), here's how to use it responsibly:

1. *Define "Emergency":* Decide in advance what constitutes an emergency. A sale at your favorite store doesn't count.

2. *The 24-Hour Rule:* Unless it's a true immediate emergency, wait 24 hours before dipping into your fund. This prevents impulse spending.

3. *Replenish It:* If you do use your emergency fund, make a plan to build it back up.

4. *Review Regularly:* As your life circumstances change, your emergency fund needs might change too. Review annually.

The Lazy Person's Emergency Fund Maintenance

Once you've built your emergency fund, maintaining it is pretty hands-off:

1. *Set It and Forget It:* Keep your automatic contributions going.

2. *Annual Check-Up:* Once a year, make sure your fund still covers 3-6 months of expenses.

Chapter 3: Lazy Budgeting - Because Math is Hard, But Being Broke is Harder

3. *Inflation Adjustment:* Every couple of years, bump up your contributions slightly to account for inflation.
4. *Interest Rate Check:* Once a year, make sure your savings account is still offering a competitive rate.

Remember, an emergency fund is like a fire extinguisher: you hope you never need it, but you'll be really glad you have it if you do. Building and maintaining an emergency fund might seem like a lot of work, but it's one of the best ways to protect your lazy lifestyle from financial disruptions.

8. Lazy Credit Management: Boost Your Score While You Snooze

Your credit score can have a big impact on your financial life, affecting everything from loan interest rates to rental applications. But managing your credit doesn't have to be a full-time job. Let's explore how to boost your credit score with minimal effort.

Understanding Your Credit Score

First, let's break down what makes up your credit score:

- Payment History (35%)
- Credit Utilization (30%)
- Length of Credit History (15%)
- Credit Mix (10%)
- New Credit (10%)

The Lazy Person's Guide to Improving Credit

1. *Automate Your Payments:*
   - Set up automatic payments for at least the minimum due on all your credit accounts.

- This ensures you never miss a payment, which is the biggest factor in your credit score.

2. *Use Credit Cards for Fixed Expenses:*
    - Put a few regular bills on your credit card (like your phone bill or streaming services).
    - Set up automatic payments to pay off the full balance each month.
    - This builds a positive payment history without requiring any extra effort.

3. *Set Up Balance Alerts:*
    - Many credit card companies allow you to set up alerts when your balance reaches a certain level.
    - This helps you keep your credit utilization low without having to constantly check your accounts.

4. *Become an Authorized User:*
    - If you have a family member or close friend with excellent credit, ask to be added as an authorized user on their card.
    - Their positive credit history can boost your score, and you don't even have to use the card.

5. *Keep Old Accounts Open:*
    - The length of your credit history matters, so keep old accounts open even if you don't use them often.

Chapter 3: Lazy Budgeting - Because Math is Hard, But Being Broke is Harder

- o To keep them active, set up a small recurring charge (like a streaming service) and automate the payments.

6. *Use a Credit Monitoring Service:*
    - o Sign up for a free credit monitoring service like Credit Karma or Credit Sesame.
    - o They'll alert you to any changes in your credit report, so you don't have to actively check.

7. *Set Calendar Reminders:*
    - o Set an annual reminder to check your full credit report at AnnualCreditReport.com.
    - o This helps you catch any errors or fraudulent activity without having to remember to check regularly.

Lazy Strategies for Specific Credit Situations

If Your Credit Score is Low:

- Consider a secured credit card. Use it for a small, fixed expense and set up automatic payments.
- Look into credit-builder loans, which are designed to help build credit history.

If You Have High Credit Card Balances:

- Set up automatic extra payments, even if it's just $20 a month.
- Consider a balance transfer card with a 0% intro APR to save on interest while you pay down the balance.

If You Don't Have Much Credit History:

- Become an authorized user on someone else's card.

- Look into credit cards designed for students or first-time cardholders.

If You Have Old Negative Items on Your Credit Report:

- Time is your friend here. Many negative items fall off after 7 years.
- Set a reminder to check your credit report after the 7-year mark to ensure these items have been removed.

The "Set It and Forget It" Credit Score Boost Plan

1. Automate all your payments.
2. Set up balance alerts for all your credit cards.
3. Put one fixed expense on each of your credit cards.
4. Sign up for a free credit monitoring service.
5. Set an annual reminder to check your full credit report.
6. If you have extra cash, set up automatic extra payments towards your highest-interest debt.

Once you've done these steps, you can largely forget about actively managing your credit. Your good habits will work in the background to gradually improve your score.

Avoiding Lazy Credit Mistakes

Even when we're trying to be hands-off with our credit, there are a few pitfalls to watch out for:

1. *Ignoring Your Statements:* While automation is great, do a quick scan of your statements each month to catch any fraudulent charges.
2. *Closing Old Accounts:* It might seem tidier to close accounts you're not using, but this can actually hurt your credit score.

3. *Applying for Too Much Credit at Once:* Each application can cause a small, temporary dip in your score. Space out applications if you need new credit.

4. *Cosigning Loans:* This might seem like an easy way to help someone out, but it puts your credit score at risk if they don't pay.

5. *Ignoring Credit Report Errors:* If you spot an error during your annual check, don't be too lazy to dispute it. It could be dragging down your score.

Remember, good credit is like a slow cooker—set it up right, and it'll do most of the work for you while you relax. With these lazy strategies, you can improve your credit score over time without breaking a sweat.

9. Taxes for Dummies (and Proud of It)

Taxes. The mere word can send shivers down the spine of even the most diligent financial planner, let alone us couch potatoes. But fear not! Even filing taxes can be approached with a lazy person's ingenuity. Let's explore how to tackle taxes with minimal effort and maximum returns.

The Lazy Person's Tax Prep

1. *Get Organized (the Easy Way):*
   - Create a "Tax Stuff" folder in your email. Throughout the year, forward any tax-related emails to this folder.
   - For physical documents, designate a single drawer or box as your "Tax Stuff" location.
   - At the end of the year, everything you need will be in one place.

2. *Use Tax Software:*

Chapter 3: Lazy Budgeting - Because Math is Hard, But Being Broke is Harder

- Programs like TurboTax, H&R Block, or TaxAct guide you through the process step-by-step.
- Many offer free versions for simple returns.

3. *Take Advantage of Free File:*
   - If your income is below $72,000, you can use the IRS Free File program to file your federal taxes for free.

4. *Consider Paying for Convenience:*
   - If your taxes are more complicated, it might be worth paying a professional.
   - The time and stress saved could be worth the cost.

Lazy Tax Deductions You Might Be Missing

1. *Standard Deduction:* For most people, taking the standard deduction is easier and often more beneficial than itemizing.
2. *Student Loan Interest:* You can deduct up to $2,500 of student loan interest, even if you don't itemize.
3. *Charitable Donations:* For 2021, you can deduct up to $300 in cash donations ($600 for married filing jointly) even if you don't itemize.
4. *Home Office Deduction:* If you're self-employed and work from home, you might be eligible for this deduction.
5. *Educator Expenses:* Teachers can deduct up to $250 for classroom supplies they purchased.
6. *State Sales Tax:* If your state doesn't have income tax, you can deduct state sales tax instead.

Chapter 3: Lazy Budgeting - Because Math is Hard, But Being Broke is Harder

The Procrastinator's Guide to April 15th

Even the best-laid lazy plans sometimes go awry. If you find yourself approaching the tax deadline without having started, here's your emergency game plan:

1. *File for an Extension:*
    - Form 4868 gives you an extra six months to file your return.
    - Remember: This is an extension to file, not to pay. If you owe taxes, you still need to estimate and pay by the original deadline to avoid penalties.

2. *Gather Your Docs:*
    - W-2s from employers
    - 1099s for any freelance work
    - 1098s for mortgage interest
    - Receipts for charitable donations
    - Last year's tax return

3. *Use the IRS Free File Fillable Forms:*
    - If you're comfortable with basic tax concepts, these forms can be a quick way to file.

4. *Consider Tax Prep Services with Late Hours:*
    - Some tax preparation services have extended hours or 24/7 online support as the deadline approaches.

5. *File Electronically:*
    - E-filing is faster and you'll get confirmation that the IRS received your return.

Chapter 3: Lazy Budgeting - Because Math is Hard, But Being Broke is Harder

Year-Round Lazy Tax Strategies

1. *Adjust Your Withholding:*
   - Use the IRS Withholding Calculator to make sure you're not having too much or too little withheld from your paycheck.
   - Aim for a small refund or a small amount owed to minimize your "interest-free loan" to the government.

2. *Automate Your Retirement Savings:*
   - Contributions to traditional 401(k)s and IRAs can reduce your taxable income.
   - Set up automatic contributions and forget about them until tax time.

3. *Use a Health Savings Account (HSA):*
   - If you have a high-deductible health plan, contribute to an HSA for triple tax benefits.

4. *Set Up a System for Business Expenses:*
   - If you're self-employed, use an app like Expensify or Receipts by Wave to automatically track and categorize expenses throughout the year.

5. *Charitable Giving:*
   - Consider setting up recurring donations to your favorite charities.
   - This spreads out your giving throughout the year and provides an easy record for tax time.

The Lazy Person's Guide to Tax Planning

1. *Automate Your Investments:*

- Set up automatic investments in tax-advantaged accounts like IRAs and 401(k)s.

2. *Use Tax-Efficient Funds:*
    - For taxable accounts, consider index funds or ETFs, which tend to be more tax-efficient than actively managed funds.

3. *Harvest Tax Losses:*
    - If you have investments that have decreased in value, consider selling them to offset capital gains.
    - Many robo-advisors offer automatic tax-loss harvesting.

4. *Bundle Deductions:*
    - If you're close to itemizing, consider bundling two years of charitable contributions into one year.

5. *Set Calendar Reminders:*
    - Set reminders for key tax dates, like estimated tax payments if you're self-employed.

When to Call in the Pros

Sometimes, even the laziest among us need to admit when a task is beyond our capabilities. Consider hiring a tax professional if:

- You've had a major life change (marriage, divorce, baby, new home)
- You've started a business
- You've inherited money or property
- You have rental property

Chapter 3: Lazy Budgeting - Because Math is Hard, But Being Broke is Harder

- You have foreign investments

Remember, the cost of a tax professional can often be offset by the deductions and credits they can find that you might have missed.

The Lazy Taxpayer's Checklist

To make sure you're on track without exerting too much effort, go through this checklist once a year:

1. Is my withholding correct?
2. Am I maximizing my retirement account contributions?
3. Have I kept good records of charitable donations?
4. Do I need to make any estimated tax payments?
5. Has my tax situation changed significantly since last year?

If you can answer these questions, you're in good shape for tax season!

10. Retirement Planning for Those Who'd Rather Not Think About It

Ah, retirement. That magical time when you can be as lazy as you want without feeling guilty. But here's the catch: to have a comfortable, worry-free retirement, you need to do some planning now. Don't worry, though – we've got some lazy-friendly strategies to help you secure your future couch time.

The Magic of Compound Interest

First, let's talk about why starting early is so important. Compound interest is like a snowball rolling down a hill – the earlier you start, the bigger it gets. Here's a simple example:

Chapter 3: Lazy Budgeting - Because Math is Hard, But Being Broke is Harder

- If you start saving $200 a month at age 25, you could have about $520,000 by age 65 (assuming a 7% annual return).
- If you wait until 35 to start, you'd only have about $245,000.

That's the power of compound interest – and it works even while you sleep!

The Lazy Person's Guide to Retirement Accounts

1. *401(k):*
    - If your employer offers a 401(k), sign up!
    - Contribute at least enough to get the full employer match (it's free money!)
    - Choose a target-date fund for a set-it-and-forget-it approach
2. *IRA (Individual Retirement Account):*
    - Open an IRA if you don't have a 401(k) or want to save more
    - Choose between Traditional (tax-deductible now) or Roth (tax-free in retirement)
    - Set up automatic monthly contributions
3. *SEP IRA or Solo 401(k):*
    - If you're self-employed, these are great options
    - They allow for higher contribution limits than regular IRAs

Lazy Investment Strategies for Retirement

1. *Target-Date Funds:*

Chapter 3: Lazy Budgeting - Because Math is Hard, But Being Broke is Harder

- Choose a fund with a date close to when you plan to retire
- The fund automatically adjusts its asset allocation as you approach retirement

2. *Index Funds:*
   - Low-cost, diversified funds that track a market index
   - Require minimal research or management

3. *Robo-Advisors:*
   - Services like Betterment or Wealthfront create and manage a diversified portfolio for you
   - They handle rebalancing and tax-loss harvesting automatically

The "Set It and Forget It" Retirement Plan

1. Sign up for your employer's 401(k) and contribute enough to get the full match
2. Open an IRA and set up automatic monthly contributions
3. Choose a target-date fund or use a robo-advisor for both accounts
4. Increase your contributions whenever you get a raise
5. Review your accounts once a year to make sure you're on track

That's it! With this plan, you can set up your retirement savings in an afternoon and then largely forget about it (except for that annual check-in).

Lazy Strategies for Catching Up

Chapter 3: Lazy Budgeting - Because Math is Hard, But Being Broke is Harder

If you're starting late, don't panic. Here are some low-effort ways to boost your retirement savings:

1. *Maximize Catch-Up Contributions:*
    - If you're 50 or older, you can contribute extra to your 401(k) and IRA
2. *HSA as a Stealth IRA:*
    - If you have a high-deductible health plan, max out your HSA
    - After age 65, you can use HSA funds for any purpose without penalty
3. *Delay Social Security:*
    - For each year you delay taking Social Security (up to age 70), your benefit increases
4. *Downsize:*
    - Consider moving to a smaller home or less expensive area in retirement
5. *Part-Time Work:*
    - Even a small amount of income in retirement can make a big difference

Common Retirement Planning Mistakes to Avoid

1. *Not Starting Early:* The best time to start was yesterday. The second-best time is now.
2. *Leaving Money on the Table:* Always get your full employer 401(k) match.
3. *Cashing Out When Changing Jobs:* Roll over your 401(k) instead of cashing it out.

Chapter 3: Lazy Budgeting - Because Math is Hard, But Being Broke is Harder

4. *Ignoring Fees:* High fees can significantly reduce your returns over time. Stick to low-cost index funds or ETFs.

5. *Not Adjusting for Inflation:* Remember that $1 million won't buy as much in 30 years as it does today.

The Lazy Retiree's Checklist

As you approach retirement, go through this checklist:

1. Do I know how much I'll need in retirement?
2. Am I on track with my savings?
3. Have I considered healthcare costs?
4. Do I understand my Social Security benefits?
5. Have I thought about where I want to live in retirement?

Remember, a little planning now can lead to a lot of lazy days later. Your future self will thank you for the effort (minimal as it may be) that you put in today.

Conclusion: Your Lazy Financial Future Starts Now

Congratulations, couch potato! You've made it through our crash course in lazy finance. Let's recap the key takeaways:

1. *Automate Everything:* From bill payments to savings, let technology do the heavy lifting.
2. *Keep It Simple:* Whether it's budgeting or investing, simpler is often better (and easier to maintain).
3. *Start Small:* Even small steps, like saving your spare change or cutting one unnecessary expense, can make a big difference over time.
4. *Use Technology:* There are apps and tools for almost every financial task. Use them to your advantage.

5. *Don't Ignore It Completely:* A little attention goes a long way. Set aside one day a year for a financial check-up.

Remember, the goal isn't to become a financial expert or to spend hours managing your money. The goal is to set up systems that work for you, so you can spend more time doing what you love (like perfecting that couch groove).

Your lazy financial journey is just beginning. As you implement these strategies, you'll find that managing your money doesn't have to be a chore. In fact, with the right approach, it can be almost as effortless as binge-watching your favorite show.

So here's to you, savvy couch potato. May your finances be healthy, your stress be low, and your remote control always be within reach. Now, go forth and conquer... or just take a well-deserved nap. You've earned it!

CHAPTER 4: COUCH INVESTING - MAKING MONEY WHILE HORIZONTAL

Welcome back, financial fledglings! You've made it to the chapter that might just change your life – or at least your bank account. We're about to dive into the world of couch investing, where we'll turn your natural inclination towards inertia into a superpower for growing wealth. Buckle up (or don't, we know moving is hard) as we explore how to make your money work harder than you do.

1. Robo-Advisors: Your New BFFs (Best Financial Friends)

Let's start with the ultimate lazy person's investment tool: robo-advisors. These digital platforms use algorithms to create and manage a diversified investment portfolio for you. It's like having a financial advisor, but without the awkward small talk or judgment about your spending habits.

Why Robo-Advisors are Perfect for Couch Potatoes:

1. *Minimal Effort:* Answer a few questions about your goals and risk tolerance, and the robo-advisor does the rest.
2. *Low Costs:* Generally cheaper than traditional financial advisors.
3. *Automatic Rebalancing:* Your portfolio stays on track without you lifting a finger.
4. *Tax-Loss Harvesting:* Some robo-advisors offer this service to help minimize your tax bill.

Top Robo-Advisors for the Discerning Lazy Investor:

1. *Betterment:*
    - Known for its user-friendly interface
    - Offers socially responsible investing options

- No minimum balance required
2. *Wealthfront:*
    - Offers a wider range of investment options, including real estate
    - Provides a free financial planning tool
    - $500 minimum investment
3. *Vanguard Digital Advisor:*
    - From the company known for low-cost index funds
    - Requires a $3,000 minimum investment
    - Good for those who want a more hands-off approach
4. *SoFi Automated Investing:*
    - No management fees
    - Access to human financial advisors at no extra cost
    - No minimum balance required

How to Get Started with a Robo-Advisor:

1. Choose a robo-advisor based on your needs and minimum investment requirements.
2. Answer the questionnaire about your financial goals and risk tolerance.
3. Link your bank account.
4. Set up automatic transfers to fund your account.
5. Sit back and watch your money grow (or don't watch – that's the beauty of it).

Pro Tip: Set up alerts to notify you of significant changes in your portfolio. This way, you can stay informed without constantly checking your account.

2. Index Funds: The Slacker's Path to Wall Street Success

If robo-advisors sound too high-tech for you, fear not! There's an even simpler way to invest: index funds. These are the ultimate "set it and forget it" investment option.

What Are Index Funds?

Index funds are mutual funds or exchange-traded funds (ETFs) designed to track a specific market index, like the S&P 500. Instead of trying to beat the market (which is hard and requires effort), index funds aim to match the market's performance.

Why Index Funds are a Couch Potato's Dream:

1. *Low Costs:* Index funds typically have lower fees than actively managed funds.
2. *Built-in Diversification:* You're investing in a broad swath of the market with one purchase.
3. *Minimal Research Required:* No need to analyze individual stocks or time the market.
4. *Historically Solid Performance:* Over the long term, index funds have often outperformed actively managed funds.

Popular Index Funds for Lazy Investors:

1. *Vanguard Total Stock Market Index Fund (VTSAX):*
    - Tracks the entire U.S. stock market
    - Very low expense ratio (0.04%)
    - Minimum investment: $3,000

2. *Fidelity ZERO Total Market Index Fund (FZROX):*
   - No minimum investment
   - Zero expense ratio (yes, you read that right)
   - Tracks the U.S. stock market
3. *SPDR S&P 500 ETF Trust (SPY):*
   - Tracks the S&P 500 index
   - Highly liquid, making it easy to buy and sell
   - No minimum investment (price of one share)
4. *iShares Core MSCI Total International Stock ETF (IXUS):*
   - Provides exposure to international stocks
   - Low expense ratio (0.09%)
   - No minimum investment (price of one share)

How to Invest in Index Funds:

1. Open a brokerage account (many offer commission-free trading on ETFs).
2. Choose your index fund(s).
3. Set up automatic investments (many brokers allow this for mutual funds, some for ETFs).
4. Reinvest dividends automatically.
5. Check your investments annually (or less often if that sounds like too much work).

The Lazy Portfolio: For the ultimate in simplicity, consider a three-fund portfolio:

- A U.S. total stock market index fund
- An international stock index fund

- A U.S. bond index fund

Adjust the percentages based on your risk tolerance, and rebalance annually. That's it!

3. Micro-Investing: Small Moves for Big Gains

For those who find even index funds too daunting (or who don't have a large lump sum to invest), micro-investing apps are here to save the day. These apps allow you to invest small amounts of money, often automatically, making it easy to start building wealth without feeling the pinch.

Why Micro-Investing is Perfect for Couch Potatoes:

1. *Low Barrier to Entry:* Start investing with as little as $5.
2. *Automatic Investing:* Many apps round up your purchases and invest the spare change.
3. *Educational:* Learn about investing without risking large sums of money.
4. *Painless Saving:* You might not even notice the small amounts being invested.

Top Micro-Investing Apps:

1. *Acorns:*
    - Rounds up your purchases and invests the difference
    - Offers a selection of pre-made portfolios based on risk tolerance
    - Fees: $1-$5 per month, depending on the plan
2. *Stash:*
    - Allows you to invest in fractional shares of stocks and ETFs

- Offers themed investment options (e.g., "Clean & Green" for eco-friendly companies)
- Fees: $1-$9 per month, depending on the plan

3. *Robinhood:*
    - Commission-free trading of stocks, ETFs, options, and cryptocurrencies
    - Allows fractional share investing
    - No fees for basic account

4. *Public:*
    - Social investing app that allows you to see what others are investing in
    - Offers fractional shares and themed investment options
    - No account minimums or commission fees

How to Get Started with Micro-Investing:

1. Choose an app that aligns with your goals and preferences.
2. Download the app and create an account.
3. Link your bank account or debit card.
4. Set up automatic investments or round-ups.
5. Watch your tiny investments grow over time.

Pro Tip: While micro-investing is a great way to start, don't rely on it as your only investment strategy long-term. As your wealth grows, consider transitioning to more comprehensive investment options.

4. Dividend Investing: Get Paid for Doing Nothing

Chapter 4: Couch Investing - Making Money While Horizontal

If the idea of earning money while you sleep appeals to you (and why wouldn't it?), dividend investing might be your cup of tea. Dividend investing involves buying stocks or funds that pay regular dividends – essentially, a share of the company's profits.

Why Dividend Investing is a Couch Potato's Dream:

1. *Passive Income:* Receive regular payments just for owning the stock.
2. *Potential for Growth:* Many dividend-paying companies are stable and may increase in value over time.
3. *Reinvestment Opportunity:* Reinvesting dividends can lead to compounding returns.
4. *Inflation Hedge:* Many companies increase their dividends over time, helping to keep pace with inflation.

Types of Dividend Investments:

1. *Individual Dividend Stocks:*
    - Pros: Ability to choose specific companies, potentially higher yields
    - Cons: Requires more research, less diversification
2. *Dividend ETFs:*
    - Pros: Instant diversification, professional management
    - Cons: Lower yields than some individual stocks, ongoing expense ratios
3. *Real Estate Investment Trusts (REITs):*
    - Pros: High yields, exposure to real estate market

- Cons: Can be volatile, complex tax implications

Lazy-Friendly Dividend ETFs:

1. *Vanguard High Dividend Yield ETF (VYM):*
   - Tracks U.S. companies with above-average dividend yields
   - Low expense ratio (0.06%)
2. *SPDR S&P Dividend ETF (SDY):*
   - Focuses on companies that have consistently increased dividends for at least 20 consecutive years
   - Expense ratio: 0.35%
3. *iShares Core High Dividend ETF (HDV):*
   - Tracks financially healthy companies with high dividend yields
   - Expense ratio: 0.08%

How to Start Dividend Investing:

1. Open a brokerage account if you don't already have one.
2. Research dividend-paying stocks or ETFs (or choose from the ones mentioned above).
3. Make your initial investment.
4. Set up dividend reinvestment (DRIP) to automatically reinvest your dividends.
5. Consider setting up automatic recurring investments to build your portfolio over time.

Chapter 4: Couch Investing - Making Money While Horizontal

Pro Tip: Don't chase the highest yields blindly. Sometimes, an extremely high dividend yield can be a red flag indicating a company in trouble.

5. Real Estate Investing for the Couch-Bound

Real estate investing might sound like it requires a lot of effort (not to mention capital), but fear not! There are ways to invest in real estate without ever leaving your couch or dealing with tenants.

Why Real Estate Investing Can Be Couch Potato-Friendly:

1. *Passive Income:* Many real estate investments provide regular cash flow.
2. *Diversification:* Real estate often moves differently from stocks and bonds, providing portfolio diversification.
3. *Potential Tax Benefits:* Real estate investments can offer tax advantages (consult a tax professional for details).
4. *Inflation Hedge:* Real estate values and rents tend to increase with inflation over time.

Lazy-Friendly Real Estate Investment Options:

1. *Real Estate Investment Trusts (REITs):*
    - What They Are: Companies that own and operate income-producing real estate
    - How to Invest: Buy shares through a brokerage account, just like stocks
    - Lazy-Friendly REIT ETFs:
        - Vanguard Real Estate ETF (VNQ)
        - Schwab US REIT ETF (SCHH)

2. *Real Estate Crowdfunding Platforms:*
    - What They Are: Online platforms that pool money from multiple investors to fund real estate projects
    - Popular Platforms:
        - Fundrise: Offers low minimum investments and a variety of investment options
        - RealtyMogul: Provides access to commercial real estate investments
        - CrowdStreet: Focuses on institutional-quality commercial real estate
3. *Real Estate Mutual Funds:*
    - What They Are: Professionally managed funds that invest in real estate securities
    - Lazy-Friendly Options:
        - Fidelity Real Estate Index Fund (FSRNX)
        - T. Rowe Price Real Estate Fund (TRREX)
4. *Real Estate Notes:*
    - What They Are: Investing in real estate debt rather than equity
    - How to Invest: Platforms like PeerStreet allow you to invest in real estate loans

How to Get Started with Lazy Real Estate Investing:

1. Research the different options to find what aligns with your goals and risk tolerance.
2. Choose a platform or brokerage to invest through.

Chapter 4: Couch Investing - Making Money While Horizontal

3. Start small and diversify across different types of real estate investments.
4. Set up automatic investments if possible.
5. Monitor your investments periodically (but not obsessively – we're aiming for lazy, remember?).

Pro Tip: While real estate can be a great addition to your portfolio, don't put all your eggs in one basket. Maintain a diversified investment strategy across different asset classes.

6. Lazy Strategies for Retirement Accounts

Retirement might seem like a long way off (or maybe it's just around the corner), but it's never too early (or late) to start planning. The good news? You can set up your retirement savings to practically run on autopilot.

Why Retirement Accounts are a Couch Potato's Best Friend:

1. *Tax Advantages:* Many retirement accounts offer tax benefits, either now or in the future.
2. *Automatic Contributions:* Set it and forget it with payroll deductions or automatic transfers.
3. *Compound Growth:* Time does the heavy lifting as your investments grow over the years.
4. *Forced Savings:* Early withdrawal penalties discourage you from dipping into your nest egg.

Types of Retirement Accounts:

1. *401(k) or 403(b):*
    - Employer-sponsored plans with high contribution limits
    - Often include employer matching (free money!)

Chapter 4: Couch Investing - Making Money While Horizontal

- o Traditional (pre-tax) or Roth (after-tax) options available

2. *Individual Retirement Account (IRA):*
   - o Open an account on your own through a brokerage
   - o Traditional (tax-deductible contributions) or Roth (tax-free withdrawals in retirement) options
   - o Lower contribution limits than 401(k)s

3. *Solo 401(k) or SEP IRA:*
   - o For self-employed individuals
   - o Higher contribution limits than traditional IRAs

4. *Health Savings Account (HSA):*
   - o Triple tax advantage: tax-deductible contributions, tax-free growth, tax-free withdrawals for medical expenses
   - o Can be used as a stealth retirement account after age 65

Lazy-Friendly Retirement Strategies:

1. The "Set It and Forget It" 401(k) Strategy:
   - o Contribute at least enough to get your full employer match
   - o Choose a target-date fund based on your expected retirement year
   - o Increase your contribution whenever you get a raise

2. The "Backdoor Roth" for High Earners:

- Contribute to a traditional IRA (without taking a tax deduction)
- Convert the contribution to a Roth IRA
- Allows high earners to indirectly contribute to a Roth IRA

3. The "HSA as Stealth IRA" Strategy:
   - Max out your HSA contributions
   - Invest the funds (many HSAs offer investment options)
   - Pay medical expenses out of pocket and save receipts
   - After age 65, you can withdraw funds for any purpose without penalty (just pay income tax)

4. The "Lazy Portfolio" for IRAs:
   - Invest in a simple three-fund portfolio:
     - Total U.S. Stock Market Index Fund
     - Total International Stock Market Index Fund
     - Total Bond Market Index Fund
   - Adjust percentages based on your risk tolerance
   - Rebalance annually

How to Implement Your Lazy Retirement Strategy:

1. If you have a 401(k), start there and contribute at least enough to get the full employer match.
2. Open an IRA (if eligible) and set up automatic contributions.

3. If you have a high-deductible health plan, open and max out an HSA.

4. Choose low-cost index funds or target-date funds for all accounts.

5. Set up automatic increases to your contributions (many 401(k) plans offer this feature).

6. Review your accounts annually and rebalance if necessary.

Pro Tip: Don't let analysis paralysis keep you from starting. It's better to start investing imperfectly than to not start at all. You can always adjust your strategy later.

7. Lazy Investing for Different Life Stages

Your investment strategy should evolve as you move through different stages of life. But don't worry – we'll keep it lazy at every stage.

The Lazy 20-Something:

1. *Focus on Building Good Habits:*
    - Start investing early, even if it's small amounts
    - Get in the habit of living below your means
    - Take full advantage of any employer 401(k) match

2. *Embrace Risk:*
    - With a long time horizon, you can afford to be aggressive
    - Consider a portfolio heavily weighted towards stocks (90% stocks, 10% bonds)

3. *Keep It Simple:*

Chapter 4: Couch Investing - Making Money While Horizontal

- Start with a target-date fund or a simple two-fund portfolio (U.S. total market and international total market)
- Set up automatic investments and forget about them

4. *Prioritize High-Interest Debt:*
   - If you have high-interest debt (like credit cards), focus on paying that off first
   - Once debt is under control, redirect that money to investments

The Lazy 30-Something:

1. *Ramp Up Savings:*
   - As your income grows, increase your savings rate
   - Aim to save 15-20% of your income for retirement

2. *Diversify:*
   - Start introducing more asset classes (like real estate or international stocks)
   - Consider a more balanced portfolio (80% stocks, 20% bonds)

3. *Take Advantage of Tax-Advantaged Accounts:*
   - Max out your 401(k) if possible
   - Consider opening a Roth IRA for tax diversification

4. *Start Thinking About Big Life Goals:*
   - If you're planning for a home purchase or kids' education, consider opening specific savings accounts for these goals

Chapter 4: Couch Investing - Making Money While Horizontal

The Lazy 40-Something:

1. *Reassess Risk Tolerance:*
    - You still have time to recover from market downturns, but you might want to start reducing risk slightly
    - Consider adjusting to a 70% stocks, 30% bonds portfolio
2. *Max Out Retirement Accounts:*
    - If you're not already maxing out your 401(k) and IRA, now's the time
    - Look into catch-up contributions if you're behind on savings
3. *Consider Tax-Efficient Investing:*
    - If you have a taxable account, focus on tax-efficient funds like index ETFs
    - Look into tax-loss harvesting strategies
4. *Start Estate Planning:*
    - Set up a will and consider establishing a trust
    - Review and update beneficiaries on all accounts

The Lazy 50-Something:

1. *Shift Towards Preservation:*
    - Start focusing more on protecting your wealth
    - Consider a more conservative portfolio (60% stocks, 40% bonds)
2. *Take Advantage of Catch-Up Contributions:*

- At age 50, you can contribute extra to your 401(k) and IRA
3. *Start Thinking About Income:*
    - Consider adding more dividend-paying stocks or bonds to your portfolio
    - Look into annuities for guaranteed income in retirement
4. *Get Serious About Healthcare Planning:*
    - Max out your HSA if you have one
    - Start researching long-term care insurance options

The Lazy Retiree:

1. *Focus on Income and Preservation:*
    - Shift towards a more conservative portfolio (40-50% stocks, 50-60% bonds)
    - Consider a bucket strategy: short-term needs in cash, medium-term in bonds, long-term in stocks
2. *Develop a Withdrawal Strategy:*
    - Consider the 4% rule or a dynamic withdrawal strategy
    - Be mindful of required minimum distributions (RMDs) from traditional retirement accounts
3. *Optimize Social Security:*
    - Decide when to start taking Social Security benefits
    - Consider strategies like "file and suspend" if applicable

4. *Stay Invested:*
   - Remember, retirement can last 30+ years. You still need growth to outpace inflation

Pro Tip: These are general guidelines. Your specific situation might call for a different approach. When in doubt, consider consulting with a financial advisor for personalized advice.

8. Lazy Investing in a Volatile Market

Market volatility can be scary, but for the lazy investor, it's just another day at the (home) office. Here's how to stay the course when the market gets choppy.

Why Lazy Investing Works in Volatile Markets:

1. *Emotion-Free:* By sticking to your plan, you avoid making rash decisions based on fear or greed.
2. *Dollar-Cost Averaging:* Regular, automatic investments mean you're buying more shares when prices are low.
3. *Long-Term Focus:* Short-term volatility matters less when you're investing for decades.

Lazy Strategies for Volatile Markets:

1. *Do Nothing:*
   - Often, the best action is inaction
   - Stick to your long-term plan and ignore the daily noise
2. *Rebalance (But Not Too Often):*
   - If your asset allocation has shifted significantly, consider rebalancing
   - Aim for once a year, or when your allocation is off by 5% or more

3. *Keep Investing:*
    - Continue your regular contributions
    - Think of volatility as a sale on stocks
4. *Increase Your Bond Allocation (If Needed):*
    - If the volatility is keeping you up at night, consider slightly increasing your bond allocation
    - Remember, this will lower your potential returns, so don't overdo it
5. *Consider Defensive Sectors:*
    - If you want to adjust your stock allocation, look into defensive sectors like utilities or consumer staples
    - These tend to be less volatile during market downturns

What Not to Do in Volatile Markets:

1. *Don't Try to Time the Market:*
    - It's nearly impossible to consistently predict market tops and bottoms
    - Trying to time the market often leads to worse performance than staying invested
2. *Don't Check Your Portfolio Constantly:*
    - Frequent checking can lead to emotional decisions
    - Set a schedule (monthly or quarterly) to review your investments
3. *Don't Panic Sell:*

- Selling during a downturn locks in your losses
- Remember, you only realize a loss when you sell

4. *Don't Neglect Your Emergency Fund:*
    - Having a solid emergency fund can prevent you from having to sell investments at a bad time

Lazy Investor's Mantra for Volatile Markets: "This too shall pass. I'm investing for the long term, and short-term volatility is just noise."

Pro Tip: If you find yourself constantly worried about market volatility, it might be a sign that your risk tolerance is lower than you thought. Consider reassessing your asset allocation during calmer times.

9. Lazy Tax Strategies for Investors

Taxes might not be the most exciting topic, but a few lazy strategies can help you keep more of your investment returns. Remember, it's not just about what you earn, but what you keep after taxes.

Why Tax Efficiency Matters:

1. *Compound Growth:* Saving on taxes means more money stays invested and compounds over time.
2. *Higher Returns:* Tax-efficient investing can significantly boost your after-tax returns.
3. *Simplified Tax Filing:* Some strategies can make your tax return easier to prepare.

Lazy Tax-Efficient Investing Strategies:

1. *Maximize Tax-Advantaged Accounts:*
    - Contribute to 401(k)s, IRAs, and HSAs before investing in taxable accounts

- These accounts offer tax benefits that can significantly boost your long-term returns

2. *Use ETFs in Taxable Accounts:*
    - ETFs are generally more tax-efficient than mutual funds due to their structure
    - They typically generate fewer capital gains distributions

3. *Consider Municipal Bonds:*
    - Interest from municipal bonds is often tax-free at the federal level
    - Can be especially beneficial for high-income investors in taxable accounts

4. *Hold Stocks for the Long Term:*
    - Long-term capital gains (on investments held over a year) are taxed at lower rates
    - Avoid frequent trading to minimize taxable events

5. *Tax-Loss Harvesting:*
    - Sell investments at a loss to offset capital gains
    - Many robo-advisors offer this service automatically

6. *Asset Location:*
    - Hold tax-inefficient investments (like bonds or REITs) in tax-advantaged accounts
    - Keep tax-efficient investments (like broad-market stock ETFs) in taxable accounts

7. *Avoid Wash Sales:*

- If you sell an investment at a loss, don't buy a substantially identical investment within 30 days before or after the sale
- This preserves your ability to claim the tax loss

8. *Donate Appreciated Securities:*
    - If you're charitably inclined, consider donating appreciated stocks instead of cash
    - You avoid capital gains tax and can still claim a deduction for the full market value

Lazy Investor's Guide to Tax-Efficient Funds:

1. *Total Market Index ETFs:*
    - Vanguard Total Stock Market ETF (VTI)
    - iShares Core S&P Total U.S. Stock Market ETF (ITOT)

2. *Tax-Managed Funds:*
    - Vanguard Tax-Managed Capital Appreciation Fund (VTCLX)
    - T. Rowe Price Tax-Efficient Equity Fund (PREFX)

3. *Municipal Bond Funds:*
    - Vanguard Tax-Exempt Bond ETF (VTEB)
    - iShares National Muni Bond ETF (MUB)

How to Implement Lazy Tax Strategies:

1. Prioritize contributions to tax-advantaged accounts.
2. For taxable accounts, choose tax-efficient funds like ETFs or tax-managed funds.
3. Set up automatic investments to avoid timing-related tax issues.

Chapter 4: Couch Investing - Making Money While Horizontal

4. Use a robo-advisor or tax software that offers tax-loss harvesting.
5. Review your investment tax strategy annually, preferably with a tax professional.

Pro Tip: Tax laws can change, so stay informed about any updates that might affect your investment strategy. Consider consulting with a tax professional for personalized advice.

10. The Lazy Investor's Guide to Staying Informed

As a lazy investor, you don't need to be glued to CNBC or reading financial newspapers every day. However, staying reasonably informed can help you make better decisions and avoid panic during market turbulence. Here's how to stay informed without it becoming a second job.

Why Staying Informed Matters:

1. *Confidence:* Understanding what's happening in the markets can help you stick to your plan.
2. *Opportunity Recognition:* Being aware of broader trends can help you identify potential opportunities.
3. *Risk Management:* Knowing about potential risks can help you adjust your strategy if needed.

Lazy Ways to Stay Informed:

1. *Use News Aggregators:*
   - Set up Google Alerts for key financial terms or companies you're interested in
   - Use apps like Flipboard or Feedly to curate financial news
2. *Follow Reputable Financial Websites:*
   - Bookmark sites like Morningstar, The Motley Fool, or Investopedia

- Check them once a week for a quick overview

3. *Subscribe to Financial Newsletters:*
   - Many offer concise, weekly summaries of important financial news
   - Examples: Morning Brew, The Hustle, Robinhood Snacks

4. *Listen to Financial Podcasts:*
   - Great for passive consumption while doing other tasks
   - Recommendations: "Planet Money," "Freakonomics Radio," "Motley Fool Money"

5. *Use Your Brokerage's Resources:*
   - Many brokerages offer research, educational materials, and market updates
   - Take advantage of these free resources

6. *Set Up Automatic Alerts:*
   - Use your brokerage's alert system to notify you of significant changes in your holdings or the broader market

7. *Annual Reports:*
   - For individual stock holdings, read the annual report (10-K) once a year
   - Focus on the business description, risk factors, and management's discussion

8. *Quarterly Portfolio Review:*
   - Set a calendar reminder to review your portfolio performance quarterly

- Compare against relevant benchmarks

What to Pay Attention To (And What to Ignore):

Pay Attention To:

- Long-term economic trends
- Major policy changes that could affect markets
- Significant geopolitical events
- Your own financial goals and risk tolerance

Ignore (or Take with a Grain of Salt):

- Daily market movements
- Short-term price targets
- Hot stock tips
- Pundit predictions about market timing

The Lazy Investor's News Diet:

1. *Daily:* Glance at headlines, but don't dive deep unless something major is happening.
2. *Weekly:* Read a financial newsletter or listen to a podcast for a broader overview.
3. *Monthly:* Check your portfolio and read any updates from your funds or brokers.
4. *Quarterly:* Do a more thorough review of your investments and rebalance if necessary.
5. *Annually:* Read annual reports for individual holdings, reassess your overall strategy.

Pro Tip: Remember, the goal is to stay informed enough to make good decisions, not to predict short-term market movements. When in doubt, stick to your long-term plan.

Chapter 4: Couch Investing - Making Money While Horizontal

Conclusion: Your Couch Investing Action Plan

Congratulations, lazy investor! You've made it through our deep dive into the world of effortless wealth-building. Let's recap with an action plan to get you started on your couch investing journey:

1. *Choose Your Lazy Investment Method:*
    - Decide between robo-advisors, index funds, or a combination of both
    - Open an account with your chosen platform
2. *Set Up Automatic Investments:*
    - Determine how much you can invest regularly
    - Set up automatic transfers from your bank account
3. *Maximize Tax Advantages:*
    - Contribute to tax-advantaged accounts like 401(k)s and IRAs
    - Consider tax-efficient funds for taxable accounts
4. *Diversify Lazily:*
    - Choose a target-date fund or a simple three-fund portfolio
    - Include U.S. stocks, international stocks, and bonds
5. *Implement Lazy Rebalancing:*
    - Set a calendar reminder to check your asset allocation annually
    - Rebalance if your allocation has drifted by 5% or more

6. *Stay Informed (But Not Too Informed):*
   - Choose one or two reliable sources for financial news
   - Set up Google Alerts for major financial terms
7. *Resist the Urge to Tinker:*
   - Remember, laziness is a virtue in investing
   - Avoid making changes based on short-term market movements
8. *Review and Adjust:*
   - Set an annual reminder to review your overall financial situation
   - Adjust your strategy if your goals or circumstances have changed significantly

Remember, the key to successful couch investing is consistency and patience. By setting up a low-effort, automated investment strategy, you're positioning yourself for long-term financial success – all while maintaining your commitment to minimal exertion.

In our next chapter, we'll explore how to turn your everyday laziness into a money-making machine with "Side Hustles for the Chronically Unmotivated." Until then, happy (lazy) investing, and may your returns always be higher than your effort!

Chapter 5: Side Hustles for the Chronically Unmotivated

Welcome back, aspiring lazy entrepreneurs! You've made it to the chapter that might just change your life – or at least your bank account. We're about to dive into the world of side hustles tailored specifically for those who prefer their income as passive as possible. Buckle up (or don't, we know moving is hard) as we explore how to make money without sacrificing your commitment to minimal effort.

1. Online Surveys: Get Paid for Your Opinions (Even the Bad Ones)

Let's start with perhaps the laziest of all side hustles: online surveys. Yes, you can actually make money by sharing your thoughts while lounging in your pajamas.

Why Online Surveys are Perfect for the Chronically Unmotivated:

1. *No Special Skills Required:* If you have opinions (and who doesn't?), you're qualified.
2. *Flexible:* Do surveys whenever you feel like it – even at 3 AM.
3. *Low Commitment:* No need to interact with actual humans.
4. *Variety:* From product testing to political polls, there's always something different.

Top Survey Sites for Lazy Money-Makers:

1. *Swagbucks:*
    - Earn points for surveys, watching videos, and online shopping
    - Points can be redeemed for gift cards or PayPal cash
    - Sign-up bonus available

2. *Survey Junkie:*
    - Focuses solely on surveys
    - Clear point system (1 point = 1 cent)
    - Low minimum payout threshold ($5)
3. *Vindale Research:*
    - Pays in cash, not points
    - Higher-paying surveys available
    - Referral program for extra earnings
4. *Opinion Outpost:*
    - Quarterly $10,000 prize draw for active members
    - Variety of reward options including PayPal and Amazon gift cards
    - Lower minimum payout threshold
5. *Pinecone Research:*
    - Invitation-only platform (exclusivity for the lazy!)
    - Fixed rate of $3 per survey
    - Product testing opportunities

How to Maximize Your Survey Earnings (with Minimal Effort):

1. *Create a Dedicated Email:* Keep your survey invitations separate from your personal email.
2. *Be Honest:* Consistency is key. Contradictory answers might get you disqualified.
3. *Fill Out Your Profile Completely:* This helps match you with relevant surveys.

4. *Set Low Expectations:* You won't get rich, but hey, it's better than nothing.
5. *Multitask:* Take surveys while watching TV or waiting in line.
6. *Use a Survey Aggregator:* Sites like Survey Police list available surveys across multiple platforms.
7. *Cash Out Regularly:* Don't let your earnings sit there – cash out as soon as you hit the minimum threshold.

Pro Tip: Be wary of survey sites that require you to pay to join. Legitimate survey sites are free to use.

2. Sell Your Stuff: One Person's Junk is Another's Treasure

Next up in our lazy money-making schemes is selling stuff you already own. It's like getting paid to declutter – a win-win for the unmotivated minimalist.

Why Selling Your Stuff is a Couch Potato's Dream:

1. *You Already Own It:* No need to create or source products.
2. *One-Time Effort:* Once it's sold, it's gone (along with your effort).
3. *Decluttering Bonus:* More space for lounging.
4. *Potential for Surprising Profits:* That old gadget might be worth more than you think.

Lazy-Friendly Platforms for Selling:

1. *Facebook Marketplace:*
    - Free to list
    - Large local audience
    - Easy to use if you're already on Facebook

Chapter 4: Couch Investing - Making Money While Horizontal

2. *eBay:*
   - Massive global audience
   - Good for niche or collectible items
   - Auction format can drive up prices
3. *Craigslist:*
   - Free to list
   - Good for large items (furniture, appliances)
   - Local pickup means no shipping hassle
4. *Poshmark:*
   - Ideal for clothing and accessories
   - Social aspect can boost sales
   - They provide a shipping label
5. *Decluttr:*
   - Specializes in electronics, CDs, DVDs, and books
   - They give you an instant offer
   - Free shipping

What to Sell (That You Probably Have Lying Around):

1. *Old Electronics:* Smartphones, tablets, laptops
2. *Clothing and Accessories:* Especially brand-name items
3. *Books:* Textbooks can be particularly valuable
4. *Furniture:* Vintage or unique pieces often sell well
5. *Collectibles:* Action figures, trading cards, coins
6. *Sports Equipment:* Exercise machines, golf clubs

7. *Musical Instruments:* Even if you never learned to play that guitar

8. *Tools:* Power tools are always in demand

The Lazy Person's Guide to Successful Selling:

1. *Take Good Photos:* This is worth the effort. Good lighting and multiple angles increase your chances of selling.

2. *Write Clear Descriptions:* Be honest about condition and include measurements for furniture.

3. *Price Competitively:* Check what similar items are selling for.

4. *Be Safe:* For local sales, meet in public places or police station parking lots.

5. *Don't Hold Items:* First come, first served is the lazy way.

6. *Use Shipping Services:* Many platforms integrate with shipping services, making it easier to send items.

7. *Bundle Items:* Sell similar items together to minimize effort.

Pro Tip: Consider hosting a virtual yard sale on Facebook Live. You can showcase multiple items in one go, and viewers can claim items in real-time.

3. Passive Income Streams: Money While You Snooze

Now we're getting to the holy grail of lazy money-making: passive income. These are ways to set up income streams that continue to pay out with minimal ongoing effort.

Why Passive Income is Perfect for the Chronically Unmotivated:

1. *Effort Front-Loading:* Do the work once, reap the benefits over time.

Chapter 4: Couch Investing - Making Money While Horizontal

2. *Scalability:* Many passive income streams can grow without proportional effort.
3. *Time Freedom:* Once set up, you're free to pursue other interests (like perfecting your couch groove).
4. *Diverse Options:* There's a passive income stream for every level of initial effort and investment.

Lazy-Friendly Passive Income Ideas:

1. *Dividend Investing:*
   - Buy shares in companies that pay regular dividends
   - Reinvest dividends for compound growth
   - Consider dividend-focused ETFs for instant diversification

2. *Real Estate Crowdfunding:*
   - Platforms like Fundrise or RealtyMogul let you invest in real estate projects
   - Low minimum investments
   - Regular income from rent payments

3. *Create a Digital Product:*
   - E-books, online courses, or printables
   - Create once, sell indefinitely
   - Platforms like Gumroad or Teachable handle sales and delivery

4. *Rent Out Storage Space:*
   - Use platforms like Neighbor to rent out your garage or spare room for storage
   - Minimal interaction required

5. *License Your Photos:*
    - Upload photos to stock photography sites like Shutterstock or Adobe Stock
    - Earn royalties each time someone uses your image
6. *Create a YouTube Channel:*
    - Make videos on topics you're knowledgeable about
    - Monetize through ads, sponsorships, and affiliate links
    - Evergreen content can generate income for years
7. *Write an eBook:*
    - Self-publish on Amazon Kindle Direct Publishing
    - One-time effort, ongoing royalties
    - Can be as short as 6,000 words for a niche topic
8. *Rent Out Your Car:*
    - Use platforms like Turo or Getaround
    - Let your car make money when you're not using it
9. *Affiliate Marketing:*
    - Promote products you use and love
    - Earn commissions on sales
    - Can be done through a blog, social media, or YouTube
10. *Create a Print-on-Demand Store:*

Chapter 4: Couch Investing - Making Money While Horizontal

- - Design t-shirts, mugs, or other items
  - Use platforms like Redbubble or Society6 to handle production and shipping
  - You just provide the designs

The Lazy Person's Guide to Setting Up Passive Income:

1. *Choose Wisely:* Pick a passive income stream that aligns with your interests and skills.
2. *Start Small:* Don't try to set up multiple streams at once. Master one before moving to the next.
3. *Automate Where Possible:* Use tools and apps to minimize ongoing work.
4. *Reinvest Early Profits:* Use initial earnings to grow your passive income stream.
5. *Be Patient:* Passive income takes time to build. Don't get discouraged if results aren't immediate.
6. *Leverage Existing Assets:* Look for ways to monetize things you already own or do.
7. *Stay Legal:* Be aware of tax implications and any necessary licenses or permits.

Pro Tip: For truly passive income, consider combining multiple low-effort streams. A diversified passive income portfolio can provide more stable earnings.

4. Microwork: Tiny Tasks for Tiny Payments

If you're looking for a side hustle that requires minimal brain power and can be done in short bursts, microwork might be your jam. These are small, simple tasks that companies need humans to complete.

Why Microwork is Great for the Unmotivated:

1. *Bite-Sized Tasks:* Most tasks take just a few minutes to complete.
2. *No Long-Term Commitment:* Do as much or as little as you want.
3. *Variety:* Different types of tasks keep things interesting.
4. *Low Pressure:* Most tasks are low-stakes and don't require special skills.

Popular Microwork Platforms:

1. *Amazon Mechanical Turk (MTurk):*
   - Wide variety of tasks called HITs (Human Intelligence Tasks)
   - Tasks can include image/audio transcription, data verification, and content moderation
   - Payment varies by task, some pay just a few cents
2. *Clickworker:*
   - Tasks include writing, translation, and data entry
   - Can include higher-paying projects like search engine evaluation
   - Available internationally
3. *Appen:*
   - Offers both microwork and longer-term projects
   - Tasks can include data collection, transcription, and translation
   - Higher pay for specialized skills

4. *Figure Eight:*
   - Focuses on AI training tasks
   - Work includes audio transcription, content moderation, and image annotation
   - Leveling system allows access to higher-paying tasks

5. *Lionbridge:*
   - Offers both microwork and more substantial online jobs
   - Tasks can include search evaluation, translation, and data entry
   - Known for higher pay rates

Types of Microwork Tasks:

1. *Data Entry:* Inputting information into databases
2. *Image Tagging:* Describing or categorizing images
3. *Transcription:* Converting audio or video to text
4. *Content Moderation:* Reviewing user-generated content for appropriateness
5. *Search Result Evaluation:* Rating the relevance of search results
6. *Sentiment Analysis:* Categorizing text as positive, negative, or neutral
7. *Translation:* Translating short phrases or sentences
8. *Survey Taking:* Providing opinions on various topics

How to Maximize Your Microwork Earnings:

1. *Create a Schedule:* Set aside specific times for microwork to build consistency.

Chapter 4: Couch Investing - Making Money While Horizontal

2. *Focus on High-Paying Tasks:* Look for tasks that offer the best pay rate for your time.

3. *Develop Efficient Systems:* Create shortcuts or templates for common tasks.

4. *Take Qualification Tests:* Many platforms offer higher-paying tasks to workers who pass qualification tests.

5. *Use Multiple Platforms:* Different platforms may have better-paying tasks at different times.

6. *Track Your Earnings:* Keep a spreadsheet to see which types of tasks are most profitable for you.

7. *Use Browser Extensions:* Some extensions can help you find and manage tasks more efficiently.

8. *Be Accurate:* Maintaining a high accuracy rate can lead to better task opportunities.

Pro Tip: While microwork won't make you rich, it can be a good way to earn money during times you'd otherwise be unproductive, like while watching TV or waiting for appointments.

5. Rent Out Your Parking Space: Asphalt Gold

If you have a parking space that you're not using all the time, why not turn it into a money-making machine? This is one of the most passive side hustles out there.

Why Parking Space Rental is Perfect for the Lazy:

1. *Truly Passive:* Once set up, there's very little ongoing work.

2. *Uses Existing Assets:* No need to buy or create anything.

3. *Consistent Income:* Especially in high-demand areas, you can count on regular payments.

4. *Low Maintenance:* Unlike renting out a room, a parking space doesn't need cleaning or repairs.

How to Rent Out Your Parking Space:

1. *Assess Your Space:*
    - Is it in a desirable location? (Near public transport, popular venues, or in a busy city center)
    - Is it easily accessible?
    - Can you legally rent it out? (Check local regulations and, if applicable, HOA rules)

2. *Determine Your Price:*
    - Research rates for similar parking spaces in your area
    - Consider offering discounts for long-term rentals

3. *Choose a Rental Platform:*
    - JustPark
    - SpotHero
    - Neighbor
    - CurbFlip

4. *Create Your Listing:*
    - Take clear photos of the space and surrounding area
    - Provide detailed information (size, security features, access instructions)
    - Be clear about any restrictions (e.g., no oversized vehicles)

Chapter 4: Couch Investing - Making Money While Horizontal

5. *Set Up Payment:*
   - Most platforms handle payment processing
   - Consider requiring a security deposit for long-term rentals
6. *Provide Access:*
   - For driveways, this might be as simple as giving an address
   - For garages, you might need to provide a key or access code

Maximizing Your Parking Space Profits:

1. *Offer Short-Term Rentals:* In some areas, you can make more by renting your space by the hour or day.
2. *Target Specific Audiences:* Near a stadium? Advertise to season ticket holders. Close to an airport? Market to frequent travelers.
3. *Bundle Services:* If you have an electric vehicle charger, include charging in the rental price.
4. *Provide Value-Adds:* Consider offering services like car washing or detailing for an additional fee.
5. *Seasonal Pricing:* Increase your rates during high-demand times (e.g., during local events or tourist season).
6. *Multiple Platforms:* List your space on several platforms to increase visibility.
7. *Referral Programs:* Some platforms offer bonuses for referring new users.

Pro Tip: If you live in an area with street cleaning or other parking restrictions, you could offer your driveway as a temporary space during these times.

Chapter 4: Couch Investing - Making Money While Horizontal

6. Pet Sitting for the Pet-Averse: Outsourced Fur Baby Care

Love the idea of extra cash but not so keen on furry friends? No problem! You can still cash in on the pet care craze without getting your hands (or furniture) dirty.

Why Pet Sitting Management is Great for the Unmotivated:

1. *Delegation is Key:* You manage the business, others do the actual pet care.
2. *Scalable:* Start small and grow as you get more clients and sitters.
3. *Flexible:* Work from home managing bookings and customer service.
4. *Recurring Revenue:* Pet owners often need regular, ongoing care.

How to Start a Pet Sitting Management Business:

1. Research Your Market:
    - Is there demand for pet care in your area?
    - What services are competitors offering?
2. Define Your Services:
    - Dog walking
    - In-home pet sitting
    - Boarding
    - Pet taxi services
3. Recruit Reliable Pet Sitters:
    - Screen candidates thoroughly (background checks are a must)
    - Look for experience and genuine love of animals

4. *Set Up Your Business:*
    - Choose a business name
    - Register your business
    - Get necessary insurance
5. *Create a Website and Online Booking System:*
    - Make it easy for clients to book and pay online
    - Showcase your sitters
6. *Marketing Your Services:*
- Use social media to showcase happy pets and testimonials
- Partner with local veterinarians and pet stores
- Offer referral bonuses to existing clients
7. *Establish Policies and Procedures:*
    - Create clear guidelines for sitters
    - Develop emergency protocols
    - Set cancellation and refund policies

Tools to Make Pet Sitting Management Easier:

1. *Scheduling Software:* Tools like Time To Pet or Rover can help manage bookings and sitter schedules.
2. *Payment Processing:* Use services like Square or Stripe for easy, secure payments.
3. *Communication Apps:* WhatsApp or Slack can keep you connected with your team of sitters.
4. *GPS Tracking:* Apps like Tractive can help sitters (and owners) keep track of dogs during walks.

5. *Customer Relationship Management (CRM):* Software like Dubsado can help manage client information and automate follow-ups.

Maximizing Profits in Pet Sitting Management:

1. *Offer Premium Services:* Charge extra for services like administering medication or caring for exotic pets.
2. *Holiday Surcharges:* Increase rates during peak times like holidays and summer vacations.
3. *Package Deals:* Offer discounts for clients who book regular, recurring services.
4. *Expand Your Offerings:* Consider adding services like pet grooming or training.
5. *Affiliate Marketing:* Earn commissions by recommending pet products to your clients.
6. *Franchise Opportunities:* Once you've established a successful model, consider franchising your business.

Pro Tip: Consider specializing in a niche market, such as exotic pet care or services for senior pets. This can help you stand out in a crowded market.

7. Laundry Service for the Perpetually Wrinkled

Doing laundry is a chore many people would gladly outsource. If you don't mind the occasional spin cycle, starting a laundry service can be a relatively low-effort way to make money.

Why a Laundry Service is Great for the Unmotivated:

1. *Low Startup Costs:* You likely already have the main equipment (washer and dryer).
2. *Flexible Schedule:* Laundry can be done at any time of day.

3. *Minimal Customer Interaction:* Most communication can be done via text or app.
4. *Recurring Clients:* People always need clean clothes.

How to Start a Lazy Laundry Service:

1. *Assess Your Capacity:*
   - How much laundry can you reasonably handle?
   - Do you need to invest in a larger capacity washer or dryer?
2. *Set Your Services and Prices:*
   - Wash and fold
   - Dry cleaning drop-off and pickup
   - Ironing services
   - Delivery options
3. *Create a Simple Business Plan:*
   - Define your target market (busy professionals, college students, families)
   - Outline your pricing strategy
   - Plan for growth and potential challenges
4. *Set Up Your Space:*
   - Designate an area for sorting and folding
   - Invest in good quality laundry baskets and hangers
   - Consider eco-friendly detergent options
5. *Develop a System:*

- Create a tagging system to keep clients' laundry separate
- Establish a clear workflow from pickup to delivery

6. *Market Your Services:*
    - Create flyers for local bulletin boards
    - Use social media to reach potential clients
    - Partner with local businesses (gyms, dorms, office buildings)

Tools to Make Your Laundry Service Easier:

1. *Scheduling Software:* Use tools like Bookafy or Acuity Scheduling for easy booking.
2. *Payment Processing:* Square or PayPal can handle transactions smoothly.
3. *Laundry Management Apps:* Apps like Washlava can help manage orders and track customer preferences.
4. *Delivery Management:* If offering delivery, use apps like Onfleet to optimize routes.

Maximizing Profits in Your Laundry Service:

1. *Offer Rush Services:* Charge a premium for same-day or next-day service.
2. *Eco-Friendly Options:* Use environmentally friendly detergents and charge a bit extra for this service.
3. *Subscription Model:* Offer discounted rates for weekly or monthly subscriptions.
4. *Partner with Local Businesses:* Offer corporate accounts to local gyms, salons, or restaurants for their towel and linen needs.

Chapter 4: Couch Investing - Making Money While Horizontal

5. *Seasonal Promotions:* Offer specials during back-to-school season or before major holidays.

6. *Referral Program:* Encourage word-of-mouth marketing by offering discounts for referrals.

Pro Tip: Consider specializing in handling delicate items or offering stain removal services to differentiate your business and justify higher prices.

8. Virtual Assistant for the Tech-Savvy Sloth

If you're comfortable with technology and have good organizational skills, becoming a virtual assistant can be a flexible and potentially lucrative side hustle.

Why Virtual Assisting is Great for the Unmotivated:

1. *Work from Home:* No need to leave your couch.

2. *Flexible Hours:* Many tasks can be done on your own schedule.

3. *Variety of Tasks:* Keeps things interesting without requiring deep expertise in any one area.

4. *Scalable:* Start with one client and grow as you're comfortable.

Types of Virtual Assistant Services:

1. *Email Management:* Sorting, responding to, and filing emails.

2. *Calendar Management:* Scheduling appointments and managing deadlines.

3. *Social Media Management:* Creating and scheduling posts, engaging with followers.

4. *Basic Bookkeeping:* Tracking expenses, invoicing clients.

5. *Travel Arrangements:* Booking flights, hotels, and creating itineraries.
6. *Data Entry:* Inputting information into spreadsheets or databases.
7. *Customer Service:* Responding to customer inquiries via email or chat.
8. *Research:* Gathering information on various topics.

How to Start as a Virtual Assistant:

1. *Assess Your Skills:*
    - What are you good at?
    - What tasks do you enjoy?
    - What software are you comfortable using?
2. *Define Your Services:*
    - Start with a few core services you're confident in
    - You can always expand your offerings later
3. *Set Your Rates:*
    - Research average rates for virtual assistants
    - Consider starting slightly lower to build your client base
4. *Create an Online Presence:*
    - Set up a simple website showcasing your services
    - Create professional social media profiles (especially LinkedIn)
5. *Find Clients:*

- Use freelance platforms like Upwork or Fiverr
- Network on LinkedIn and in relevant Facebook groups
- Reach out to small business owners in your network

Tools to Make Virtual Assisting Easier:

1. *Project Management:* Trello or Asana for task tracking
2. *Time Tracking:* Toggl or RescueTime to log hours
3. *Communication:* Slack or Zoom for client interactions
4. *File Sharing:* Dropbox or Google Drive for document management
5. *Password Management:* LastPass or 1Password for secure access to client accounts

Maximizing Profits as a Virtual Assistant:

1. *Specialize:* Focus on a specific industry or type of client (e.g., real estate agents, coaches, authors).
2. *Offer Packages:* Create service bundles for common client needs.
3. *Upsell:* Once you've proven your value, offer additional services to existing clients.
4. *Continuous Learning:* Stay updated on new tools and technologies to increase your value.
5. *Automate:* Use tools like Zapier to automate repetitive tasks, allowing you to take on more clients.
6. *Subcontract:* As you grow, consider hiring other VAs to work under you.

Pro Tip: Create templates and standard operating procedures (SOPs) for common tasks. This will save you time and ensure consistency in your work.

9. Freelance Writing for the Wordsmith Wannabe

If you have a way with words (or at least a passing acquaintance with grammar), freelance writing can be a flexible and potentially lucrative side hustle.

Why Freelance Writing is Great for the Unmotivated:

1. *Work from Anywhere:* All you need is a computer and internet connection.
2. *Flexible Hours:* Write when inspiration strikes (or when the deadline looms).
3. *Variety of Topics:* Write about subjects you're interested in or learn about new ones.
4. *Scalable:* Start small with shorter pieces and work up to longer, higher-paying projects.

Types of Freelance Writing:

1. *Blog Posts:* Short, informative articles for websites.
2. *Website Copy:* Creating content for business websites.
3. *Social Media Content:* Crafting engaging posts for various platforms.
4. *Product Descriptions:* Writing compelling descriptions for e-commerce sites.
5. *Email Newsletters:* Creating content for email marketing campaigns.
6. *eBooks:* Longer form content, often used for lead generation.

7. *Technical Writing:* Creating user manuals, how-to guides, etc.
8. *Ghostwriting:* Writing content that will be published under someone else's name.

How to Start Freelance Writing:

1. *Identify Your Niche:*
    - What topics are you knowledgeable about?
    - What kind of writing do you enjoy?
2. *Create a Portfolio:*
    - Write sample pieces in your chosen niche
    - Consider starting a blog to showcase your writing
3. *Set Your Rates:*
    - Research average rates for your type of writing
    - Consider charging per word or per project
4. *Find Clients:*
    - Use freelance platforms like Upwork, Fiverr, or ProBlogger
    - Reach out to businesses in your niche
    - Network with other freelancers for referrals
5. *Develop a Writing Process:*
    - Create an outline before writing
    - Use tools like Grammarly for proofreading
    - Set personal deadlines ahead of client deadlines

Tools to Make Freelance Writing Easier:

1. *Writing Software:* Scrivener or Google Docs for composing
2. *Grammar Checkers:* Grammarly or Hemingway App for proofreading
3. *Productivity Tools:* Focus@Will or for background music to enhance concentration
4. *Research Tools:* Evernote or Pocket for saving and organizing research
5. *Plagiarism Checkers:* Copyscape to ensure originality

Maximizing Profits in Freelance Writing:

1. *Specialize:* Become an expert in a high-paying niche (e.g., technical writing, financial content).
2. *Upsell:* Offer additional services like SEO optimization or social media promotion.
3. *Create Templates:* Develop templates for common types of content to speed up your writing process.
4. *Repurpose Content:* With client permission, adapt content for different platforms to maximize your earnings.
5. *Offer Packages:* Bundle services (e.g., blog post + social media content) for higher value deals.
6. *Continuous Learning:* Stay updated on SEO best practices and content marketing trends to increase your value.

Pro Tip: Consider creating a course or ebook about writing to create a passive income stream alongside your freelance work.

10. Online Tutoring for the Reluctant Scholar

Chapter 4: Couch Investing - Making Money While Horizontal

If you excel in a particular subject but the thought of teaching in a classroom makes you want to hide under your bed, online tutoring might be the perfect side hustle for you.

Why Online Tutoring is Great for the Unmotivated:

1. *Work from Home:* No need to travel to students.
2. *Flexible Schedule:* Choose your own hours.
3. *One-on-One Interaction:* Less stressful than managing a full classroom.
4. *Use Existing Knowledge:* Leverage what you already know.

Subjects You Could Tutor Online:

1. *Academic Subjects:* Math, Science, English, History, etc.
2. *Test Prep:* SAT, ACT, GRE, GMAT, etc.
3. *Languages:* English as a Second Language (ESL) is in high demand.
4. *Music:* Instrument lessons or music theory.
5. *Computer Skills:* Programming, web design, software use.
6. *Arts and Crafts:* Painting, knitting, photography, etc.
7. *Professional Skills:* Business writing, public speaking, Excel, etc.

How to Start Online Tutoring:

1. *Identify Your Subject(s):*
    - What are you knowledgeable and passionate about?
    - What subjects are in high demand?

Chapter 4: Couch Investing - Making Money While Horizontal

2. *Get Certified (If Necessary):*
   - Some subjects or platforms may require certifications
   - Even if not required, certifications can boost your credibility
3. *Choose Your Platform:*
   - Use established tutoring platforms like VIPKid, Chegg, or TutorMe
   - Or go independent with video conferencing tools like Zoom
4. *Create a Compelling Profile:*
   - Highlight your expertise and experience
   - Consider creating a short intro video
5. *Set Your Rates:*
   - Research average rates for your subject and experience level
   - Consider offering an introductory rate to attract initial students
6. *Prepare Your Space:*
   - Ensure you have a quiet area with good lighting
   - Invest in a quality webcam and microphone

Tools to Make Online Tutoring Easier:

1. *Video Conferencing:* Zoom or Skype for live sessions
2. *Interactive Whiteboard:* Bitpaper or Miro for visual explanations

3. *Document Sharing:* Google Docs for collaborative work
4. *Scheduling:* Calendly for easy booking
5. *Payment Processing:* PayPal or Stripe for independent tutors

Maximizing Profits in Online Tutoring:

1. *Specialize:* Focus on high-demand, high-paying subjects or tests.
2. *Group Sessions:* Offer small group tutoring for a lower per-student rate but higher overall earnings.
3. *Create Study Materials:* Develop and sell study guides or practice tests.
4. *Record Sessions:* With student permission, record sessions to create a library of tutorials you can sell.
5. *Offer Packages:* Sell bundles of sessions at a discount to encourage commitment.
6. *Referral Program:* Offer discounts to students who refer new clients.

Pro Tip: Consider creating a YouTube channel with free tutorials. This can serve as both marketing for your tutoring services and a potential source of ad revenue.

Conclusion: Your Lazy Side Hustle Action Plan

Congratulations, aspiring lazy entrepreneur! You've made it through our deep dive into side hustles for the chronically unmotivated. Let's recap with an action plan to get you started on your journey to effortless income:

1. *Assess Your Assets:*
    - What skills do you have?

- What resources (time, space, equipment) are available to you?

2. *Choose Your Hustle:*
    - Pick one (or a few) side hustles that align with your skills and resources
    - Start with the one that requires the least upfront effort or investment
3. *Set Up Your Systems:*
    - Create any necessary accounts or profiles
    - Invest in basic tools or equipment if needed
4. *Start Small:*
    - Begin with a manageable workload
    - Gradually increase as you become more comfortable
5. *Automate and Optimize:*
    - Look for ways to streamline your processes
    - Use tools and apps to minimize manual work
6. *Track Your Earnings:*
    - Keep a record of your income from each side hustle
    - This will help you focus on the most profitable ventures
7. *Reinvest or Expand:*
    - Use early profits to improve your side hustle
    - Or start a new, complementary hustle

Chapter 4: Couch Investing - Making Money While Horizontal

Remember, the key to a successful lazy side hustle is finding a balance between effort and reward. Don't be afraid to try different things until you find what works best for you.

In our next chapter, we'll explore how to boost your credit score without breaking a sweat in "Credit Score Hacking: Boost Your Numbers Without Lifting a Finger." Until then, happy (lazy) hustling, and may your bank account grow as effortlessly as your to-do list!

CHAPTER 6: CREDIT SCORE HACKING: BOOST YOUR NUMBERS WITHOUT LIFTING A FINGER

Welcome back, financial fledglings! You've made it to the chapter that might just change your life – or at least your creditworthiness. We're about to dive into the world of credit score hacking, where we'll turn your natural inclination towards inertia into a superpower for boosting those all-important three digits. Buckle up (or don't, we know moving is hard) as we explore how to make your credit score soar with minimal effort.

1. The Authorized User Trick: Piggyback Your Way to Better Credit

Let's start with perhaps the laziest way to boost your credit score: becoming an authorized user on someone else's credit card. It's like hitching a ride on someone else's good credit habits without having to do any of the work yourself.

Why the Authorized User Trick is Perfect for the Chronically Unmotivated:

1. *Minimal Effort Required:* You don't even need to use the card.
2. *Quick Results:* Can see an impact on your credit score in as little as 30 days.
3. *No Financial Responsibility:* You're not legally responsible for the debt.
4. *Learn by Example:* See how responsible credit use affects a credit score.

How the Authorized User Trick Works:

1. *Find a Credit Mentor:* This should be someone with excellent credit and a long history of on-time payments.

2. *Get Added:* Your credit mentor adds you as an authorized user on their credit card account.
3. *Reap the Benefits:* The entire account history typically gets added to your credit report.
4. *Monitor Your Progress:* Watch as your credit score potentially improves.

Choosing the Right Credit Mentor:

- Look for someone with:
    - A long credit history (ideally 10+ years)
    - Perfect or near-perfect payment history
    - Low credit utilization (under 30%)
    - High credit limit

Best Practices for Authorized Users:

1. *Don't Actually Use the Card:* Remember, the goal is to benefit from the account history, not to spend.
2. *Monitor the Account:* Keep an eye on the account to ensure it continues to be managed responsibly.
3. *Have an Exit Strategy:* Discuss in advance how and when you'll be removed from the account.
4. *Consider Multiple Mentors:* If possible, become an authorized user on more than one account to diversify your credit profile.

Potential Pitfalls to Watch Out For:

1. *Negative Impact:* If your credit mentor mismanages the account, it could hurt your credit score.

2. *Relationship Strain:* Money matters can complicate relationships. Make sure expectations are clear from the start.

3. *Limited Benefit:* Some credit scoring models may give less weight to authorized user accounts.

4. *Removal Shock:* Your score might dip when you're eventually removed from the account.

Pro Tip: Some credit card issuers don't report authorized users to the credit bureaus. Check with the issuer to ensure they do before going through the process.

2. Disputing Like a Boss: Clean Up Your Credit Report from Your Recliner

Next up in our lazy credit-boosting arsenal is the art of credit report disputes. It's like spring cleaning for your credit report, but you can do it without ever leaving your favorite spot on the couch.

Why Disputing is a Couch Potato's Dream:

1. *It's Free:* No need to pay for credit repair services.

2. *Can Be Done Online:* Many disputes can be filed through credit bureau websites.

3. *Potentially Big Impact:* Removing a single negative item can significantly boost your score.

4. *Legal Right:* The Fair Credit Reporting Act gives you the right to dispute inaccurate information.

Types of Items to Dispute:

1. *Inaccurate Personal Information:* Wrong name spellings, addresses, or employment info.

2. *Accounts That Aren't Yours:* Could be due to identity theft or mixed files.

Chapter 6: Credit Score Hacking: Boost Your Numbers Without Lifting a Finger

3. *Incorrect Account Statuses:* Closed accounts reported as open, or vice versa.

4. *Outdated Negative Information:* Most negative items should fall off after 7 years.

5. *Duplicate Accounts:* The same account reported multiple times.

6. *Incorrect Payment History:* Late payments that were actually on time.

7. *Incorrect Balances or Credit Limits:* These can affect your credit utilization ratio.

The Lazy Person's Guide to Disputing:

1. *Get Your Free Credit Reports:* Visit AnnualCreditReport.com to get free reports from all three major bureaus.

2. *Review for Errors:* Look for any inaccuracies or items you don't recognize.

3. *Gather Evidence:* Collect any documents that support your dispute (payment records, identity theft reports, etc.).

4. *File Your Dispute:*

    o Online: Use the credit bureaus' online dispute forms.

    o By Mail: Send a dispute letter along with copies (not originals) of your evidence.

5. *Wait for Results:* The bureau has 30 days to investigate and respond.

6. *Review the Outcome:* If the dispute is resolved in your favor, the item should be removed or corrected.

7. *Rinse and Repeat:* If necessary, dispute with other bureaus or directly with the creditor.

Tips for Successful Disputes:

1. *Be Specific:* Clearly identify which item you're disputing and why.
2. *Keep Records:* Save copies of all correspondence and note dates of any phone calls.
3. *Follow Up:* If you don't hear back within 30 days, contact the bureau.
4. *Consider a Goodwill Letter:* For late payments, try writing a goodwill letter to the creditor asking for removal.
5. *Don't Dispute Everything at Once:* Space out your disputes to avoid raising red flags.

Pro Tip: Set calendar reminders to check your credit reports regularly. You're entitled to one free report from each bureau annually, so you could stagger them and check one every four months.

3. The Magic of On-Time Payments (And How to Never Miss One Again)

Now, we're getting to the heart of credit score improvement: on-time payments. But don't worry, we're going to make this as effortless as possible.

Why On-Time Payments are Crucial (Even for the Lazy):

1. *Biggest Factor:* Payment history accounts for about 35% of your FICO score.
2. *Long-Lasting Impact:* Late payments can stay on your credit report for up to 7 years.

Chapter 6: Credit Score Hacking: Boost Your Numbers Without Lifting a Finger

3. *Builds Trust:* Consistent on-time payments show lenders you're reliable.
4. *Avoid Fees:* Late payments often come with hefty fees.

The Lazy Person's Guide to Never Missing a Payment:

1. *Automate Everything:* Set up automatic payments for all your bills.
2. *Use Credit Card Autopay:* For variable bills, set up automatic payments on your credit card, then set up autopay for the credit card bill.
3. *Set Up Alerts:* Enable text or email alerts for due dates and low balances.
4. *Use Round-Up Apps:* Apps like Digit or Qapital can round up your purchases and set aside money for bills.
5. *Create a Bill Payment Calendar:* Use Google Calendar or a similar app to visualize all your due dates.
6. *Consolidate Due Dates:* Many creditors will let you change your due date. Try to align all your bills around the same time.
7. *Maintain a Buffer:* Keep a small cushion in your checking account to cover any unexpected expenses.

Tools to Make On-Time Payments Effortless:

1. *Mint:* Tracks all your accounts and bills in one place.
2. *Prism:* Aggregates all your bills and lets you pay them from one app.
3. *Bill Pay through Your Bank:* Many banks offer free bill pay services.

4. *PayPal:* Can be used to set up recurring payments for many bills.

   5. *IFTTT (If This Then That):* Create custom reminders and automations.

What to Do If You Miss a Payment:

   1. *Act Fast:* If you realize you've missed a payment, make it as soon as possible.

   2. *Contact the Creditor:* Explain the situation and ask if they can waive the late fee.

   3. *Request a Goodwill Adjustment:* If it's your first late payment, ask if they'll remove it from your credit report.

   4. *Set Up Safeguards:* Use this as a learning experience and set up systems to prevent future missed payments.

Pro Tip: Consider setting up autopay for the minimum payment on credit cards, then manually pay more if you can. This ensures you never miss a payment, even if you can't pay in full.

4. Credit Utilization: The Art of Looking Good While Doing Nothing

Credit utilization is like the Goldilocks of credit factors – you want it to be just right. The good news? Once you set it up correctly, you can mostly forget about it.

Why Credit Utilization Matters (Even to the Lazy):

   1. *Major Impact:* It accounts for about 30% of your FICO score.

2. *Quick Changes:* Unlike other factors, utilization can change rapidly, affecting your score month-to-month.
3. *Easy to Control:* With a few strategies, you can optimize your utilization without much ongoing effort.

The Ideal Credit Utilization:

- Aim for 30% or less of your total available credit.
- For the best scores, shoot for 10% or less.
- But don't go to 0% – using some credit shows you can manage it responsibly.

Lazy Strategies for Optimizing Credit Utilization:

1. *Request Credit Limit Increases:*
   - Higher limits = lower utilization (if spending stays the same)
   - Many issuers let you request increases online or through their app
2. *Set Up Balance Alerts:*
   - Get notified when your balance reaches a certain percentage of your limit
3. *Use Multiple Cards:*
   - Spread your spending across several cards to keep individual utilizations low
4. *Pay Mid-Cycle:*
   - Make a payment before your statement closes to lower reported utilization
5. *Keep Old Accounts Open:*
   - More available credit = lower overall utilization

Chapter 6: Credit Score Hacking: Boost Your Numbers Without Lifting a Finger

6. *Use a Personal Loan for Debt Consolidation:*
   - Can lower utilization and simplify payments

Advanced (But Still Lazy) Utilization Tactics:

1. *The AZEO Method:*
   - All Zero Except One
   - Pay all but one card to zero before the statement closes
   - Leave a small balance (1-2% of the limit) on one card

2. *Credit Cycling:*
   - Use your card heavily early in the billing cycle
   - Pay it off before the statement closes
   - Shows high usage to the card issuer but low utilization to credit bureaus

3. *The 5/24 Strategy:*
   - Keep overall utilization under 5%, but let one card report 24%
   - This combo has been shown to boost scores in some models

Tools to Help Manage Utilization:

1. *Credit Karma:* Tracks your utilization and simulates how changes might affect your score
2. *Mint:* Provides an overview of all your credit accounts and balances
3. *Most Credit Card Apps:* Offer balance alerts and easy payments

Chapter 6: Credit Score Hacking: Boost Your Numbers Without Lifting a Finger

What to Do If Your Utilization is Too High:

1. *Snowball Method:* Focus on paying down the card with the lowest balance first
2. *Avalanche Method:* Focus on the highest interest rate card first
3. *Balance Transfer:* Move high-balance debts to a 0% intro APR card
4. *Ask for a Limit Increase:* A quick call or online request can sometimes do the trick

Pro Tip: If you're applying for a major loan soon, pay down your credit card balances about two months before applying. This gives time for the lower utilization to be reported and reflected in your score.

5. The Credit Mix Magic: Diversify Your Credit Portfolio from Your Couch

Credit mix might only account for 10% of your FICO score, but hey, when we're aiming for credit score perfection, every point counts. And the best part? Once you set up a good credit mix, you can pretty much forget about it.

Why Credit Mix Matters (Even to the Lazy):

1. *Shows Versatility:* Demonstrates you can handle different types of credit.
2. *Improves Score:* A diverse credit mix can boost your score.
3. *Opens Opportunities:* Having experience with various credit types can make future approvals easier.

Types of Credit to Mix In:

1. *Revolving Credit:* Credit cards, store cards, home equity lines of credit

2. *Installment Loans:* Personal loans, auto loans, student loans, mortgages

3. *Open Credit:* Charge cards (like some American Express cards)

4. *Service Credit:* Utilities, cell phone plans (these don't always report to credit bureaus)

The Lazy Person's Guide to Improving Credit Mix:

1. *Take Stock:* Review your current credit mix. What's missing?

2. *Add a Credit Card:* If you only have installment loans, consider adding a credit card.

3. *Consider a Small Personal Loan:* If you only have revolving credit, a small personal loan can diversify your mix.

4. *Use Existing Accounts:* Sometimes just using dormant accounts can improve your mix.

5. *Become an Authorized User:* Get added to someone else's diverse credit accounts.

6. *Look into Credit-Builder Loans:* These loans are designed to help build credit history.

Lazy Strategies for Each Credit Type:

1. *Revolving Credit:*
    - Set up a small recurring charge on a credit card (like a streaming service)
    - Enable autopay for the full balance

2. *Installment Loans:*

Chapter 6: Credit Score Hacking: Boost Your Numbers Without Lifting a Finger

- If you're considering a major purchase, opting for a loan instead of paying cash can diversify your mix
- Set up autopay to ensure on-time payments

3. *Open Credit:*
   - Some charge cards automatically pay in full each month, requiring minimal effort

4. *Service Credit:*
   - Check if your utility companies report to credit bureaus
   - If they do, just paying your regular bills helps your credit mix

Tools to Help Manage Your Credit Mix:

1. *Credit Karma:* Provides an overview of your credit mix and suggests improvements
2. *Experian Boost:* Can add utility and phone bills to your Experian credit report
3. *Self:* Offers credit-builder loans and a secured credit card in one package

What Not to Do When Improving Credit Mix:

1. *Don't Open Accounts You Don't Need:* Only add new credit if it makes sense for your financial situation.
2. *Avoid High-Interest Debt:* Don't take on expensive debt just to improve your mix.
3. *Don't Close Old Accounts:* Keeping accounts open (even if unused) can help your credit history length.
4. *Don't Overextend Yourself:* Only take on new credit you can comfortably manage.

Chapter 6: Credit Score Hacking: Boost Your Numbers Without Lifting a Finger

Pro Tip: If you're considering adding a new type of credit, look for options with no annual fee and low interest rates. This way, even if you rarely use it, it won't cost you anything to keep it open.

6. The Length of Credit History Hack: Time Is On Your Side

When it comes to the length of your credit history, laziness is actually a virtue. The longer your accounts stay open, the better it is for your credit score. So sit back, relax, and let time do the work for you.

Why Length of Credit History Matters (Even to the Lazy):

1. *Shows Stability:* A long credit history demonstrates you're a stable borrower.
2. *Improves Score:* Accounts for about 15% of your FICO score.
3. *Builds Trust:* Lenders like to see a track record of responsible credit use over time.

What Factors into Length of Credit History:

1. *Age of Your Oldest Account:* The longer, the better.
2. *Average Age of All Your Accounts:* A higher average is generally better.
3. *Age of Specific Types of Accounts:* Having long-standing accounts of different types can be beneficial.
4. *How Long It's Been Since You Used Certain Accounts:* Recently used accounts may be weighted more heavily.

The Lazy Person's Guide to Maximizing Credit History Length:

1. *Keep Old Accounts Open:* Resist the urge to close old credit cards, even if you rarely use them.

2. *Use It or Lose It:* Make a small purchase on old cards occasionally to keep them active.

3. *Become an Authorized User:* Get added to an older account to potentially boost your average account age.

4. *Think Twice Before Opening New Accounts:* New accounts will lower your average account age.

5. *Be Patient:* Sometimes, the best strategy is simply to wait and let your accounts age naturally.

6. *Set It and Forget It:* Put a small recurring charge on old credit cards and set up autopay.

Strategies for Different Credit History Situations:

1. For Those with a Short Credit History:
    - Become an authorized user on an older account
    - Consider a secured credit card if you can't get approved for traditional cards
    - Look into credit-builder loans

2. For Those with a Medium-Length History:
    - Focus on keeping all your current accounts open and in good standing
    - Be selective about opening new accounts

3. For Those with a Long Credit History:
    - Maintain your oldest accounts, even if you don't use them often
    - Consider consolidating newer, unused accounts

Chapter 6: Credit Score Hacking: Boost Your Numbers Without Lifting a Finger

Tools to Help Manage Your Credit History Length:

1. *Credit Karma:* Shows the age of your oldest and newest accounts, as well as your average account age
2. *AnnualCreditReport.com:* Provides free access to your credit reports, which include account opening dates
3. *ExtraCredit:* Offers features to help you build and maintain a strong credit history

What Not to Do When Managing Credit History Length:

1. *Don't Close Old Accounts:* Even if you're not using them, keep them open to maintain your length of credit history.
2. *Avoid Churning Credit Cards:* While sign-up bonuses are tempting, constantly opening new cards can lower your average account age.
3. *Don't Ignore Old Accounts:* Inactive accounts may be closed by the issuer, so use them occasionally.
4. *Don't Cosign Lightly:* Cosigning a loan will add a new account to your credit history, potentially lowering your average account age.

Pro Tip: If you must close a credit card, try to close your newest one rather than your oldest. And if an issuer closes an old, unused account, consider calling them to see if they'll reopen it.

7. The New Credit Conundrum: How to Grow Your Credit Without Hurting Your Score

New credit can be a double-edged sword. On one hand, it can increase your available credit and potentially improve your credit mix. On the other, it can lower your average

Chapter 6: Credit Score Hacking: Boost Your Numbers Without Lifting a Finger

account age and result in hard inquiries on your credit report. Let's explore how to navigate this conundrum with minimal effort.

Why New Credit Matters (Even to the Lazy):

1. *Short-Term Impact:* New credit applications can temporarily lower your score.

2. *Long-Term Benefit:* Successfully managing new credit can improve your score over time.

3. *Shows Lenders Your Current Situation:* Recent credit activity gives lenders insight into your current creditworthiness.

Factors Related to New Credit:

1. *Number of Recently Opened Accounts:* Too many new accounts in a short time can be a red flag.

2. *Number of Hard Inquiries:* Each application for credit typically results in a hard inquiry, which can slightly lower your score.

3. *Time Since Last Credit Account Opening:* Lenders like to see that you're not constantly seeking new credit.

4. *Re-establishment of Credit After Payment Problems:* Opening new accounts after past credit issues can show you're back on track.

The Lazy Person's Guide to Managing New Credit:

1. *Space Out Applications:* Wait at least six months between credit applications when possible.

2. *Research Before Applying:* Use pre-qualification tools to gauge your approval odds without a hard inquiry.

3. *Leverage Existing Relationships:* Your current bank or credit card issuers may offer pre-approved offers.

4. *Consider Authorized User Status:* Get the benefit of a new account without the hard inquiry.

5. *Time Your Applications:* If you need to apply for multiple forms of credit, do it within a short timeframe (2-4 weeks) so the inquiries may be treated as a single inquiry for scoring purposes.

6. *Let Inquiries Age:* Hard inquiries typically only affect your score for 12 months, so sometimes the best strategy is to wait it out.

Strategies for Different New Credit Situations:

1. *For Those Building Credit:*
    - Start with a secured credit card or become an authorized user
    - Graduate to unsecured cards as your credit improves
    - Space out applications to avoid too many inquiries

2. *For Those with Established Credit:*
    - Be selective about new credit applications
    - Take advantage of pre-approved offers from existing creditors
    - Consider the long-term value of a new account, not just sign-up bonuses

3. *For Those Recovering from Credit Issues:*
    - Look for secured or credit-builder products
    - Show responsible use of new credit to improve your score over time

Chapter 6: Credit Score Hacking: Boost Your Numbers Without Lifting a Finger

- Be patient – time is a crucial factor in credit recovery

Tools to Help Manage New Credit:

1. *Credit Karma:* Offers Approval Odds to help you gauge your chances before applying
2. *CardMatch:* Shows personalized credit card offers without affecting your credit score
3. *AnnualCreditReport.com:* Check your credit reports to see recent inquiries and new accounts

What Not to Do When Managing New Credit:

1. *Don't Apply for Multiple Cards at Once:* This can look like desperation for credit to lenders.
2. *Avoid Applying for Credit Right Before a Major Loan:* New credit applications can lower your score right when you need it most.
3. *Don't Fall for the "More Cards = Better Credit" Myth:* Quality of credit management matters more than quantity of accounts.
4. *Don't Apply for Store Cards Just for a One-Time Discount:* The long-term impact on your credit might not be worth the savings.

Pro Tip: If you're denied for a credit card, call the reconsideration line. Sometimes a human review can overturn an automatic denial, saving you from having to apply elsewhere and incur another hard inquiry.

8. The Credit Monitoring Mastery: Keeping an Eye on Your Score Without Obsessing

Credit monitoring is crucial for maintaining and improving your credit score, but it doesn't have to be a full-time job.

Chapter 6: Credit Score Hacking: Boost Your Numbers Without Lifting a Finger

Let's explore how to keep tabs on your credit with minimal effort.

Why Credit Monitoring Matters (Even to the Lazy):

1. *Catch Errors Early:* Spot and dispute inaccuracies before they can do serious damage.
2. *Detect Fraud:* Quickly identify suspicious activity that could indicate identity theft.
3. *Track Progress:* See how your credit-building efforts are paying off over time.
4. *Stay Informed:* Know your credit status before applying for loans or credit cards.

The Lazy Person's Guide to Credit Monitoring:

1. *Use Free Credit Monitoring Services:* Sites like Credit Karma, Credit Sesame, and WalletHub offer free credit score updates and monitoring.
2. *Set Up Alerts:* Most credit monitoring services allow you to set up notifications for significant changes to your credit report.
3. *Check Your Free Annual Credit Reports:* Use AnnualCreditReport.com to get your free reports from each bureau once a year.
4. *Leverage Credit Card Issuer Tools:* Many credit cards now offer free credit score access and basic monitoring.
5. *Use a Password Manager:* Safely store login information for various credit monitoring sites to make checking your credit hassle-free.
6. *Set Calendar Reminders:* Schedule periodic check-ins to review your credit in more depth.

Chapter 6: Credit Score Hacking: Boost Your Numbers Without Lifting a Finger

Types of Credit Monitoring to Consider:

1. *Basic Credit Score Monitoring:*
    - Free services that provide regular updates to your credit score
    - Examples: Credit Karma, Credit Sesame
2. *Credit Report Monitoring:*
    - Services that track changes to your full credit report
    - Examples: Experian CreditWorks, TransUnion Credit Monitoring
3. *Identity Theft Monitoring:*
    - More comprehensive services that monitor your personal information across the web
    - Examples: LifeLock, Identity Guard
4. *Dark Web Monitoring:*
    - Advanced monitoring that scans the dark web for your personal information
    - Often included in premium identity theft protection services

Tools for Effortless Credit Monitoring:

1. *Credit Karma:* Free credit scores, reports, and monitoring from TransUnion and Equifax
2. *Experian:* Free FICO score and basic monitoring of your Experian credit report
3. *CreditWise from Capital One:* Free TransUnion credit score and report monitoring (available even if you're not a Capital One customer)

4. *Mint:* Free credit score monitoring integrated with budgeting tools

   5. *MyFICO:* Paid service offering FICO scores from all three bureaus and comprehensive monitoring

What to Monitor:

   1. *Credit Score Changes:* Look for significant fluctuations.

   2. *New Accounts:* Make sure all new accounts were opened by you.

   3. *Hard Inquiries:* Check that all credit applications were initiated by you.

   4. *Account Balances and Payments:* Ensure reported information is accurate.

   5. *Negative Items:* Watch for any new negative marks on your report.

   6. *Personal Information:* Verify that all personal details are correct.

How Often to Check:

   1. *Credit Scores:* Monthly is usually sufficient for most people.

   2. *Credit Reports:* At least once a year, or once every four months if you stagger your free annual reports.

   3. *Alerts:* Set these up to notify you immediately of significant changes.

What to Do If You Spot an Issue:

   1. *For Errors:* File a dispute with the credit bureau reporting the inaccuracy.

2. *For Fraud:* Place a fraud alert on your credit reports and consider a credit freeze.

3. *For Negative (But Accurate) Information:* Focus on improving your credit habits going forward.

Pro Tip: Don't obsess over small, short-term fluctuations in your credit score. Focus on the overall trend over time and major changes that might indicate a problem.

9. The Debt Payoff Paradigm: Snowballs, Avalanches, and Other Effortless Strategies

Paying off debt is a crucial step in improving your credit score, but it doesn't have to be painful or require constant attention. Let's explore some lazy-friendly strategies for debt payoff.

Why Debt Payoff Matters (Even to the Lazy):

1. *Improves Credit Utilization:* Paying down debt lowers your credit utilization ratio, boosting your score.

2. *Builds Positive Payment History:* Consistent payments improve your credit over time.

3. *Reduces Financial Stress:* Less debt means fewer bills to manage and less interest to pay.

4. *Frees Up Future Income:* Once debt is paid off, you have more money for other financial goals (or lazy pursuits).

The Lazy Person's Guide to Debt Payoff:

1. *Choose a Strategy:* Pick a debt payoff method that aligns with your personality and goals.

2. *Automate Payments:* Set up automatic payments for at least the minimum on all debts.

Chapter 6: Credit Score Hacking: Boost Your Numbers Without Lifting a Finger

3. *Use Windfalls Wisely:* Apply unexpected money (tax refunds, bonuses, gifts) to debt.
4. *Consider Balance Transfers:* Move high-interest debt to a 0% intro APR card to save on interest.
5. *Negotiate Lower Interest Rates:* A single phone call to your creditors could save you money over time.
6. *Use Debt Payoff Apps:* Let technology track your progress and motivate you.

Popular Debt Payoff Strategies:

1. *Debt Snowball:*
    - Focus on paying off the smallest debt first
    - Provides quick wins for motivation
    - Good for those who need to see progress to stay motivated
2. *Debt Avalanche:*
    - Focus on the highest interest rate debt first
    - Saves the most money in interest over time
    - Ideal for those who are motivated by long-term savings
3. *Debt Consolidation:*
    - Combine multiple debts into one loan or balance transfer card
    - Simplifies payments and potentially lowers interest rates
    - Good for those who feel overwhelmed by multiple payments
4. *Debt Snowflaking:*

Chapter 6: Credit Score Hacking: Boost Your Numbers Without Lifting a Finger

- o Apply small, unexpected savings to debt
- o Can be combined with other strategies
- o Perfect for those who want to make progress without changing their budget

5. *Debt Chunking:*
   - o Pay off debt in large chunks using windfalls or savings
   - o Can make significant progress quickly
   - o Ideal for those with irregular income or who receive large bonuses

Tools for Effortless Debt Payoff:

1. *Undebt.it:* Free debt snowball and avalanche calculator and tracking
2. *Tally:* App that manages credit card payments and helps you pay off debt faster
3. *Debt Payoff Planner:* App that creates a debt payoff plan and tracks progress
4. *Digit:* Automatically saves small amounts and can apply them to debt
5. *You Need A Budget (YNAB):* Budgeting app with debt payoff features

Lazy Hacks for Faster Debt Payoff:

1. *Round Up Payments:* If your minimum payment is $37, pay $40. Small increases add up over time.
2. *Make Bi-Weekly Payments:* Instead of one monthly payment, make half the payment every two weeks. You'll make an extra payment each year without really noticing.

Chapter 6: Credit Score Hacking: Boost Your Numbers Without Lifting a Finger

3. *Use Cash Back Rewards:* Apply any cash back from credit cards directly to your debt.

4. *Set Up Payment Reminders:* Use calendar alerts or apps to remind you when payments are due.

5. *Utilize the Spare Change:* Use apps like Acorns or Qapital to round up purchases and apply the difference to debt.

What to Do If You're Struggling with Debt Payoff:

1. *Consider Credit Counseling:* Non-profit credit counseling agencies can provide advice and may help negotiate with creditors.

2. *Look Into Income-Driven Repayment Plans:* For student loans, these plans can make payments more manageable.

3. *Explore Hardship Programs:* Many creditors offer temporary hardship programs with reduced interest rates or payments.

4. *Consider a Side Hustle:* Even a small amount of extra income can accelerate debt payoff.

5. *Don't Be Afraid to Seek Help:* If you're feeling overwhelmed, talk to a financial advisor or therapist specializing in financial stress.

Pro Tip: Create a visual representation of your debt payoff journey. Something as simple as a paper chain where you remove a link for each $100 paid off can be surprisingly motivating.

10. The Credit Score Maintenance Mode: Keeping Your Score High with Minimal Effort

Chapter 6: Credit Score Hacking: Boost Your Numbers Without Lifting a Finger

Congratulations! You've improved your credit score. Now, how do you maintain it without constant vigilance? Let's explore how to keep your credit score high on autopilot.

Why Maintenance Matters (Even to the Lazy):

1. *Preserves Hard Work:* Keeps your improved score from slipping.
2. *Opens Opportunities:* A consistently high score means better terms on future credit.
3. *Reduces Stress:* Knowing your credit is in good shape provides peace of mind.
4. *Saves Time:* Maintaining is easier than rebuilding credit from scratch.

The Lazy Person's Guide to Credit Score Maintenance:

1. *Set It and Forget It:* Automate all bill payments to ensure on-time payments.
2. *Use Alerts:* Set up balance and payment due alerts to stay on top of your accounts without constant checking.
3. *Implement the AZEO Strategy:* Allow one card to report a small balance while paying others in full.
4. *Keep Old Accounts Active:* Set up a small recurring charge on older credit cards to keep them active.
5. *Limit Hard Inquiries:* Only apply for new credit when necessary.
6. *Use Credit Monitoring:* Sign up for a free credit monitoring service to catch any issues early.
7. *Periodically Review Credit Reports:* Check your full credit reports once a year for any errors.

Chapter 6: Credit Score Hacking: Boost Your Numbers Without Lifting a Finger

Maintenance Strategies for Different Credit Score Ranges:

1. *For Excellent Credit (750+):*
    - Focus on maintaining current habits
    - Be selective about new credit applications
    - Consider using credit cards for all purchases (and paying in full) to maximize rewards
2. *For Good Credit (700-749):*
    - Look for opportunities to lower credit utilization
    - Consider requesting credit limit increases
    - Be patient – length of credit history will improve naturally over time
3. *For Fair Credit (650-699):*
    - Continue to pay down any existing debt
    - Look for opportunities to diversify credit mix
    - Be extra vigilant about on-time payments

Tools for Effortless Credit Score Maintenance:

1. *Mint:* Integrates credit score monitoring with budgeting tools
2. *CreditWise:* Provides TransUnion VantageScore 3.0 and credit report monitoring
3. *Experian Boost:* Allows you to add utility and streaming service payments to your Experian credit report
4. *FICO Score Simulator:* Helps predict how different actions might affect your score
5. *Credit Karma:* Offers free credit monitoring and score tracking from two bureaus

Chapter 6: Credit Score Hacking: Boost Your Numbers Without Lifting a Finger

Lazy Hacks for Long-Term Credit Health:

1. *The "Set a Calendar Reminder" Trick:* Set an annual reminder to review your full credit reports and overall credit strategy.

2. *The "Credit Limit Increase" Ritual:* Once a year, request credit limit increases on your cards to keep utilization low.

3. *The "Rotation" Method:* Rotate which credit card you use for small purchases to keep all accounts active.

4. *The "Autopay and Forget" Approach:* Set up autopay for the full balance on all credit cards, then use them like debit cards.

5. *The "Lazy Person's Credit Mix":* Maintain one installment loan (like a car loan or personal loan) alongside 2-3 credit cards for an optimal credit mix.

What to Watch Out For in Maintenance Mode:

1. *Complacency:* Don't ignore your credit just because it's good. Set up monitoring to catch any issues.

2. *Lifestyle Inflation:* As your credit improves and you qualify for higher limits, resist the urge to overspend.

3. *Closing Old Accounts:* Keep old accounts open to maintain a long average age of accounts.

4. *Cosigning:* Be cautious about cosigning loans, as it can impact your credit if the primary borrower doesn't pay.

5. *Identity Theft:* Even with good credit, you're not immune to fraud. Stay vigilant.

Chapter 6: Credit Score Hacking: Boost Your Numbers Without Lifting a Finger

Pro Tip: Create a "credit maintenance" email folder. Direct all credit-related emails (statements, alerts, etc.) to this folder for easy reference and organization.

Conclusion: Your Lazy Credit Score Action Plan

Congratulations, credit score optimizer! You've made it through our deep dive into effortless credit improvement. Let's recap with an action plan to get you started on your journey to a better credit score:

1. *Assess Your Current Situation:*
    - Get your free credit reports from AnnualCreditReport.com
    - Sign up for a free credit monitoring service
2. *Set Up Your Lazy Credit Foundation:*
    - Automate all bill payments
    - Set up balance and due date alerts for all credit accounts
3. *Implement Quick Wins:*
    - Become an authorized user on a responsible person's credit card
    - Request credit limit increases on existing cards
4. *Develop Your Lazy Debt Payoff Strategy:*
    - Choose between the snowball or avalanche method
    - Set up automatic extra payments towards your target debt
5. *Optimize Your Credit Mix:*

- Ensure you have a mix of credit card and installment accounts
- Consider a credit-builder loan if needed

6. *Establish Your Maintenance Routine:*
    - Set calendar reminders for annual credit check-ups
    - Implement the AZEO strategy for optimal credit utilization

7. *Protect Your Progress:*
    - Set up fraud alerts or consider a credit freeze
    - Be cautious about applying for new credit

Remember, the key to lazy credit optimization is setting up systems that work for you in the background. Once you've implemented these strategies, you can largely sit back and watch your credit score improve over time.

In our next chapter, we'll explore how to tackle taxes with minimal effort in "Taxes for Dummies (and Proud of It)." Until then, happy credit building, and may your score always be higher than your stress levels!

CHAPTER 7: TAXES FOR DUMMIES (AND PROUD OF IT)

Welcome back, financial fledglings! You've made it to the chapter that might just save you money and headaches: taxes. Don't worry, we're going to make this as painless as possible. We'll explore how to tackle your taxes with minimal effort and maximum returns. So sit back, relax, and let's dive into the world of lazy tax management.

1. Free File Alliance: Because Paying for Tax Software is So Last Year

Let's start with perhaps the laziest way to file your taxes: using free software provided by the IRS and its partners. Yes, you read that right – free!

Why Free File is Perfect for the Chronically Unmotivated:

1. *It's Free:* No need to shell out money for tax software.
2. *User-Friendly:* Designed for people who aren't tax experts.
3. *Accessible:* Can be done from the comfort of your couch.
4. *Accurate:* These programs are designed to catch common errors.

How Free File Works:

The Free File program is a partnership between the IRS and tax software companies. Here's how to use it:

1. *Check Eligibility:* Free File is available to taxpayers with an Adjusted Gross Income (AGI) of $73,000 or less (as of 2023).
2. *Choose a Provider:* Visit the IRS Free File website and select a participating company.

Chapter 7: Taxes for Dummies (and Proud of It)

3. *Create an Account:* You'll need to set up an account with the provider you choose.
4. *Answer Questions:* The software will guide you through a series of questions about your income and deductions.
5. *Review and File:* Once you've entered all your information, review for accuracy and submit.

Popular Free File Options:

1. *TurboTax Free Edition:*
   - Known for its user-friendly interface
   - Good for simple returns
2. *H&R Block Free Online:*
   - Offers a robust free version
   - Includes unemployment income reporting
3. *TaxAct Free Edition:*
   - Provides free phone support
   - Includes a price-lock guarantee
4. *FreeTaxUSA:*
   - Offers free federal filing for all income levels
   - State returns for a low fee
5. *Credit Karma Tax:*
   - Completely free for both federal and state returns
   - Includes audit support

Tips for Using Free File:

1. *Gather Your Documents:* Have all your W-2s, 1099s, and other tax documents ready before you start.

2. *Take Your Time:* There's no need to rush. You can save your progress and come back later.

3. *Double-Check Your Work:* Even though the software checks for errors, it's always good to review everything yourself.

4. *Don't Assume You Don't Qualify:* Even if you've paid for software in the past, check if you're eligible for Free File this year.

5. *Consider State Taxes:* Some providers offer free state returns, while others charge a fee. Factor this in when choosing a provider.

What to Watch Out For:

1. *Upsells:* Some providers may try to get you to upgrade to paid versions. Stick to the free version if it meets your needs.

2. *Eligibility Changes:* The income threshold for Free File can change from year to year. Always check the current year's requirements.

3. *Limited Support:* Free versions may not offer as much support as paid versions. Be prepared to do a bit more research on your own if you have questions.

Pro Tip: If your income is just over the Free File limit, look for ways to reduce your AGI, such as contributing to a traditional IRA or increasing 401(k) contributions. This could bring you under the threshold and allow you to use Free File.

2. Deductions You Didn't Know You Could Take

Now that we've covered how to file for free, let's talk about ways to keep more of your hard-earned money. There are many deductions available that you might not be aware of.

Chapter 7: Taxes for Dummies (and Proud of It)

Remember, every dollar you deduct is a dollar less of taxable income!

Why Deductions Matter (Even to the Lazy):

1. *Save Money:* Deductions reduce your taxable income, potentially lowering your tax bill.
2. *Reward Good Behavior:* Many deductions incentivize financially responsible actions.
3. *Customize Your Taxes:* Deductions allow you to tailor your tax return to your specific situation.

Common Deductions You Might Be Missing:

1. *Student Loan Interest:*
   - You can deduct up to $2,500 of interest paid on student loans.
   - This is an "above-the-line" deduction, meaning you can take it even if you don't itemize.
2. *State Sales Tax:*
   - If your state doesn't have income tax, you can deduct state sales tax instead.
   - The IRS provides tables to help you estimate this if you didn't keep all your receipts.
3. *Charitable Donations:*
   - Donations to qualified organizations are deductible if you itemize.
   - Don't forget non-cash donations, like clothes or household items given to Goodwill.
4. *Job Search Expenses:*

Chapter 7: Taxes for Dummies (and Proud of It)

- If you're looking for a job in your current field, expenses like resume preparation and travel to interviews may be deductible.

5. *Self-Employed Health Insurance:*
    - If you're self-employed, you can deduct 100% of your health insurance premiums.

6. *Moving Expenses for Military:*
    - Active-duty military members can deduct unreimbursed moving expenses for a military-ordered move.

7. *Educator Expenses:*
    - K-12 teachers can deduct up to $250 for unreimbursed classroom supplies.

8. *Energy-Efficient Home Improvements:*
    - Installing solar panels, wind turbines, or geothermal heat pumps can lead to substantial tax credits.

9. *Medical Expenses:*
    - If your medical expenses exceed 7.5% of your AGI, you can deduct the amount over that threshold.

10. *Gambling Losses:*
    - If you itemize, you can deduct gambling losses up to the amount of your winnings.

The Lazy Person's Guide to Maximizing Deductions:

1. *Use Tax Software:* Most tax software will ask you questions to determine which deductions you qualify for.

Chapter 7: Taxes for Dummies (and Proud of It)

2. *Keep Digital Records:* Use apps like Expensify or Evernote to easily track deductible expenses throughout the year.

3. *Set Up Separate Accounts:* Use a separate credit card or bank account for potentially deductible expenses to make tracking easier.

4. *Automate Charitable Giving:* Set up recurring donations to your favorite charities to ensure you have deductions come tax time.

5. *Use a Health Savings Account (HSA):* Contributions are tax-deductible, and withdrawals for qualified medical expenses are tax-free.

What to Watch Out For:

1. *Eligibility Requirements:* Many deductions have specific eligibility criteria. Make sure you qualify before claiming a deduction.

2. *Documentation:* Keep receipts and records for any deductions you claim. Digital copies are fine for most purposes.

3. *Standard vs. Itemized Deduction:* Calculate whether itemizing or taking the standard deduction will save you more money.

4. *Phase-Outs:* Some deductions phase out at higher income levels. Be aware of these limitations.

Pro Tip: Consider bunching deductions. If you're close to the threshold for itemizing, try to concentrate deductible expenses in a single tax year. For example, make two years' worth of charitable contributions in December of one year and January of the next.

3. The Procrastinator's Guide to April 15th

Chapter 7: Taxes for Dummies (and Proud of It)

Alright, let's face it. Despite our best intentions, sometimes we find ourselves staring down the barrel of the tax deadline without having done a thing. Don't panic! Here's how to handle your taxes when you've waited until the last minute.

Why Last-Minute Filing Happens (Even to the Best of Us):

1. *Busy Lives:* Sometimes taxes just fall to the bottom of the to-do list.
2. *Anxiety:* Fear of owing money or making mistakes can lead to procrastination.
3. *Missing Documents:* Waiting on that one last form can delay the whole process.
4. *Complexity:* If your tax situation is complicated, it's easy to put it off.

The Lazy Person's Last-Minute Tax Plan:

1. *File for an Extension:*
    - Form 4868 gives you an extra six months to file.
    - Remember: This is an extension to file, not to pay. If you owe taxes, you still need to estimate and pay by the original deadline to avoid penalties.
2. *Gather Your Documents:*
    - W-2s from employers
    - 1099s for any freelance work or investments
    - Receipts for deductible expenses
    - Last year's tax return
3. *Choose Your Filing Method:*
    - Free File (if you qualify)

- Tax software (many offer last-minute deals)
- Tax preparer (some offer extended hours near the deadline)

4. *Consider Filing Electronically:*
   - E-filing is faster and you'll get confirmation that the IRS received your return.
   - Many e-file options are available up until midnight on tax day.

5. *Pay What You Can:*
   - If you can't pay your full tax bill, pay as much as you can to minimize penalties and interest.
   - Look into IRS payment plans for the remainder.

Last-Minute Filing Tips:

1. *Use the IRS Free File Fillable Forms:* If you're comfortable with basic tax concepts, these forms can be a quick way to file.
2. *Take Advantage of 24/7 Options:* Many online tax preparation services offer round-the-clock support as the deadline approaches.
3. *Don't Forget State Taxes:* Many states have the same filing deadline as federal taxes.
4. *Double-Check Everything:* When rushing, it's easy to make mistakes. Take a few extra minutes to review your return.
5. *Keep Proof of Filing:* If e-filing, save the confirmation. If mailing, use certified mail for proof of timely filing.

What to Do If You Miss the Deadline:

Chapter 7: Taxes for Dummies (and Proud of It)

1. *File As Soon As Possible:* The longer you wait, the more penalties and interest can accrue.
2. *Pay What You Can:* Even a partial payment can help reduce penalties.
3. *Look Into First-Time Penalty Abatement:* If you have a clean tax history, you might qualify for penalty relief.
4. *Consider Professional Help:* A tax professional can help you navigate late filing and minimize negative consequences.

Pro Tip: Set a reminder for next year to start your taxes earlier. Even gathering documents a month before the deadline can make the process much less stressful.

4. Navigating the Gig Economy: Taxes for Side Hustlers

In today's world, many of us have side hustles or gig work in addition to our regular jobs. While this can be great for your bank account, it can complicate your taxes. Let's break down how to handle taxes for your side hustle without breaking a sweat.

Why Gig Economy Taxes Matter (Even to the Lazy):

1. *Avoid Surprises:* Proper planning prevents a shocking tax bill.
2. *Stay Legal:* The IRS takes self-employment income seriously.
3. *Maximize Deductions:* Gig work often comes with deductible expenses.
4. *Future Benefits:* Properly reported income can increase your Social Security benefits later.

The Lazy Person's Guide to Gig Economy Taxes:

1. *Keep Good Records:*

- Use apps like QuickBooks Self-Employed or Hurdlr to track income and expenses.
- Take photos of receipts with your phone for easy record-keeping.

2. *Understand Your Tax Forms:*
   - You'll likely receive 1099 forms from companies you worked for.
   - If you earned $400 or more from self-employment, you need to report it.

3. *Pay Quarterly Estimated Taxes:*
   - If you expect to owe $1,000 or more in taxes, you should make quarterly payments.
   - Use Form 1040-ES to calculate and pay these taxes.

4. *Know Your Deductions:*
   - Common deductions include mileage, home office, supplies, and part of your phone and internet bills.
   - Keep track of these expenses throughout the year.

5. *Consider a Separate Bank Account:*
   - Use a dedicated account for your gig income and expenses to simplify tracking.

Common Deductions for Gig Workers:

1. *Mileage:* If you drive for your gig, you can deduct either actual expenses or use the standard mileage rate.

2. *Home Office:* If you have a dedicated space for your gig work, you may be able to deduct a portion of your rent or mortgage interest.

3. *Equipment:* Computers, cameras, or other equipment used for your gig can be deductible.

4. *Health Insurance Premiums:* Self-employed individuals can often deduct their health insurance costs.

5. *Retirement Contributions:* Contributions to a SEP IRA or Solo 401(k) can be deductible.

6. *Professional Development:* Courses or conferences related to your gig work may be deductible.

Tools for Effortless Gig Economy Tax Management:

1. *QuickBooks Self-Employed:* Tracks income, expenses, and mileage; estimates quarterly taxes.

2. *Stride Tax:* Free app for tracking mileage and expenses.

3. *TurboTax Self-Employed:* Includes a feature to search for industry-specific deductions.

4. *Wave:* Free accounting software good for freelancers and small businesses.

5. *MileIQ:* Automatic mileage tracking app.

What to Watch Out For:

1. *Mixing Personal and Business Expenses:* Keep them separate to avoid headaches at tax time.

2. *Underreporting Income:* Report all your income, even if you didn't receive a 1099 for it.

3. *Overstating Deductions:* Be honest about your deductions. Inflating them can lead to audits.

Chapter 7: Taxes for Dummies (and Proud of It)

4. *Forgetting About Self-Employment Tax:* This is an additional 15.3% tax on your net earnings.

5. *Missing Quarterly Payments:* These are due April 15, June 15, September 15, and January 15.

Pro Tip: Consider setting aside 25-30% of your gig income for taxes. This should cover both income tax and self-employment tax for most people.

5. Tax-Advantaged Accounts: Your Lazy Path to a Lower Tax Bill

One of the easiest ways to reduce your tax bill is to take advantage of tax-advantaged accounts. These accounts allow you to save money on taxes now or in the future, often while saving for important goals like retirement or healthcare.

Why Tax-Advantaged Accounts Matter (Even to the Lazy):

1. *Automatic Savings:* Many of these accounts can be funded through automatic payroll deductions.

2. *Lower Taxable Income:* Contributions to some accounts can reduce your taxable income for the year.

3. *Tax-Free Growth:* Money in these accounts can grow tax-free.

4. *Future Benefits:* You're saving on taxes while also saving for important life goals.

Types of Tax-Advantaged Accounts:

1. *Traditional 401(k):*
   - Contributions are pre-tax, reducing your taxable income.
   - Withdrawals in retirement are taxed as ordinary income.

Chapter 7: Taxes for Dummies (and Proud of It)

- o Many employers offer matching contributions (free money!).

2. Roth 401(k):
    - o Contributions are after-tax.
    - o Withdrawals in retirement are tax-free.
    - o Good option if you expect to be in a higher tax bracket in retirement.

3. Traditional IRA:
    - o Contributions may be tax-deductible, depending on your income and whether you have a work retirement plan.
    - o Withdrawals in retirement are taxed as ordinary income.

4. Roth IRA:
    - o Contributions are after-tax.
    - o Withdrawals in retirement are tax-free.
    - o Income limits apply for direct contributions.

5. Health Savings Account (HSA):
    - o Triple tax advantage: contributions are tax-deductible, grow tax-free, and withdrawals for qualified medical expenses are tax-free.
    - o Must have a high-deductible health plan to contribute.

6. 529 College Savings Plan:
    - o Contributions grow tax-free.
    - o Withdrawals for qualified education expenses are tax-free.

Chapter 7: Taxes for Dummies (and Proud of It)

- Some states offer tax deductions for contributions.

The Lazy Person's Guide to Tax-Advantaged Accounts:

1. *Start with Your Employer's Plan:*
- If your employer offers a 401(k) with matching, contribute at least enough to get the full match.
- Set up automatic contributions from your paycheck.

2. *Open an IRA:*
   - Choose between Traditional and Roth based on your current and expected future tax brackets.
   - Set up automatic monthly contributions from your bank account.

3. *Consider an HSA:*
   - If you have a high-deductible health plan, max out your HSA contributions.
   - Many HSAs allow you to invest the funds, potentially leading to tax-free growth.

4. *Use a 529 for Education Savings:*
   - If you have kids (or plan to), open a 529 plan.
   - Some plans allow automatic contributions from your bank account.

5. *Maximize Your Contributions:*
   - Try to contribute the maximum allowed to each account type.
   - If you can't max out everything, prioritize accounts with employer matching, then HSAs, then IRAs.

Chapter 7: Taxes for Dummies (and Proud of It)

Lazy Hacks for Tax-Advantaged Accounts:

1. *The "Increase with Every Raise" Trick:* Every time you get a raise, increase your 401(k) contribution by 1%.
2. *The "Round Up" Method:* If you're contributing $420 per month to your IRA, round it up to $500. You'll barely notice the difference.
3. *The "Windfall" Strategy:* Commit to putting any unexpected money (tax refunds, bonuses, gifts) into tax-advantaged accounts.
4. *The "Auto-Escalation" Feature:* Many 401(k) plans offer this. It automatically increases your contribution percentage each year.
5. *The "Catch-Up" Reminder:* Set a calendar reminder for your 50th birthday to start making catch-up contributions to your retirement accounts.

What to Watch Out For:

1. *Contribution Limits:* Each account type has annual contribution limits. Don't exceed them.
2. *Income Limits:* Some accounts (like Roth IRAs) have income limits for contributions.
3. *Early Withdrawal Penalties:* Most of these accounts have penalties if you withdraw money before retirement age.
4. *Required Minimum Distributions (RMDs):* Traditional 401(k)s and IRAs require you to start taking distributions at age 72.

Pro Tip: If you're maxing out your 401(k) and still want to save more, look into the "Backdoor Roth IRA" strategy. This allows high earners to indirectly contribute to a Roth IRA.

6. The Joy of Tax Credits: Free Money for the Taking

Chapter 7: Taxes for Dummies (and Proud of It)

While deductions are great, tax credits are even better. Why? Because they reduce your tax bill dollar for dollar. Let's explore some tax credits you might be missing out on.

Why Tax Credits Matter (Even to the Lazy):

1. *Direct Reduction:* Credits reduce your tax bill directly, not just your taxable income.
2. *Some are Refundable:* Certain credits can result in a refund even if you don't owe taxes.
3. *Reward Specific Actions:* Many credits incentivize behaviors the government wants to encourage.

Common Tax Credits You Might Be Missing:

1. *Earned Income Tax Credit (EITC):*
    o   For low to moderate income workers
    o   Can result in a significant refund
    o   Often overlooked, especially by workers without children
2. *Child Tax Credit:*
    o   Up to $2,000 per qualifying child under 17
    o   Partially refundable
3. *Child and Dependent Care Credit:*
    o   For expenses related to care for children under 13 or disabled dependents
    o   Up to $3,000 for one qualifying individual, $6,000 for two or more
4. *American Opportunity Tax Credit:*
    o   For college expenses
    o   Up to $2,500 per eligible student

- Partially refundable
5. *Lifetime Learning Credit:*
    - Also for education expenses, but with no limit on years claimed
    - Up to $2,000 per tax return
6. *Retirement Savings Contributions Credit (Saver's Credit):*
    - For low to moderate income taxpayers who contribute to retirement accounts
    - Up to $1,000 for single filers, $2,000 for married filing jointly
7. *Residential Energy Efficient Property Credit:*
    - For installation of solar, wind, geothermal, or fuel cell technology in your home
    - Up to 30% of the cost

The Lazy Person's Guide to Maximizing Tax Credits:

1. *Use Tax Software:* Most tax software will ask you questions to determine which credits you qualify for.
2. *Keep Good Records:* Save receipts and documentation for expenses that might qualify for credits.
3. *Plan Ahead:* Some credits require action during the tax year, not just at tax time.
4. *Check Income Limits:* Many credits phase out at higher income levels. Know where you stand.
5. *Consider Timing:* If you're close to qualifying for a credit, consider timing income or expenses to become eligible.

Chapter 7: Taxes for Dummies (and Proud of It)

Lazy Hacks for Tax Credit Maximization:

1. *The "Education Bunching" Strategy:* If you're in school, consider bunching tuition payments into a single tax year to maximize education credits.

2. *The "Dependent Care FSA" Combo:* Use a Dependent Care FSA in conjunction with the Child and Dependent Care Credit for maximum tax savings.

3. *The "Saver's Credit" Boost:* If you're close to the income limit for the Saver's Credit, consider making an IRA contribution to lower your AGI and qualify.

4. *The "Solar Panel" Play:* If you've been considering solar panels, the tax credit can significantly reduce the cost.

5. *The "EITC Awareness" Check:* Even if you didn't qualify for the EITC last year, check again. Life changes like marriage, divorce, or having a child can affect eligibility.

What to Watch Out For:

1. *Credit Phaseouts:* Many credits reduce or disappear as your income increases.

2. *Documentation Requirements:* Keep records to prove your eligibility for credits.

3. *Refundable vs. Non-refundable:* Understand which credits can result in a refund and which can only reduce your tax to zero.

4. *Eligibility Changes:* Tax laws change. A credit you qualified for last year might not be available this year.

Pro Tip: If you're self-employed or have variable income, estimate your taxes quarterly. This can help you project your income and plan for credits you might be eligible for.

7. The Art of the Extension: Buying Time Without Buying Trouble

Sometimes, despite our best intentions (and our love for procrastination), we just can't get our taxes done by the deadline. That's where tax extensions come in. Let's explore how to use them effectively.

Why Extensions Matter (Even to the Lazy):

1. *Stress Reduction:* Gives you more time to gather documents and prepare your return.
2. *Avoid Penalties:* Filing an extension helps you avoid the late filing penalty.
3. *Accuracy:* More time can mean a more accurate return, potentially saving you from amendments later.

The Basics of Tax Extensions:

- An extension gives you an additional 6 months to file your return.
- The extension deadline is typically October 15th.
- An extension to file is NOT an extension to pay. You still need to estimate and pay any taxes owed by the original deadline (usually April 15th).

The Lazy Person's Guide to Filing an Extension:

1. *Use Form 4868:* This is the Application for Automatic Extension of Time To File U.S. Individual Income Tax Return.
2. *File Electronically:* You can e-file an extension for free using many tax software programs or the IRS Free File site.
3. *Estimate Your Tax Liability:* You'll need to estimate what you owe (if anything) when filing the extension.

Chapter 7: Taxes for Dummies (and Proud of It)

4. *Pay What You Can:* If you can't pay the full amount you estimate you owe, pay as much as possible to reduce penalties and interest.

5. *State Extensions:* Check if your state requires a separate extension request. Some states automatically grant an extension if you receive a federal one, but not all do.

Lazy Hacks for Extension Filing:

1. *The "Overestimate" Strategy:* When in doubt, slightly overestimate your tax liability. You can get any overpayment back when you file your actual return.

2. *The "Payment Method" Trick:* Paying with a credit card counts as filing an extension request. Just be sure the convenience fee doesn't outweigh the benefits.

3. *The "Previous Year" Shortcut:* If your income and deductions are similar to last year, use last year's tax liability as an estimate.

4. *The "Automatic Extension" Loophole:* If you're out of the country on the tax deadline, you automatically get two extra months to file and pay without requesting an extension.

What to Watch Out For:

1. *Extension to File, Not Pay:* Remember, you still need to pay your estimated taxes by the original deadline.

2. *Penalties and Interest:* If you don't pay enough with your extension, you may owe penalties and interest.

3. *Refunds:* If you're owed a refund, you're just delaying getting your money by filing an extension.

4. *Special Situations:* Some tax situations (like foreign income) have different rules for extensions.

Chapter 7: Taxes for Dummies (and Proud of It)

Pro Tip: If you're self-employed, use the extension period to max out your retirement contributions. You have until the extended deadline to make SEP IRA or Solo 401(k) contributions for the previous tax year.

8. The Audit Survival Guide: Keeping Cool When the IRS Comes Knocking

The word "audit" strikes fear into the hearts of many taxpayers. But with the right preparation and attitude, an audit doesn't have to be a nightmare. Let's explore how to handle an audit with minimal stress.

Why Audit Preparedness Matters (Even to the Lazy):

1. *Peace of Mind:* Knowing you're prepared can reduce anxiety about potential audits.
2. *Time Savings:* Good record-keeping makes responding to an audit much faster.
3. *Financial Protection:* Being prepared can help you avoid unnecessary payments or penalties.

Types of IRS Audits:

1. *Mail Audit:* The most common type. The IRS requests additional information via mail.
2. *Office Audit:* You're asked to bring certain documents to an IRS office.
3. *Field Audit:* The rarest type. An IRS agent comes to your home or business.

The Lazy Person's Guide to Audit Preparedness:

1. *Keep Good Records:*
    - Use apps or software to track income and expenses.

- Keep receipts (digital copies are fine) for at least 3 years after filing.

2. *Be Honest on Your Return:*
    - Report all income, even if you didn't receive a form for it.
    - Only claim deductions and credits you're eligible for.

3. *Respond Promptly to IRS Notices:*
    - Don't ignore IRS mail. Open it promptly and respond within the given timeframe.

4. *Know Your Rights:*
    - Familiarize yourself with the Taxpayer Bill of Rights.
    - You have the right to professional and courteous treatment by IRS employees.

5. *Consider Professional Help:*
    - If you're audited, consider hiring a tax professional to represent you.

What to Do If You're Audited:

1. *Don't Panic:* Most audits are conducted by mail and are often resolved easily.
2. *Gather Your Documents:* Collect all relevant financial records for the tax year in question.
3. *Respond Timely:* Adhere to all deadlines provided by the IRS.
4. *Be Concise:* Provide only the information requested. Don't volunteer additional information.

5. *Consider Professional Representation:* A tax attorney or CPA can handle communications with the IRS on your behalf.

6. *Know Your Rights:* You have the right to appeal the audit findings if you disagree.

Lazy Hacks for Audit-Proofing Your Taxes:

1. *The "Separate Account" Strategy:* Use a dedicated bank account or credit card for business expenses to simplify tracking.

2. *The "Real-Time" Recording Method:* Use apps to record expenses as they happen, rather than trying to remember at tax time.

3. *The "Explanation" Approach:* If you have unusual items on your return, include a brief explanation with your filing. This can head off potential questions.

4. *The "Consistency" Key:* Be consistent in how you report income and claim deductions from year to year. Major changes can trigger audits.

5. *The "Round Numbers" Red Flag:* Avoid rounding all your numbers. Exact figures suggest accurate record-keeping.

What to Watch Out For:

1. *Audit Triggers:* Be aware of common audit triggers like high deductions relative to income, home office deductions, and hobby losses.

2. *Statute of Limitations:* The IRS generally has 3 years to audit a return, but this can be extended in some cases.

3. *Correspondence Scams:* Be wary of audit notifications by email or phone. The IRS initiates most contacts by mail.

Chapter 7: Taxes for Dummies (and Proud of It)

4. *Your Rights:* You have the right to end an interview and speak to a supervisor if you feel uncomfortable.

Pro Tip: If you're self-employed or have a complex tax situation, consider having a CPA review your return before filing. The cost could be worth it for the peace of mind and potential audit prevention.

9. Tax Planning for Life Changes: Navigating Big Transitions with Minimal Stress

Life is full of changes, and many of these changes can have significant tax implications. Let's explore how to handle major life transitions without letting taxes add to your stress.

Why Tax Planning for Life Changes Matters (Even to the Lazy):

1. *Avoid Surprises:* Understanding tax implications in advance can prevent unexpected tax bills.
2. *Maximize Benefits:* Many life changes come with new tax benefits you'll want to take advantage of.
3. *Reduce Stress:* Knowing you're prepared can make big life changes less overwhelming.

Common Life Changes with Tax Implications:

1. *Getting Married:*
    - New filing status options
    - Potential "marriage penalty" or bonus
    - Need to adjust withholding
2. *Having a Child:*
    - New dependent to claim
    - Child Tax Credit
    - Child and Dependent Care Credit

Chapter 7: Taxes for Dummies (and Proud of It)

3. *Buying a Home:*
   - Mortgage interest deduction
   - Property tax deduction
   - Possible energy efficiency credits
4. *Changing Jobs:*
   - Adjusting withholding
   - Dealing with retirement account rollovers
   - Possible moving expense deductions (for military)
5. *Starting a Business:*
   - New deductions for business expenses
   - Self-employment tax considerations
   - Estimated tax payments
6. *Retiring:*
   - Taxation of Social Security benefits
   - Required Minimum Distributions from retirement accounts
   - Possible change in tax bracket

The Lazy Person's Guide to Tax Planning for Life Changes:

1. *Use Life Change Checklists:* Many tax software providers offer checklists for major life changes. Use these to ensure you're not missing anything.
2. *Adjust Your Withholding:* Use the IRS Withholding Calculator to ensure you're having the right amount withheld from your paycheck after a major change.

Chapter 7: Taxes for Dummies (and Proud of It)

3. *Consult a Professional:* For major changes like starting a business or retiring, a one-time consultation with a tax professional can save you a lot of hassle.

4. *Set Calendar Reminders:* Many tax implications of life changes aren't immediate. Set reminders to revisit your tax situation a few months after the change.

5. *Take Advantage of Software Features:* Many tax preparation software options allow you to plan for future scenarios. Use these features to see how life changes might affect your taxes.

Lazy Hacks for Life Change Tax Planning:

1. *The "New Job" Withholding Trick:* When starting a new job, slightly overwithhold for the first few months to make up for any under-withholding from your previous job.

2. *The "New Baby" Credit Check:* As soon as you have a child, check if you're eligible for the Earned Income Tax Credit. Your new dependent might qualify you even if you weren't eligible before.

3. *The "Home Purchase" Deduction Tracker:* Set up a simple spreadsheet or use an app to track home-related expenses that might be tax-deductible.

4. *The "Business Start-Up" Expense Log:* From day one of your new business, use an app like QuickBooks Self-Employed to automatically categorize and track all business expenses.

5. *The "Retirement Rollover" Simplifier:* When changing jobs, consider a direct rollover of your 401(k) to avoid tax complications.

What to Watch Out For:

Chapter 7: Taxes for Dummies (and Proud of It)

1. *Timing Matters:* For tax purposes, your status on December 31st is generally what counts for the whole year.
2. *State Tax Implications:* Don't forget to consider how life changes might affect your state taxes, especially if you're moving to a new state.
3. *Social Security Impact:* Some life changes, like marriage or retirement, can affect your Social Security benefits and their taxation.
4. *Alternative Minimum Tax (AMT):* Major life changes can sometimes trigger AMT. Be aware of this possibility.

Pro Tip: Create a "tax implications" note on your phone. Whenever you experience a life change, jot down potential tax effects to remember come tax time.

10. The Lazy Person's Year-Round Tax Strategy

While it's tempting to think about taxes only when April rolls around, a little bit of year-round attention can make tax time much less stressful. Let's explore how to keep your taxes in check throughout the year with minimal effort.

Why Year-Round Tax Planning Matters (Even to the Lazy):

1. *Stress Reduction:* Spreading tax tasks throughout the year makes tax season less overwhelming.
2. *Better Decision Making:* Awareness of your tax situation can help you make better financial decisions year-round.
3. *Avoid Surprises:* Regular check-ins can prevent unexpected tax bills.

The Lazy Person's Monthly Tax To-Do List:

1. *January:*

- Gather tax documents as they arrive
- Schedule an appointment with a tax preparer if needed

2. *February:*
    - Continue collecting tax documents
    - Start organizing receipts and records

3. *March:*
    - Begin preparing your tax return or provide documents to your preparer
    - Contribute to IRAs for the previous year if you haven't maxed them out

4. *April:*
    - File your tax return or an extension
    - Pay any taxes owed
    - Make first quarter estimated tax payment if self-employed

5. *May:*
    - Review your withholdings and adjust if necessary
    - Start tax planning for the current year

6. *June:*
    - Make second quarter estimated tax payment if self-employed
    - Revisit your tax strategy mid-year

7. *July:*

- If you filed an extension, start gathering remaining documents
8. *August:*
    - Check your withholdings again and adjust if needed
9. *September:*
    - Make third quarter estimated tax payment if self-employed
    - If you filed an extension, finish preparing your return
10. *October:*
    - File your tax return if you got an extension
    - Start year-end tax planning
11. *November:*
    - Review potential year-end tax moves (like tax-loss harvesting)
12. *December:*
    - Make last-minute tax-saving moves (charitable donations, max out 401(k), etc.)
    - Gather receipts and start organizing for next tax season

Lazy Hacks for Year-Round Tax Management:

1. *The "Tax Folder" Email Rule:* Set up an email rule to automatically file tax-related emails into a specific folder throughout the year.
2. *The "Receipt App" Habit:* Use an app like Expensify to snap pictures of receipts immediately, then toss the paper.

3. *The "Withholding Check-Up" Reminder:* Set a calendar reminder for May and August to review and adjust your tax withholdings.

4. *The "Quarterly Review" Routine:* Spend 15 minutes at

Chapter 7: Taxes for Dummies (and Proud of It)

The end of each quarter reviewing your tax situation and making any necessary adjustments.

5. *The "Financial App" Dashboard:* Use a financial app like Mint or Personal Capital that integrates with your accounts and provides a tax overview.

Tools for Effortless Year-Round Tax Management:

1. *TurboTax Year-Round Tax Planner:* Helps you stay on top of tax-saving opportunities throughout the year.
2. *IRS2Go App:* Official IRS app for checking refund status, making payments, and accessing tax records.
3. *QuickBooks Self-Employed:* Tracks income and expenses year-round, estimates quarterly taxes.
4. *TaxCaster:* Free app that lets you estimate your taxes at any point during the year.
5. *H&R Block MyBlock:* Provides year-round access to tax documents and support.

What to Watch Out For:

1. *Life Changes:* Major life events can significantly impact your taxes. Be sure to reassess when these occur.
2. *Tax Law Changes:* Stay informed about any tax law changes that might affect you.
3. *Income Fluctuations:* If your income varies significantly, you may need to adjust withholdings or estimated payments.
4. *Recordkeeping Lapses:* Don't let too much time pass between organizing your tax records. Little and often is easier than all at once.

Pro Tip: Create a simple "tax diary" where you jot down major financial events or decisions throughout the year. This can be invaluable when preparing your taxes or planning for the future.

Conclusion: Your Lazy Tax Action Plan

Congratulations, tax novice! You've made it through our deep dive into effortless tax management. Let's recap with an action plan to get you started on your journey to stress-free taxes:

1. *Assess Your Current Situation:*
    - Gather your most recent tax return and any major financial changes since then
    - Sign up for a free tax estimation tool
2. *Set Up Your Lazy Tax Foundation:*
    - Create a dedicated email folder for tax-related documents
    - Download a receipt-tracking app
    - Set up calendar reminders for key tax dates
3. *Implement Quick Wins:*
    - Adjust your withholdings if needed
    - Check if you qualify for often-overlooked credits like the EITC
    - Set up automatic contributions to tax-advantaged accounts
4. *Develop Your Year-Round Strategy:*
    - Choose a day each month to review your tax situation
    - Set quarterly reminders to check on estimated taxes if self-employed

- Plan ahead for known life changes

5. *Prepare for Next Tax Season:*
    - Start a folder (physical or digital) for next year's tax documents
    - Research free filing options you might qualify for
    - Consider if you need to consult a tax professional

Remember, the key to lazy tax management is setting up systems that work for you in the background. Once you've implemented these strategies, you can largely sit back and let your tax management run on autopilot.

In our next chapter, we'll explore how to plan for retirement without breaking a sweat in "Retirement Planning for Those Who'd Rather Not Think About It." Until then, happy tax optimizing, and may your refunds be large and your tax bills small!

CHAPTER 8: RETIREMENT PLANNING FOR THOSE WHO'D RATHER NOT THINK ABOUT IT

Welcome back, financial fledglings! You've made it to the chapter that might just secure your future: retirement planning. Don't worry, we're going to make this as painless as possible. We'll explore how to set yourself up for a comfortable retirement with minimal effort and maximum returns. So sit back, relax, and let's dive into the world of lazy retirement planning.

1. 401(k)s: Free Money You're Probably Ignoring

Let's start with perhaps the laziest way to save for retirement: the 401(k). If your employer offers this, you're potentially leaving free money on the table by not taking full advantage of it.

Why 401(k)s are Perfect for the Chronically Unmotivated:

1. *Automatic Savings:* Contributions are deducted directly from your paycheck.
2. *Employer Matching:* Many companies match a portion of your contributions (free money!).
3. *Tax Benefits:* Traditional 401(k) contributions are pre-tax, reducing your taxable income.
4. *Set It and Forget It:* Once set up, it requires minimal maintenance.

How 401(k)s Work:

1. *Contribution Limits:* As of 2023, you can contribute up to $22,500 per year ($30,000 if you're 50 or older).
2. *Investment Options:* Your plan will offer a selection of investment options, typically mutual funds.
3. *Vesting:* Employer contributions might be subject to a vesting schedule.

Chapter 8: Retirement Planning for Those Who'd Rather Not Think About It

4. *Withdrawals:* Generally, you can't withdraw without penalty before age 59½.

The Lazy Person's Guide to Maximizing Your 401(k):

1. *Get the Full Match:* At a minimum, contribute enough to get your full employer match.
2. *Automate Increases:* Many plans offer an auto-increase feature. Use it to gradually increase your contributions each year.
3. *Choose a Target-Date Fund:* If available, these funds automatically adjust their asset allocation as you approach retirement.
4. *Consider a Roth 401(k):* If your employer offers this option, it might be beneficial if you expect to be in a higher tax bracket in retirement.
5. *Don't Cash Out:* When changing jobs, resist the temptation to cash out. Instead, roll over your 401(k) to your new employer's plan or an IRA.

Lazy Hacks for 401(k) Success:

1. *The "Raise" Trick:* Every time you get a raise, increase your 401(k) contribution by half the raise amount.
2. *The "Bonus" Boost:* Allocate a portion of any bonuses or windfalls to your 401(k).
3. *The "Age-Based" Contribution:* Set your contribution percentage to half your age (e.g., 15% at age 30).
4. *The "Rounding Up" Method:* If you're contributing 6% of your salary, round it up to 10%.
5. *The "Set It and Forget It" Approach:* Choose a target-date fund based on your expected retirement year and let it do the work for you.

What to Watch Out For:

1. *High Fees:* Some 401(k) plans have high administrative fees or expensive fund options. Be aware of the costs.
2. *Inadequate Savings:* Don't assume the default contribution rate is enough. It often isn't.
3. *Ignoring Asset Allocation:* Even with target-date funds, periodically review your investment mix to ensure it aligns with your risk tolerance.
4. *Forgetting Old 401(k)s:* Keep track of 401(k)s from previous employers and consider consolidating them.

Pro Tip: If you're maxing out your 401(k) and want to save more, look into a backdoor Roth IRA or, if you're self-employed, a Solo 401(k).

2. IRAs: Not Just for Your Grandpa Anymore

While 401(k)s are great, they're not the only game in town. Individual Retirement Accounts (IRAs) offer another excellent way to save for retirement, often with more investment options and potentially lower fees.

Why IRAs Matter (Even to the Lazy):

1. *More Control:* You choose where to open your IRA and what to invest in.
2. *Lower Fees:* Often have lower fees than 401(k) plans.
3. *Tax Benefits:* Traditional IRAs offer tax-deductible contributions, while Roth IRAs offer tax-free withdrawals in retirement.
4. *Flexibility:* Can be opened in addition to a 401(k) for extra savings.

Types of IRAs:

1. *Traditional IRA:*
    - Contributions may be tax-deductible

Chapter 8: Retirement Planning for Those Who'd Rather Not Think About It

- Withdrawals in retirement are taxed as ordinary income
- Required Minimum Distributions (RMDs) start at age 72

2. *Roth IRA:*
   - Contributions are made with after-tax dollars
   - Qualified withdrawals in retirement are tax-free
   - No RMDs during the owner's lifetime

3. *SEP IRA:*
   - For self-employed individuals and small business owners
   - Higher contribution limits than traditional or Roth IRAs

4. *SIMPLE IRA:*
   - For small businesses with 100 or fewer employees
   - Employer must make contributions

The Lazy Person's Guide to IRA Success:

1. *Choose Your IRA Type:* Consider your current tax bracket and expected retirement tax bracket.
2. *Open an Account:* Choose a provider with low fees and a wide range of investment options.
3. *Set Up Automatic Contributions:* Arrange for monthly transfers from your checking account.
4. *Choose Your Investments:* Consider low-cost index funds or target-date funds for easy diversification.

Chapter 8: Retirement Planning for Those Who'd Rather Not Think About It

5. *Max It Out If Possible:* As of 2023, you can contribute up to $6,500 per year ($7,500 if you're 50 or older).

Lazy Hacks for IRA Optimization:

1. *The "Tax Refund" Redirect:* Use your tax refund to fund your IRA each year.

2. *The "Birthday" Contribution:* Make an extra IRA contribution each year as a birthday gift to your future self.

3. *The "Spousal" IRA:* If you're married and one spouse doesn't work, you can still contribute to an IRA for them.

4. *The "Backdoor" Roth:* If your income is too high for direct Roth contributions, consider the backdoor Roth strategy.

5. *The "Sweep" Account:* Set up your checking account to automatically transfer any balance over a certain amount to your IRA.

What to Watch Out For:

1. *Contribution Deadlines:* You have until the tax filing deadline (usually April 15) to make IRA contributions for the previous year.

2. *Income Limits:* There are income limits for deducting traditional IRA contributions and for contributing to Roth IRAs.

3. *Early Withdrawal Penalties:* Generally, you'll face a 10% penalty (plus taxes) for withdrawing from an IRA before age 59½.

4. *Required Minimum Distributions:* Traditional IRAs require you to start taking distributions at age 72.

Chapter 8: Retirement Planning for Those Who'd Rather Not Think About It

Pro Tip: If you're self-employed, look into a SEP IRA or Solo 401(k). These allow for much higher contribution limits than traditional or Roth IRAs.

3. The Magic of Compound Interest: Time Does the Heavy Lifting

Now that we've covered the basic retirement accounts, let's talk about why starting early is so crucial. The magic of compound interest means that even small contributions can grow into a substantial nest egg over time.

Why Compound Interest Matters (Even to the Lazy):

1. *Effortless Growth:* Your money makes money, which then makes more money.
2. *Time is Your Friend:* The longer your money compounds, the more dramatic the effects.
3. *Reduces Pressure:* Starting early means you can save less each month and still reach your goals.

How Compound Interest Works:

Imagine you invest $1,000 and earn 7% interest annually:

- After 1 year, you'd have $1,070
- After 10 years, you'd have $1,967
- After 30 years, you'd have $7,612

Now imagine you add $100 per month to that initial $1,000:

- After 10 years, you'd have $17,308
- After 30 years, you'd have $122,709

The Lazy Person's Guide to Harnessing Compound Interest:

1. *Start Now:* The earlier you start, the more time your money has to grow.

Chapter 8: Retirement Planning for Those Who'd Rather Not Think About It

2. *Automate Your Savings:* Set up automatic transfers to your investment accounts.
3. *Reinvest Dividends:* Many brokerages offer automatic dividend reinvestment.
4. *Don't Touch It:* Resist the urge to withdraw money. Let it grow.
5. *Increase Contributions Over Time:* Even small increases can make a big difference over the long term.

Lazy Hacks for Maximizing Compound Interest:

1. *The "Latte Factor":* Redirect small, regular expenses (like a daily coffee) to your investments.
2. *The "Raise" Allocation:* Dedicate a portion of each raise to increased retirement contributions.
3. *The "Windfall" Rule:* Commit to investing a set percentage of any unexpected money (bonuses, tax refunds, gifts).
4. *The "Rounding Down" Trick:* If your checking account balance is $2,543, transfer the $43 to your investment account.
5. *The "Age-Based" Saving:* Save a percentage of your income equal to your age (e.g., 30% at age 30).

What to Watch Out For:

1. *Inflation:* Remember that inflation will erode the purchasing power of your money over time.
2. *Fees:* High fees can significantly reduce the effects of compound interest. Opt for low-cost index funds when possible.
3. *Market Volatility:* The stock market doesn't go up in a straight line. Be prepared for ups and downs.

4. *Lifestyle Creep:* As your income grows, resist the urge to spend it all. Keep increasing your savings rate.

Pro Tip: Use a compound interest calculator to see the potential growth of your investments. Seeing the numbers can be a powerful motivator to save more.

4. Asset Allocation: Diversification for the Disinterested

Asset allocation is a fancy term for "don't put all your eggs in one basket." It's crucial for managing risk in your retirement portfolio, but it doesn't have to be complicated.

Why Asset Allocation Matters (Even to the Lazy):

1. *Risk Management:* Helps protect your portfolio from major losses.
2. *Potential for Better Returns:* Different asset classes perform differently at different times.
3. *Peace of Mind:* A well-diversified portfolio can help you sleep better at night.

Basic Asset Classes:

1. *Stocks:* Ownership in companies, higher risk but potential for higher returns.
2. *Bonds:* Loans to companies or governments, generally lower risk and lower returns.
3. *Cash:* Includes savings accounts and money market funds, very low risk but low returns.
4. *Real Estate:* Can include REITs (Real Estate Investment Trusts) or physical property.

The Lazy Person's Guide to Asset Allocation:

1. *Use Your Age:* A simple rule of thumb is to subtract your age from 110 to get your stock percentage. The rest goes to bonds.

Chapter 8: Retirement Planning for Those Who'd Rather Not Think About It

2. *Consider Target-Date Funds:* These automatically adjust your asset allocation as you approach retirement.

3. *Use Broad Market Index Funds:* These provide instant diversification across many stocks or bonds.

4. *Rebalance Annually:* Once a year, adjust your portfolio back to your target allocation.

5. *Don't Forget International:* Consider allocating a portion of your portfolio to international stocks and bonds.

Lazy Hacks for Easy Asset Allocation:

1. *The "Three-Fund Portfolio":* Use just three funds - a U.S. total stock market fund, an international stock fund, and a U.S. bond fund.

2. *The "Set It and Forget It" Approach:* Choose a target-date fund based on your expected retirement year and let it handle asset allocation for you.

3. *The "Robo-Advisor" Route:* Use a robo-advisor service that automatically creates and manages a diversified portfolio for you.

4. *The "Core and Explore" Strategy:* Put 90% of your portfolio in broad market index funds and use the remaining 10% for individual stocks or sectors you're interested in.

5. *The "Periodic Table" Method:* Each year, invest in the previous year's worst-performing asset class. This naturally buys low and rebalances your portfolio.

What to Watch Out For:

1. *Overcomplicating Things:* You don't need dozens of funds to be well-diversified.

Chapter 8: Retirement Planning for Those Who'd Rather Not Think About It

2. *Ignoring Fees:* High-fee funds can significantly eat into your returns over time.

3. *Emotional Decisions:* Stick to your allocation plan even when markets are volatile.

4. *Forgetting to Rebalance:* Set a calendar reminder to rebalance your portfolio annually.

Pro Tip: Consider your overall financial picture when determining asset allocation. For example, if you have a pension or rental properties, you might be able to take more risk in your investment portfolio.

5. Social Security: What You Need to Know (But Were Too Lazy to Ask)

Social Security can be a crucial part of your retirement income, but it's often misunderstood. Let's break down what you need to know without getting bogged down in the details.

Why Social Security Matters (Even to the Lazy):

1. *Guaranteed Income:* It provides a base level of income in retirement that you can't outlive.

2. *Inflation Protection:* Benefits are adjusted for inflation over time.

3. *Additional Benefits:* Includes disability and survivor benefits.

Social Security Basics:

1. *Eligibility:* You need 40 "credits" (about 10 years of work) to be eligible.

2. *Benefit Amount:* Based on your 35 highest-earning years.

3. *Full Retirement Age (FRA):* Between 66 and 67, depending on your birth year.

Chapter 8: Retirement Planning for Those Who'd Rather Not Think About It

4. *Early vs. Late Claiming:* You can claim as early as 62 (with reduced benefits) or as late as 70 (with increased benefits).

The Lazy Person's Guide to Maximizing Social Security:

1. *Work at Least 35 Years:* This ensures you don't have zeros averaged into your benefit calculation.

2. *Consider Delaying:* If you can afford to, waiting until age 70 to claim can significantly increase your benefit.

3. *Check Your Earnings Record:* Periodically review your Social Security statement to ensure all your earnings are correctly reported.

4. *Coordinate with Your Spouse:* If you're married, consider strategies to maximize your combined benefits.

5. *Don't Rely Solely on Social Security:* It's designed to replace only about 40% of your pre-retirement income.

Lazy Hacks for Social Security Success:

1. *The "Bridge" Strategy:* If you can afford it, use savings to delay claiming Social Security until age 70 for a higher lifetime benefit.

2. *The "Spousal Benefit" Play:* If you're married, one spouse might be able to claim a spousal benefit while letting their own benefit grow.

3. *The "Ex-Spouse" Bonus:* If you were married for at least 10 years, you might be eligible for benefits based on your ex-spouse's record.

4. *The "Do-Over" Option:* If you claim early and regret it, you have 12 months to withdraw your application and repay benefits.

5. *The "Working in Retirement" Trick:* If you claim before FRA and continue working, your benefits might be temporarily reduced, but they'll be recalculated later.

What to Watch Out For:

1. *Taxes on Benefits:* Up to 85% of your Social Security benefits may be taxable, depending on your overall income.

2. *Windfall Elimination Provision (WEP):* If you have a pension from a job not covered by Social Security, your benefits might be reduced.

3. *Government Pension Offset (GPO):* This can reduce Social Security spousal or survivor benefits for government workers with pensions.

4. *Claiming Too Early:* While you can claim at 62, your benefit will be permanently reduced.

Pro Tip: Use the Social Security Administration's online calculators to estimate your benefits under different claiming scenarios. This can help you make an informed decision about when to claim.

6. The 4% Rule: A Lazy Person's Guide to Retirement Withdrawals

When it comes to retirement planning, one of the biggest questions is: "How much can I safely withdraw from my savings each year?" Enter the 4% rule, a simple guideline that can help even the laziest among us plan for retirement income.

Why the 4% Rule Matters (Even to the Lazy):

1. *Simple to Understand:* It provides a straightforward way to estimate how much you need to save.

2. *Flexible:* Can be adjusted based on your specific circumstances.

Chapter 8: Retirement Planning for Those Who'd Rather Not Think About It

3. *Longevity:* Designed to make your money last for a 30-year retirement.

How the 4% Rule Works:

The basic idea is that you can withdraw 4% of your retirement savings in the first year of retirement, then adjust that amount for inflation each subsequent year. For example:

- If you have $1 million saved, you could withdraw $40,000 in your first year of retirement.
- The next year, if inflation is 2%, you'd withdraw $40,800.
- This continues, adjusting for inflation each year.

The Lazy Person's Guide to Using the 4% Rule:

1. *Estimate Your Retirement Expenses:* Think about what you'll need annually in retirement.
2. *Calculate Your Savings Goal:* Multiply your annual expenses by 25. This is roughly how much you need to save to use the 4% rule.
3. *Consider Other Income Sources:* Factor in Social Security, pensions, or other income when determining how much you need from your savings.
4. *Be Flexible:* In good market years, you might be able to withdraw a bit more. In down years, you might need to cut back.
5. *Reassess Periodically:* Every few years, check if your withdrawal rate is still sustainable based on your portfolio's performance.

Lazy Hacks for 4% Rule Success:

1. *The "Reverse" 4% Rule:* To estimate how much you need to save, multiply your desired annual retirement income by 25.

2. *The "Buffer" Strategy:* Aim to save a bit more than the 4% rule suggests to give yourself a safety margin.

3. *The "Bucket" Approach:* Divide your portfolio into near-term (cash), medium-term (bonds), and long-term (stocks) buckets to weather market volatility.

4. *The "Floor and Upside" Method:* Use guaranteed income sources (like Social Security and annuities) to cover basic expenses, then use the 4% rule for discretionary spending.

5. *The "Variable" Withdrawal Strategy:* Adjust your withdrawals based on market performance, taking out less in down years and more in good years.

What to Watch Out For:

1. *Market Volatility:* The 4% rule assumes historical market returns, which aren't guaranteed.

2. *Longer Retirements:* If you retire early or live longer than expected, you might need to use a lower withdrawal rate.

3. *Inflation:* High inflation can erode the purchasing power of your withdrawals over time.

4. *Sequence of Returns Risk:* Poor market performance early in retirement can deplete your savings faster than expected.

Pro Tip: Consider using a "dynamic" withdrawal strategy that adjusts based on market performance and your portfolio balance. This can help your money last longer and potentially allow for higher withdrawals in good years.

7. Catch-Up Contributions: It's Never Too Late to Boost Your Savings

If you've reached your 50s and feel like you're behind on retirement savings, don't panic! The IRS allows "catch-up" contributions to help older savers boost their retirement accounts.

Why Catch-Up Contributions Matter (Even to the Lazy):

1. *Extra Savings Opportunity:* Allows you to contribute more to tax-advantaged accounts.
2. *Tax Benefits:* Additional contributions to traditional accounts can lower your current tax bill.
3. *Make Up for Lost Time:* Helps if you started saving late or had to reduce savings during certain life events.

How Catch-Up Contributions Work:

Once you turn 50, you can contribute extra money to various retirement accounts:

- 401(k), 403(b), and most 457 plans: Additional $7,500 per year (as of 2023)
- Traditional and Roth IRAs: Additional $1,000 per year
- SIMPLE IRA: Additional $3,500 per year

The Lazy Person's Guide to Catch-Up Contributions:

1. *Automate It:* If possible, set up automatic contributions to take advantage of catch-up limits.
2. *Prioritize Accounts:* If you can't max out everything, prioritize accounts with the highest catch-up limits or best employer matches.
3. *Use Windfalls:* Dedicate bonuses, tax refunds, or other unexpected money to catch-up contributions.
4. *Reassess Your Budget:* Look for areas where you can cut back to increase your retirement savings.

5. *Consider a Roth:* Roth catch-up contributions can be particularly valuable if you expect to be in a higher tax bracket in retirement.

Lazy Hacks for Maximizing Catch-Up Contributions:

1. *The "Automatic Increase" Trick:* Set up your 401(k) to automatically increase your contribution percentage each year.
2. *The "Age-Based" Contribution:* Increase your savings rate by 1% each year after 50.
3. *The "Downsize" Strategy:* If you're an empty nester, consider downsizing your home and redirecting the savings to catch-up contributions.
4. *The "Side Hustle" Boost:* Use income from a part-time job or side gig solely for catch-up contributions.
5. *The "Spousal IRA" Play:* If you're married and one spouse isn't working, you can still make catch-up contributions to an IRA for them.

What to Watch Out For:

1. *Contribution Limits:* Make sure you're aware of the total contribution limits, including catch-up amounts.
2. *Income Limits:* Remember that there are income limits for deducting traditional IRA contributions and for contributing to Roth IRAs.
3. *Tax Implications:* Consider whether traditional or Roth contributions are more beneficial for your tax situation.
4. *Don't Neglect Other Financial Goals:* While retirement saving is important, don't sacrifice emergency savings or paying off high-interest debt.

Pro Tip: If you're self-employed, look into a Solo 401(k). These plans have higher contribution limits than traditional 401(k)s and allow for significant catch-up contributions.

8. Health Savings Accounts (HSAs): The Secret Weapon of Lazy Retirement Planning

Health Savings Accounts (HSAs) are often overlooked in retirement planning, but they offer a triple tax advantage that makes them a powerful tool for the savvy (but lazy) saver.

Why HSAs Matter (Even to the Lazy):

1. *Triple Tax Advantage:* Contributions are tax-deductible, grow tax-free, and withdrawals for qualified medical expenses are tax-free.

2. *Flexibility:* After age 65, you can withdraw funds for any purpose without penalty (though you'll pay income tax on non-medical withdrawals).

3. *No Required Minimum Distributions:* Unlike traditional IRAs and 401(k)s, HSAs don't require you to start withdrawing at a certain age.

How HSAs Work:

- You must have a high-deductible health plan (HDHP) to contribute to an HSA.

- For 2023, you can contribute up to $3,850 for individual coverage or $7,750 for family coverage.

- If you're 55 or older, you can make an additional $1,000 catch-up contribution.

The Lazy Person's Guide to Maximizing HSAs:

1. *Max It Out:* If possible, contribute the maximum amount each year.

2. *Invest Your HSA Funds:* Many HSAs allow you to invest your balance in mutual funds or other investments.

3. *Pay Medical Expenses Out-of-Pocket:* If you can afford to, pay current medical expenses out-of-pocket and let your HSA grow.

4. *Keep Your Receipts:* You can reimburse yourself for medical expenses years after they occur, as long as you have the receipts.

5. *Use It as a Retirement Account:* Consider your HSA as an additional retirement account, especially if you've maxed out your other options.

Lazy Hacks for HSA Success:

1. *The "Payroll Deduction" Trick:* Contribute to your HSA through payroll deductions to save on FICA taxes.

2. *The "Lump Sum" Strategy:* If you can, contribute a lump sum at the beginning of the year to maximize tax-free growth.

3. *The "Shoebox" Method:* Keep all medical receipts in a shoebox (or digital folder). You can reimburse yourself tax-free at any time in the future.

4. *The "Medicare Premium" Play:* In retirement, you can use HSA funds tax-free to pay Medicare premiums.

5. *The "Family Contribution" Loophole:* If you're on a family HDHP, you can contribute the family maximum even if it's just you and one child.

What to Watch Out For:

1. *Eligibility:* Make sure your health plan qualifies as a high-deductible health plan.

2. *State Taxes:* While HSAs offer federal tax benefits, not all states offer the same tax advantages.

3. *Fees:* Some HSA providers charge monthly maintenance fees or investment fees. Shop around for low-cost options.

4. *Non-Medical Withdrawals:* Before age 65, non-medical withdrawals incur a 20% penalty plus income tax.

Pro Tip: If you're eligible for both an HSA and a 401(k) with employer match, prioritize getting the full 401(k) match first, then max out your HSA, then return to maxing out your 401(k).

9. Long-Term Care: Planning for the "What Ifs" Without Losing Sleep

Long-term care is often the elephant in the room when it comes to retirement planning. It's not fun to think about, but ignoring it could derail even the best-laid retirement plans.

Why Long-Term Care Planning Matters (Even to the Lazy):

1. *Cost Protection:* Long-term care can quickly deplete retirement savings.

2. *Peace of Mind:* Knowing you have a plan can reduce anxiety about the future.

3. *Family Protection:* Relieves potential burden on family members.

Long-Term Care Basics:

- Includes services like in-home care, assisted living, or nursing home care.
- Medicare generally doesn't cover long-term care.
- As of 2021, the median annual cost for a private room in a nursing home was over $100,000.

The Lazy Person's Guide to Long-Term Care Planning:

Chapter 8: Retirement Planning for Those Who'd Rather Not Think About It

1. *Start Early:* The younger and healthier you are, the cheaper long-term care insurance will be.

2. *Consider Hybrid Policies:* These combine life insurance or annuities with long-term care coverage.

3. *Self-Insure:* If you have significant assets, you might choose to set aside funds specifically for potential long-term care needs.

4. *Look into State Partnership Programs:* These programs allow you to keep more of your assets if you exhaust your long-term care insurance and need Medicaid.

5. *Explore Alternatives:* Consider options like continuing care retirement communities or home modifications that might reduce the need for formal long-term care.

Lazy Hacks for Long-Term Care Planning:

1. *The "LTC Annuity" Strategy:* Consider a deferred annuity with a long-term care rider. It provides income if you need care, or to your heirs if you don't.

2. *The "HSA for LTC" Approach:* If you have an HSA, you can use it tax-free to pay long-term care insurance premiums (within limits).

3. *The "Life Insurance Conversion" Trick:* Some life insurance policies allow you to convert part of the death benefit into long-term care coverage.

4. *The "Shared Care" Option:* If you're married, look into shared care policies that allow you to share a pool of benefits.

5. *The "Medicaid Planning" Strategy:* Consult with an elder law attorney about strategies to protect assets while still qualifying for Medicaid if needed.

What to Watch Out For:

Chapter 8: Retirement Planning for Those Who'd Rather Not Think About It

1. *Policy Exclusions:* Understand what conditions or situations your long-term care insurance doesn't cover.
2. *Premium Increases:* Long-term care insurance premiums can increase over time. Make sure you can afford potential increases.
3. *Elimination Periods:* Most policies have a waiting period before benefits kick in. Make sure you can cover costs during this time.
4. *Inflation Protection:* Without this feature, your coverage may not keep pace with rising care costs.

Pro Tip: Consider long-term care insurance as part of your overall retirement plan, not in isolation. It should work in conjunction with your other retirement savings and income sources.

10. Estate Planning: Leaving a Legacy (Without the Headache)

Estate planning might sound like something only for the wealthy, but everyone should have at least a basic plan in place. Don't worry, we'll keep it simple and lazy-friendly.

Why Estate Planning Matters (Even to the Lazy):

1. *Control:* Ensures your assets are distributed according to your wishes.
2. *Family Protection:* Can prevent family disputes and protect vulnerable family members.
3. *Tax Efficiency:* Proper planning can minimize estate taxes for larger estates.
4. *Incapacity Planning:* Addresses who makes decisions if you're unable to.

Estate Planning Basics:

- Will: Directs how your assets should be distributed after death.
- Trust: Can provide more control over asset distribution and potentially avoid probate.
- Power of Attorney: Designates someone to make financial decisions if you're incapacitated.
- Healthcare Directive: Specifies your healthcare wishes if you're unable to communicate them.

The Lazy Person's Guide to Estate Planning:

1. *Start with a Will:* At minimum, create a basic will. Many online services make this process simple.
2. *Name Beneficiaries:* Ensure all your financial accounts and insurance policies have up-to-date beneficiary designations.
3. *Consider a Trust:* If you have significant assets or want more control, look into setting up a revocable living trust.
4. *Create Powers of Attorney:* Designate someone you trust to make financial and healthcare decisions if you're unable to.
5. *Review and Update:* Set a reminder to review your estate plan every few years or after major life events.

Lazy Hacks for Estate Planning Success:

1. *The "Online Will" Option:* Use reputable online services like LegalZoom or Nolo to create basic estate planning documents.
2. *The "Letter of Instruction":* Write a letter to your executor explaining where to find important documents and any specific wishes not covered in your will.

3. *The "Password Manager" Trick:* Use a password manager to securely store login information for all your accounts. Share access with a trusted person.

4. *The "Guardianship" Nomination:* If you have minor children, nominate a guardian in your will to ensure they're cared for according to your wishes.

5. *The "Digital Assets" Plan:* Include instructions for handling your digital assets (social media accounts, cryptocurrencies, etc.) in your estate plan.

What to Watch Out For:

1. *DIY Limitations:* While online tools can be great for simple situations, complex estates may require professional help.

2. *Outdated Plans:* Life changes like marriage, divorce, or having children can necessitate updates to your estate plan.

3. *State Laws:* Estate laws vary by state. Ensure your plan complies with your state's requirements.

4. *Probate:* Without proper planning, your estate may have to go through probate, which can be time-consuming and costly.

Pro Tip: Consider setting up a "legacy drawer" or digital folder with all important documents and information your loved ones might need. Include your will, insurance policies, account information, and any final wishes.

Conclusion: Your Lazy Retirement Planning Action Plan

Congratulations, future retiree! You've made it through our deep dive into effortless retirement planning. Let's recap with an action plan to get you started on your journey to a comfortable retirement:

1. *Assess Your Current Situation:*

- Estimate your current retirement savings
- Check if you're getting your full 401(k) match
- Review your Social Security statement

2. *Set Up Your Lazy Retirement Foundation:*
    - Automate contributions to your 401(k) or IRA
    - Choose a target-date fund or simple index fund portfolio
    - Set up an HSA if you're eligible

3. *Implement Quick Wins:*
    - Increase your retirement contributions by 1%
    - Review and update your beneficiary designations
    - Check if you're eligible for catch-up contributions

4. *Develop Your Long-Term Strategy:*
    - Use online calculators to estimate how much you need to save
    - Consider your Social Security claiming strategy
    - Think about potential long-term care needs

5. *Protect Your Future:*
    - Create a basic estate plan (will, power of attorney, healthcare directive)
    - Review your insurance needs (life, disability, long-term care)
    - Set up a system for organizing important documents

Chapter 8: Retirement Planning for Those Who'd Rather Not Think About It

Remember, the key to lazy retirement planning is setting up systems that work for you in the background. Once you've implemented these strategies, you can largely sit back and let your retirement plan run on autopilot.

In our next chapter, we'll explore how to tackle homeownership without breaking a sweat in "Homeownership: The Ultimate Adulting Move (With Minimal Effort)." Until then, happy retirement planning, and may your golden years be as comfortable as your favorite recliner!

Bonus Section: Retirement Planning FAQs for the Chronically Unmotivated

To wrap up this chapter, let's address some common questions that might be lingering in your mind:

1. *Q: How much do I really need to save for retirement?* A: While everyone's needs are different, a common rule of thumb is to aim for 10-15 times your annual salary by retirement age. But even saving a little is better than nothing!

2. *Q: Is it too late to start saving if I'm already in my 40s or 50s?* A: It's never too late! Take advantage of catch-up contributions and consider working a few years longer if needed.

3. *Q: Should I pay off my mortgage before retiring?* A: It depends on your specific situation. Having a paid-off home can reduce retirement expenses, but if your mortgage rate is low, you might be better off investing that money instead.

4. *Q: Do I need to worry about retirement if I love my job and plan to work forever?* A: It's great to love your job, but it's wise to save for retirement anyway. Health issues or job loss could force an earlier retirement than planned.

5. Q: *Is a 401(k) enough, or do I need other retirement accounts too?* A: While a 401(k) is a great start, diversifying with an IRA and taxable accounts can provide more flexibility and tax diversification in retirement.

6. Q: *Should I focus on paying off debt or saving for retirement?* A: If you have high-interest debt, prioritize paying that off. But if you have low-interest debt, consider doing both - pay down debt while also saving for retirement.

7. Q: *How do I know if I'm on track for retirement?* A: Use online retirement calculators or consult with a financial advisor. Many 401(k) providers also offer tools to check if you're on track.

8. Q: *What if the stock market crashes right before I retire?* A: This is why it's important to adjust your asset allocation as you near retirement. Consider keeping 1-2 years of expenses in cash or short-term bonds to weather market downturns.

9. Q: *Should I count on Social Security for my retirement?* A: While Social Security will likely be around in some form, it's best to think of it as a supplement to your own savings rather than your primary source of retirement income.

10. Q: *Is a target-date fund all I need for my retirement investments?* A: For many people, a target-date fund can be a simple, one-stop solution. However, as your savings grow, you might benefit from a more tailored approach.

Remember, the most important step in retirement planning is simply to start. Even small actions can make a big difference over time. So pat yourself on the back for making it through this chapter - you're already ahead of many of your peers!

CHAPTER 9: HOMEOWNERSHIP: THE ULTIMATE ADULTING MOVE (WITH MINIMAL EFFORT)

Welcome back, aspiring homeowners! You've made it to the chapter that might just change your living situation: homeownership. Don't worry, we're going to make this as painless as possible. We'll explore how to navigate the world of real estate and become a homeowner without breaking a sweat (or the bank). So sit back, relax, and let's dive into the world of lazy homeownership.

1. Rent vs. Buy: A Lazy Person's Analysis

Before we jump into the nitty-gritty of buying a home, let's tackle the age-old question: should you rent or buy? This decision can have a huge impact on your financial future, but don't worry – we'll break it down in true lazy fashion.

Why the Rent vs. Buy Decision Matters (Even to the Lazy):

1. *Long-Term Financial Impact:* This decision can significantly affect your wealth over time.
2. *Lifestyle Implications:* Owning and renting come with different responsibilities and freedoms.
3. *Flexibility:* Renting generally offers more flexibility, while buying provides more stability.

Factors to Consider in the Rent vs. Buy Decision:

1. *Time Horizon:* How long do you plan to stay in one place?
2. *Market Conditions:* Are home prices and rents rising or falling in your area?
3. *Financial Readiness:* Do you have savings for a down payment and closing costs?
4. *Job Stability:* Is your income reliable?

Chapter 9: Homeownership: The Ultimate Adulting Move (With Minimal Effort)

5. *Maintenance Skills/Interests:* Are you willing and able to handle home maintenance?

The Lazy Person's Guide to the Rent vs. Buy Decision:

1. *Use Online Calculators:* Tools like the New York Times Rent vs. Buy Calculator can do the math for you.

2. *Consider the 5-Year Rule:* Generally, buying makes more sense if you plan to stay put for at least 5 years.

3. *Factor in Hidden Costs:* Remember to include property taxes, insurance, and maintenance in your homeownership calculations.

4. *Think About Opportunity Costs:* Consider what else you could do with the money that would go into a down payment.

5. *Evaluate Your Lifestyle:* Do you value the freedom to move easily, or do you prefer to put down roots?

Lazy Hacks for the Rent vs. Buy Decision:

1. *The "Rent Your Ideal Home" Trick:* Before buying, try renting a similar home in your desired area to see if you like the lifestyle.

2. *The "1% Rule":* If monthly rent is less than 1% of the home's purchase price, renting might be cheaper.

3. *The "Mock Mortgage" Strategy:* While renting, set aside the difference between your rent and estimated mortgage payment. If you can do this comfortably, you might be ready to buy.

4. *The "Maintenance Reality Check":* Talk to homeowner friends about their maintenance experiences and costs.

Chapter 9: Homeownership: The Ultimate Adulting Move (With Minimal Effort)

5. *The "Future Planning" Approach:* Consider your future plans (career changes, family plans) when deciding between renting and buying.

What to Watch Out For:

1. *Market Timing:* Don't try to time the real estate market perfectly – it's nearly impossible.

2. *Peer Pressure:* Don't buy just because "everyone else is doing it" or you feel you should.

3. *Overlooking Costs:* Remember to factor in all costs of homeownership, not just the mortgage payment.

4. *Ignoring the Intangibles:* Consider non-financial factors like the desire to customize your space or the stress of being responsible for repairs.

Pro Tip: If you're on the fence, consider "house hacking" – buying a multi-unit property, living in one unit, and renting out the others. This can be a way to dip your toes into homeownership while still generating rental income.

2. Down Payment Hacks for the Savings-Challenged

One of the biggest hurdles to homeownership is saving up for a down payment. But don't worry, we've got some lazy-friendly strategies to help you build that nest egg.

Why Down Payments Matter (Even to the Lazy):

1. *Lower Monthly Payments:* A larger down payment means a smaller mortgage and lower monthly payments.

2. *Better Loan Terms:* You might qualify for better interest rates with a larger down payment.

3. *Avoid PMI:* With 20% down, you can typically avoid private mortgage insurance.

Chapter 9: Homeownership: The Ultimate Adulting Move (With Minimal Effort)

The Basics of Down Payments:

- Conventional loans typically require 3-20% down.
- FHA loans can require as little as 3.5% down.
- VA loans and USDA loans may offer 0% down options for those who qualify.

The Lazy Person's Guide to Saving for a Down Payment:

1. *Automate Your Savings:* Set up automatic transfers to a high-yield savings account dedicated to your down payment fund.
2. *Use Windfalls Wisely:* Commit to putting any tax refunds, bonuses, or gifts towards your down payment.
3. *Cut One Major Expense:* Rather than micromanaging your budget, find one big expense to cut (like car payments or dining out).
4. *Consider Down Payment Assistance Programs:* Many states and cities offer programs to help first-time homebuyers.
5. *Look into 401(k) Loans:* While not ideal, you may be able to borrow from your 401(k) for a down payment.

Lazy Hacks for Boosting Your Down Payment Savings:

1. *The "Round-Up" Trick:* Use apps like Acorns or Qapital to round up your purchases and save the difference.
2. *The "Side Hustle" Boost:* Use a low-effort side gig (like renting out a parking space) specifically for your down payment fund.
3. *The "Savings Challenge":* Try the 52-week savings challenge, where you save $1 the first week, $2 the second week, and so on.

4. *The "Family Gift" Strategy:* If you have family members who want to help, look into using gift funds for your down payment.

5. *The "Windfall Rule":* Commit to saving a set percentage (like 90%) of any unexpected money you receive.

Creative Down Payment Sources:

1. *Crowdfunding:* Platforms like Feather the Nest allow you to crowdfund your down payment.

2. *Employer Assistance:* Some employers offer down payment assistance as a benefit.

3. *Sell Stuff:* Have a major decluttering session and sell items you no longer need.

4. *Rent Out a Room:* If you're currently renting, consider getting a roommate and saving the extra rent.

5. *Borrow from Your IRA:* First-time homebuyers can withdraw up to $10,000 from an IRA without penalty.

What to Watch Out For:

1. *Don't Deplete Your Emergency Fund:* Make sure you still have savings for unexpected expenses after buying.

2. *Beware of High-Interest Debt:* Don't use credit cards or high-interest loans for your down payment.

3. *Gift Funds Rules:* If using gift funds, be aware of lender requirements for documenting the gift.

4. *Down Payment Source Restrictions:* Some loan programs have restrictions on where your down payment can come from.

Chapter 9: Homeownership: The Ultimate Adulting Move (With Minimal Effort)

Pro Tip: Consider whether a larger down payment is always better. Sometimes, it might make more sense to make a smaller down payment and keep more cash on hand for emergencies or investments.

3. Mortgages Made Easy: Let the Experts Do the Heavy Lifting

Navigating the world of mortgages can feel overwhelming, but it doesn't have to be. Let's break down how to get a mortgage without breaking a sweat.

Why Understanding Mortgages Matters (Even to the Lazy):

1. *Save Money:* The right mortgage can save you thousands over the life of the loan.
2. *Avoid Pitfalls:* Understanding your mortgage helps you avoid predatory lending practices.
3. *Budget Accurately:* Knowing your true costs helps you budget for homeownership.

Types of Mortgages:

1. *Conventional Loans:* Not backed by the government, typically require good credit.
2. *FHA Loans:* Government-backed loans with more lenient credit requirements.
3. *VA Loans:* For veterans and active-duty military, often with no down payment required.
4. *USDA Loans:* For rural and some suburban homebuyers, can offer 0% down.

The Lazy Person's Guide to Getting a Mortgage:

1. *Check Your Credit:* Use a free service like Credit Karma to see where you stand.

Chapter 9: Homeownership: The Ultimate Adulting Move (With Minimal Effort)

2. *Get Pre-Approved:* This gives you a clear idea of what you can afford and strengthens your offer.

3. *Compare Lenders:* Use a service like Zillow or Bankrate to compare mortgage rates and terms.

4. *Consider a Mortgage Broker:* They can do the shopping around for you.

5. *Gather Your Documents:* Have pay stubs, tax returns, and bank statements ready to go.

Lazy Hacks for Mortgage Success:

1. *The "Rate Lock" Strategy:* Once you find a good rate, ask about locking it in.

2. *The "Points" Consideration:* Evaluate whether paying points to lower your interest rate makes sense for your situation.

3. *The "Pre-Approval Letter" Trick:* Get pre-approved by multiple lenders within a 14-day window to minimize the impact on your credit score.

4. *The "Automated Underwriting" Advantage:* Ask lenders if they use automated underwriting, which can speed up the process.

5. *The "Appraisal Waiver" Option:* Some lenders may waive the appraisal requirement, saving you time and money.

Key Mortgage Terms to Understand:

- *Principal:* The amount you borrow.
- *Interest:* The cost of borrowing money.
- *Escrow:* An account for property taxes and insurance.

Chapter 9: Homeownership: The Ultimate Adulting Move (With Minimal Effort)

- *PMI:* Private Mortgage Insurance, required if you put less than 20% down.
- *DTI:* Debt-to-Income ratio, a key factor in mortgage approval.

What to Watch Out For:

1. *Adjustable Rates:* Be cautious with adjustable-rate mortgages (ARMs) – the low initial rate can increase significantly.
2. *Prepayment Penalties:* Some mortgages charge a fee if you pay off the loan early.
3. *Hidden Fees:* Ask for a detailed breakdown of all fees associated with the mortgage.
4. *Borrowing Too Much:* Just because you're approved for a certain amount doesn't mean you should borrow that much.

Pro Tip: Consider a 15-year mortgage if you can afford the higher payments. You'll pay much less in interest over the life of the loan and build equity faster.

4. House Hunting for the Horizontally Inclined

Now comes the fun part – finding your dream home! But don't worry, we'll show you how to do it without wearing yourself out.

Why Smart House Hunting Matters (Even to the Lazy):

1. *Save Time:* Efficient house hunting means less time traipsing through unsuitable homes.
2. *Find the Right Fit:* A well-chosen home means less need for changes or moves later.
3. *Avoid Buyer's Remorse:* Thorough hunting reduces the chances of regretting your purchase.

Chapter 9: Homeownership: The Ultimate Adulting Move (With Minimal Effort)

The Lazy Person's Guide to House Hunting:

1. *Know Your Must-Haves:* Make a short list of non-negotiable features.
2. *Use Online Tools:* Sites like Zillow, Redfin, and Realtor.com can help you filter homes based on your criteria.
3. *Virtual Tours:* Many listings now offer virtual tours, allowing you to see homes without leaving your couch.
4. *Work with a Realtor:* Let a professional do the legwork of finding suitable homes.
5. *Set Up Alerts:* Most real estate sites allow you to set up notifications for new listings that meet your criteria.

Lazy Hacks for Efficient House Hunting:

1. *The "Drive-By" Trick:* Before scheduling a showing, drive by the house and neighborhood at different times of day.
2. *The "Google Street View" Preview:* Use Google Street View to virtually explore the neighborhood.
3. *The "Open House Blitz":* If you must leave the house, plan to hit multiple open houses in one day.
4. *The "Friend Reconnaissance":* If you have friends in your target neighborhood, ask them for insider info.
5. *The "Lifestyle Mapping" Strategy:* Use Google Maps to check the distance to your frequent destinations (work, gym, favorite restaurants) from potential homes.

What to Look for When House Hunting:

Chapter 9: Homeownership: The Ultimate Adulting Move (With Minimal Effort)

1. *Location:* Consider commute times, school districts, and neighborhood amenities.
2. *Condition:* Look for signs of good maintenance or potential costly repairs.
3. *Layout:* Think about how the layout fits your lifestyle.
4. *Natural Light:* Check the home's orientation and window placement.
5. *Storage:* Ensure there's enough space for your stuff.
6. *Potential:* Consider whether the home has room to grow with you.

What to Watch Out For:

1. *Falling in Love:* Don't get so enamored with a home that you overlook major issues.
2. *Overlooking the Neighborhood:* The perfect house in the wrong neighborhood isn't perfect.
3. *Ignoring Future Needs:* Consider how the home will fit your life 5-10 years from now.
4. *Fixation on Cosmetics:* Don't be swayed by staging – focus on the bones of the house.

Pro Tip: Create a simple scorecard for each home you view, rating it on your most important criteria. This can help you make a more objective decision when it's time to choose.

5. The Art of the Lazy Offer: Negotiating Without the Stress

You've found a home you love – now it's time to make an offer. Don't worry, we'll show you how to negotiate like a pro without breaking a sweat.

Why Smart Negotiation Matters (Even to the Lazy):

Chapter 9: Homeownership: The Ultimate Adulting Move (With Minimal Effort)

1. *Save Money:* Good negotiation can save you thousands on your home purchase.
2. *Get What You Want:* Negotiation isn't just about price – it can cover repairs, appliances, and more.
3. *Avoid Regrets:* Proper negotiation ensures you're happy with the deal long-term.

The Lazy Person's Guide to Making an Offer:

1. *Know the Market:* Understand whether you're in a buyer's or seller's market.
2. *Let Your Realtor Lead:* They have experience and can often handle most of the negotiation for you.
3. *Start Reasonable:* An outrageously low offer might offend the seller and end negotiations.
4. *Have Your Pre-Approval Ready:* This shows you're a serious buyer.
5. *Be Prepared to Walk Away:* Don't get so attached that you make a bad deal.

Lazy Hacks for Effective Negotiation:

1. *The "Odd Number" Trick:* Instead of offering $300,000, try $298,500. It seems more carefully considered.
2. *The "Closing Cost" Strategy:* If the seller won't budge on price, ask them to cover some closing costs.
3. *The "Inspection Contingency" Leverage:* Use issues found in the inspection to negotiate repairs or price reductions.
4. *The "Appraisal Gap" Coverage:* In a hot market, offer to cover a gap between appraised value and purchase price (up to a limit) to make your offer stand out.

5. *The "Escalation Clause" Tactic:* In a competitive market, include a clause that automatically increases your offer up to a set amount if other offers come in.

What to Negotiate Besides Price:

1. *Closing Date:* A flexible closing date can be attractive to sellers.

2. *Repairs:* Ask the seller to make necessary repairs before closing.

3. *Appliances/Fixtures:* Specify which items you want included in the sale.

4. *Home Warranty:* Ask the seller to provide a home warranty.

5. *Contingencies:* Negotiate terms that protect you, like a financing contingency.

What to Watch Out For:

1. *Emotional Attachment:* Don't let your love for the home cloud your judgment.

2. *Neglecting Due Diligence:* Always get a professional inspection, even if you're waiving the contingency.

3. *Ignoring Market Conditions:* Your negotiation strategy should adapt to whether it's a buyer's or seller's market.

4. *Focusing Only on Price:* Remember that terms can be just as important as the final price.

Pro Tip: If you're in a multiple offer situation, consider writing a personal letter to the seller explaining why you love the home. Sometimes an emotional connection can tip the scales in your favor, even if your offer isn't the highest.

6. The Inspection: Finding Flaws Without Flexing a Muscle

Chapter 9: Homeownership: The Ultimate Adulting Move (With Minimal Effort)

The home inspection is a crucial step in the home buying process. It's your chance to uncover any potential issues before you commit to the purchase. Let's explore how to navigate this step with minimal stress.

Why the Inspection Matters (Even to the Lazy):

1. *Avoid Costly Surprises:* Uncover potential issues before you buy.

2. *Negotiation Leverage:* Use inspection findings to negotiate repairs or price.

3. *Peace of Mind:* Know what you're getting into before you close.

The Lazy Person's Guide to Home Inspections:

1. *Hire a Pro:* This is not the time for DIY. Hire a certified professional inspector.

2. *Be Present:* Attend the inspection if possible. It's a great way to learn about your potential new home.

3. *Ask Questions:* Don't be afraid to ask the inspector to explain things you don't understand.

4. *Get a Written Report:* Ensure you receive a detailed written report of the findings.

5. *Prioritize Issues:* Not all problems are created equal. Focus on major issues like structural problems or water damage.

Lazy Hacks for Inspection Success:

1. *The "Rainy Day" Trick:* If possible, schedule the inspection on a rainy day to check for water issues.

2. *The "Specialist" Strategy:* For older homes or those with specific concerns, consider bringing in specialists (like

a structural engineer or roofer) along with the general inspector.

3. *The "Photo Documentation" Approach:* Ask your inspector to take plenty of photos, especially of any issues found.

4. *The "Future Maintenance" Question:* Ask your inspector about anticipated maintenance needs in the next 5-10 years.

5. *The "Re-Inspection" Clause:* If the seller agrees to make repairs, include a clause allowing you to re-inspect after the work is done.

Key Areas the Inspection Should Cover:

1. *Foundation and Structure*
2. *Roof and Gutters*
3. *Electrical Systems*
4. *Plumbing*
5. *HVAC Systems*
6. *Windows and Doors*
7. *Insulation and Ventilation*
8. *Exterior Siding and Trim*
9. *Interior Walls, Ceilings, and Floors*
10. *Basement and Crawl Spaces*

What to Watch Out For:

1. *Rushed Inspections:* A thorough inspection of an average-sized home should take 2-3 hours.

Chapter 9: Homeownership: The Ultimate Adulting Move (With Minimal Effort)

2. *Overlooking the Age of Major Systems:* Ask about the expected lifespan of big-ticket items like the roof, HVAC, and water heater.

3. *Ignoring Small Issues:* While focus on major problems, don't completely disregard smaller issues as they can add up.

4. *Skipping Specialized Inspections:* In some cases, you might need additional inspections for things like pests, mold, or radon.

Pro Tip: Create a simple checklist of questions to ask your inspector, including the condition and estimated remaining life of major home systems and any red flags they've noticed.

7. Closing Time: Sealing the Deal Without Breaking a Sweat

You're in the home stretch! The closing process is where you finalize the purchase and officially become a homeowner. Here's how to navigate this final stage with minimal stress.

Why a Smooth Closing Matters (Even to the Lazy):

1. *Avoid Last-Minute Hiccups:* A well-prepared closing reduces the chance of unexpected issues.

2. *Save Time:* Good preparation can make the closing process quicker and smoother.

3. *Peace of Mind:* Understanding the process helps reduce stress and anxiety.

The Lazy Person's Guide to Closing:

1. *Review Documents in Advance:* Ask for closing documents ahead of time so you can review them at your leisure.

Chapter 9: Homeownership: The Ultimate Adulting Move (With Minimal Effort)

2. *Bring the Right Items:* Make sure you have your ID, any required cashier's checks, and any other necessary documents.

3. *Use a Closing Checklist:* Many real estate websites offer closing checklists. Use one to make sure you don't forget anything.

4. *Understand the Costs:* Know what you're expected to pay at closing and how (usually a cashier's check or wire transfer).

5. *Plan for Time:* Closings can take a few hours. Don't schedule anything important immediately after.

Lazy Hacks for a Smooth Closing:

1. *The "Pre-Signing" Trick:* Some lenders allow you to pre-sign certain documents, reducing time at the closing table.

2. *The "Mobile Notary" Option:* In some areas, you can have a notary come to you for closing, allowing you to sign documents from the comfort of your current home.

3. *The "Final Walk-Through" Timing:* Schedule your final walk-through the morning of closing to ensure any agreed-upon repairs have been completed.

4. *The "Utility Transfer" Reminder:* Set calendar reminders to transfer utilities to your name a few days before closing.

5. *The "Post-Closing File" Preparation:* Bring a folder to store all your closing documents neatly in one place.

Key Players at Closing:

1. *You (the Buyer)*

Chapter 9: Homeownership: The Ultimate Adulting Move (With Minimal Effort)

2. *Seller (or Seller's Attorney)*
3. *Your Real Estate Agent*
4. *Closing Attorney or Escrow Agent*
5. *Lender's Representative*
6. *Title Company Representative*

What to Expect at Closing:

1. *Sign Lots of Documents:* You'll be signing many legal documents, including your mortgage agreement.
2. *Pay Closing Costs:* This includes things like attorney fees, title insurance, and prepaid property taxes.
3. *Receive Important Documents:* You'll get copies of everything you sign, plus the deed and keys to your new home.
4. *Transfer of Funds:* The purchase funds will be transferred to the seller.

What to Watch Out For:

1. *Last-Minute Changes:* Be wary of any changes to agreed-upon terms at the closing table.
2. *Rushing Through Documents:* Take your time to understand what you're signing. Don't be afraid to ask questions.
3. *Forgetting Important Items:* Double-check that you have all necessary documents and funds before heading to closing.
4. *Skipping the Final Walk-Through:* Always do a final walk-through to ensure the home is in the expected condition.

Chapter 9: Homeownership: The Ultimate Adulting Move (With Minimal Effort)

Pro Tip: Consider scheduling your closing for earlier in the week and earlier in the month. This can provide a buffer if there are any last-minute issues that need to be resolved.

8. Moving for Minimalists: Relocate Without the Hassle

Congratulations, you're a homeowner! Now comes the "fun" part – moving. But don't worry, we've got some lazy-friendly tips to make your move as painless as possible.

Why Efficient Moving Matters (Even to the Lazy):

1. *Save Time and Energy:* A well-planned move is less exhausting and time-consuming.
2. *Reduce Stress:* Organized moving minimizes the chaos and anxiety of relocation.
3. *Protect Your Stuff:* Proper packing and moving techniques help prevent damage to your belongings.

The Lazy Person's Guide to Moving:

1. *Declutter First:* The less you have to move, the easier it is. Be ruthless in getting rid of things you don't need.
2. *Start Early:* Begin packing non-essential items weeks in advance.
3. *Hire Professionals:* If your budget allows, professional movers can save you a lot of effort.
4. *Use Proper Supplies:* Invest in good quality boxes, packing tape, and bubble wrap to make packing easier and safer.
5. *Label Everything:* Clearly label each box with its contents and the room it belongs in.

Lazy Hacks for Easy Moving:

Chapter 9: Homeownership: The Ultimate Adulting Move (With Minimal Effort)

1. *The "Suitcase" Trick:* Pack a suitcase like you're going on a trip, with everything you'll need for the first few days in your new home.
2. *The "Trash Bag" Wardrobe:* Leave clothes on hangers and cover them with trash bags for easy transport and unpacking.
3. *The "Box in Box" Method:* Keep small items in dresser drawers or storage containers, then move these as-is.
4. *The "Color Code" System:* Assign each room a color and use colored tape or stickers to label boxes accordingly.
5. *The "First Open" Box:* Pack a clearly marked box with essential items you'll need immediately in your new home (toilet paper, basic tools, phone chargers, etc.).

Moving Day Survival Kit:

1. *Snacks and Water:* Keep energy up and stay hydrated.
2. *Basic Cleaning Supplies:* For last-minute touch-ups.
3. *Toolkit:* For assembling furniture or minor repairs.
4. *First Aid Kit:* Just in case.
5. *Important Documents:* Keep these with you, not in the moving truck.
6. *Chargers:* For phones and other essential devices.

What to Watch Out For:

1. *Underestimating Time:* Moving almost always takes longer than you think. Build in buffer time.

Chapter 9: Homeownership: The Ultimate Adulting Move (With Minimal Effort)

2. *Forgetting to Update Your Address:* Create a checklist of places to update your address (bank, employer, subscriptions, etc.).

3. *Neglecting to Transfer Utilities:* Arrange for utilities to be connected at your new home before you move in.

4. *Packing Hazardous Items:* Some items (like cleaning chemicals) shouldn't be packed and moved. Dispose of these properly.

Pro Tip: Consider a "hybrid" move where you pack everything yourself but hire movers just for loading and unloading the truck. This can be a cost-effective middle ground between a full-service move and a completely DIY approach.

9. Home Maintenance for the Motivation-Challenged

Owning a home comes with the responsibility of maintaining it. But don't worry – with a little planning, you can keep your home in good shape without becoming a full-time handyman.

Why Home Maintenance Matters (Even to the Lazy):

1. *Prevent Costly Repairs:* Regular maintenance can prevent small issues from becoming big, expensive problems.

2. *Preserve Home Value:* A well-maintained home retains its value better.

3. *Improve Comfort and Safety:* Proper maintenance keeps your home comfortable and safe to live in.

The Lazy Person's Guide to Home Maintenance:

1. *Create a Schedule:* Make a calendar of regular maintenance tasks, spread out over the year.

Chapter 9: Homeownership: The Ultimate Adulting Move (With Minimal Effort)

2. *Set Reminders:* Use your phone or a home management app to remind you of maintenance tasks.
3. *Build a Relationship with Professionals:* Find reliable professionals for tasks you can't (or don't want to) do yourself.
4. *Invest in Quality:* Buying quality appliances and materials can reduce the frequency of repairs and replacements.
5. *Learn Basic DIY:* Knowing how to do simple tasks like changing air filters or unclogging drains can save you money and time.

Lazy Hacks for Effortless Home Maintenance:

1. *The "Seasonal" Approach:* Group maintenance tasks by season to make them more manageable.
2. *The "One Room at a Time" Method:* Focus on maintaining one room or area of your home each month.
3. *The "Subscription" Strategy:* Sign up for subscription services that automatically send you replacement items (like air filters) when it's time to change them.
4. *The "Multi-Tasking" Trick:* Combine maintenance tasks with other activities. For example, check your smoke detectors when you change your clocks for daylight savings.
5. *The "Home Warranty" Option:* Consider a home warranty to cover repairs and replacements of major systems and appliances.

Essential Home Maintenance Tasks:

Chapter 9: Homeownership: The Ultimate Adulting Move (With Minimal Effort)

1. *HVAC:* Change filters regularly, schedule professional servicing annually.
2. *Plumbing:* Check for leaks, clean drains, test water pressure.
3. *Roof:* Inspect for damage, clean gutters.
4. *Appliances:* Clean and maintain according to manufacturer instructions.
5. *Exterior:* Check for paint damage, cracks in foundation, wood rot.
6. *Safety Devices:* Test smoke and carbon monoxide detectors, check fire extinguishers.
7. *Pest Control:* Regular inspections and preventive treatments.

What to Watch Out For:

1. *Ignoring Small Problems:* Small issues can quickly become big, expensive ones if ignored.
2. *Skipping Professional Inspections:* Some systems, like HVAC and chimneys, need regular professional inspection.
3. *Forgetting About Unseen Areas:* Don't neglect areas you can't easily see, like the attic or crawl spaces.
4. *Neglecting Outdoor Maintenance:* Your home's exterior needs care too, including landscaping and drainage systems.

Pro Tip: Create a home maintenance binder or digital folder where you keep all important information about your home, including appliance manuals, warranty information, and records of repairs and improvements.

10. Home Improvements for the Horizontally Inclined

Chapter 9: Homeownership: The Ultimate Adulting Move (With Minimal Effort)

Want to increase your home's value or just make it more comfortable? Home improvements don't have to be a huge hassle. Here's how to approach home improvements with minimal effort.

Why Smart Home Improvements Matter (Even to the Lazy):

1. *Increase Home Value:* The right improvements can boost your home's resale value.
2. *Enhance Comfort:* Improvements can make your home more enjoyable to live in.
3. *Save Money:* Some improvements, like energy-efficient upgrades, can save you money in the long run.

The Lazy Person's Guide to Home Improvements:

1. *Start Small:* Begin with manageable projects that make a big impact, like painting or updating hardware.
2. *Focus on High-ROI Projects:* Prioritize improvements that offer the best return on investment, like kitchen or bathroom updates.
3. *Hire Professionals:* For complex projects, hiring pros can save you time and ensure quality results.
4. *Plan Carefully:* Good planning can prevent costly mistakes and reduce stress.
5. *Consider Long-Term Benefits:* Choose improvements that will benefit you now and in the future.

Lazy Hacks for Effortless Home Improvements:

1. *The "One Room at a Time" Approach:* Focus on improving one room or area at a time to avoid feeling overwhelmed.

2. *The "Facelift" Strategy:* Sometimes, small changes like new paint, hardware, or lighting can transform a space without major renovations.

3. *The "Multi-Purpose" Upgrade:* Choose improvements that serve multiple purposes, like adding insulation (which improves comfort and energy efficiency).

4. *The "Smart Home" Investment:* Install smart home devices that can save energy and make your life easier.

5. *The "Curb Appeal" Focus:* Prioritize exterior improvements that boost curb appeal for a big impact with relatively little effort.

High-Impact, Low-Effort Improvements:

1. *Paint:* A fresh coat of paint can transform a room or your home's exterior.

2. *Hardware Updates:* New doorknobs, cabinet handles, and light switches can update a space quickly.

3. *Landscaping:* Simple landscaping improvements can boost curb appeal significantly.

4. *Energy-Efficient Upgrades:* Replacing old appliances or adding insulation can improve comfort and save money.

5. *Smart Home Devices:* Things like smart thermostats or lighting can add convenience and efficiency.

What to Watch Out For:

1. *Over-Improving:* Be careful not to improve beyond what's standard for your neighborhood, as you might not recoup the cost.

Chapter 9: Homeownership: The Ultimate Adulting Move (With Minimal Effort)

2. *Neglecting Necessary Repairs:* Address any structural or system issues before cosmetic improvements.

3. *DIY Disasters:* Know your limits. Some projects are best left to professionals.

4. *Ignoring Permits:* Make sure you obtain necessary permits for any major improvements.

Pro Tip: Before starting any major improvement project, research its potential return on investment. Some improvements, like a minor kitchen remodel or adding a wood deck, typically offer good returns.

Conclusion: Your Lazy Homeownership Action Plan

Congratulations, future homeowner! You've made it through our deep dive into effortless homeownership. Let's recap with an action plan to get you started on your journey to lazy homeownership:

1. *Assess Your Readiness:*
    - Check your credit score and savings
    - Use online calculators to estimate how much home you can afford
    - Decide if you're ready for the responsibilities of homeownership

2. *Prepare for the Purchase:*
    - Get pre-approved for a mortgage
    - Start saving for a down payment and closing costs
    - Research first-time homebuyer programs in your area

3. *Begin Your Home Search:*

Chapter 9: Homeownership: The Ultimate Adulting Move (With Minimal Effort)

- Define your must-haves and nice-to-haves
- Set up online alerts for homes that meet your criteria
- Find a reliable real estate agent to help with your search

4. *Make a Smart Offer:*
    - Research comparable home prices in the area
    - Factor in potential repair or renovation costs
    - Be prepared for negotiation

5. *Navigate the Closing Process:*
    - Schedule a professional home inspection
    - Review all closing documents carefully
    - Prepare for closing costs and don't forget to do a final walk-through

6. *Plan Your Move:*
    - Start decluttering and packing early
    - Consider hiring movers or renting a truck
    - Don't forget to change your address and set up utilities

7. *Set Up Your Home Maintenance Plan:*
    - Create a maintenance calendar
    - Find reliable local professionals for tasks you can't do yourself
    - Start a home maintenance fund for future repairs and improvements

Chapter 9: Homeownership: The Ultimate Adulting Move (With Minimal Effort)

Remember, the key to lazy homeownership is setting up systems that work for you in the background. Once you've implemented these strategies, you can largely sit back and enjoy your new home without constant stress and effort.

Bonus Section: Homeownership FAQs for the Chronically Unmotivated

To wrap up this chapter, let's address some common questions that might be lingering in your mind:

1. Q: *Is it really cheaper to buy than rent in the long run?* A: Often, yes, but it depends on factors like how long you plan to stay in the home, the local real estate market, and how much you're able to put down. Use online rent vs. buy calculators to compare in your specific situation.

2. Q: *How much do I really need for a down payment?* A: While 20% is often cited as ideal, many loans allow for much lower down payments. FHA loans can require as little as 3.5% down, and some conventional loans allow for 3% down payments.

3. Q: *Can I buy a home with bad credit?* A: It's possible, but challenging. FHA loans have lower credit requirements, and some lenders specialize in loans for those with less-than-perfect credit. However, you'll likely face higher interest rates.

4. Q: *How long does the home buying process usually take?* A: From start to finish, buying a home typically takes 2-3 months, but it can vary widely depending on your local market and individual circumstances.

5. Q: *Do I really need a real estate agent?* A: While it's possible to buy a home without an agent, having one can make the process much easier, especially for first-

Chapter 9: Homeownership: The Ultimate Adulting Move (With Minimal Effort)

time buyers. Plus, the seller typically pays the buyer's agent commission.

6. Q: *What's the difference between a fixed-rate and adjustable-rate mortgage?* A: A fixed-rate mortgage keeps the same interest rate for the life of the loan, while an adjustable-rate mortgage (ARM) can change over time based on market conditions.

7. Q: *How much should I budget for home maintenance?* A: A common rule of thumb is to budget 1% of your home's value annually for maintenance and repairs. So for a $300,000 home, you'd set aside $3,000 per year.

8. Q: *What's the deal with property taxes?* A: Property taxes vary widely by location and are typically based on the assessed value of your home. They're often included in your mortgage payment and held in an escrow account.

9. Q: *Do I need to buy homeowners insurance?* A: Yes, most mortgage lenders require it. Even if they didn't, it's a crucial protection for what's likely your largest asset.

10. Q: *What if I decide I don't like the house after I buy it?* A: This is why it's crucial to do your due diligence before purchasing. Once you've closed on the home, it's yours. That's why things like careful house hunting, thorough inspections, and final walk-throughs are so important.

Remember, homeownership is a big step, but it doesn't have to be overwhelming. Take it one step at a time, use the lazy-friendly strategies we've discussed, and don't be afraid to ask for help when you need it. Happy house hunting!

CHAPTER 10: TRAVEL ON A SHOESTRING (WHILE WEARING SLIPPERS)

Welcome back, aspiring lazy travelers! You've made it to the chapter that might just change your vacation game: budget travel. Don't worry, we're going to make this as painless as possible. We'll explore how to see the world (or at least a small part of it) without breaking the bank or breaking a sweat. So sit back, relax, and let's dive into the world of shoestring travel for the chronically unmotivated.

1. Credit Card Points: Your Ticket to Free Vacations

Let's start with perhaps the laziest way to fund your travels: credit card points. Yes, you can actually turn your everyday spending into free flights and hotel stays.

Why Credit Card Points Matter (Even to the Lazy):

1. *Free Travel:* Points can be redeemed for flights, hotels, and more.
2. *Everyday Earnings:* You earn points on purchases you'd make anyway.
3. *Sign-Up Bonuses:* Many cards offer large bonuses just for signing up and meeting a spending requirement.
4. *Additional Perks:* Travel cards often come with benefits like travel insurance and airport lounge access.

Types of Travel Rewards Cards:

1. *Airline Co-Branded Cards:* Earn miles with a specific airline.
2. *Hotel Co-Branded Cards:* Earn points with a specific hotel chain.
3. *Flexible Points Cards:* Earn points that can be transferred to multiple airlines and hotels.

Chapter 10: Travel on a Shoestring (While Wearing Slippers)

4. *Cash Back Cards:* Earn cash back that can be applied to travel expenses.

The Lazy Person's Guide to Credit Card Points:

1. *Choose the Right Card:* Pick a card that aligns with your spending habits and travel goals.

2. *Put Everything on the Card:* Use your card for all possible expenses to maximize point earnings.

3. *Pay in Full:* Always pay your balance in full each month to avoid interest charges.

4. *Hit the Minimum Spend:* Make sure you meet the minimum spending requirement to earn sign-up bonuses.

5. *Set Up Autopay:* Ensure you never miss a payment by setting up automatic payments.

Lazy Hacks for Maximizing Credit Card Points:

1. *The "Category Bonus" Trick:* Use different cards for different spending categories to maximize points.

2. *The "Authorized User" Boost:* Add a trusted family member as an authorized user to earn points on their spending too.

3. *The "Shopping Portal" Strategy:* Use your card issuer's online shopping portal for extra points on purchases.

4. *The "Retention Offer" Play:* Call your card issuer before cancelling to see if they'll offer bonus points to keep you.

5. *The "Point Pooling" Method:* If allowed, combine points with a spouse or family member for bigger rewards.

Popular Travel Rewards Cards for Lazy Travelers:

Chapter 10: Travel on a Shoestring (While Wearing Slippers)

1. *Chase Sapphire Preferred:* Flexible points, good sign-up bonus, travel protections.
2. *Capital One Venture:* Easy-to-use miles, good for infrequent travelers.
3. *American Express Gold Card:* Great for foodies, with bonus points on dining and groceries.
4. *Citi Double Cash:* Simple 2% cash back on everything, can be applied to travel.

What to Watch Out For:

1. *Annual Fees:* Make sure the card's benefits outweigh any annual fee.
2. *Temptation to Overspend:* Don't buy things you don't need just to earn points.
3. *Devaluation:* Points can lose value over time, so don't hoard them for too long.
4. *Blackout Dates:* Some rewards programs have restrictions on when you can use points.

Pro Tip: Consider the "Chase Trifecta" - using the Chase Sapphire Reserve, Chase Freedom Unlimited, and Chase Freedom Flex in combination can maximize your point earnings across all spending categories.

2. House Sitting: Live Like a Local (For Free)

Next up in our lazy travel arsenal is house sitting. It's a fantastic way to stay in destinations around the world for free while experiencing life as a local.

Why House Sitting Matters (Even to the Lazy):

1. *Free Accommodation:* Stay in homes for free in exchange for taking care of the property and often pets.

Chapter 10: Travel on a Shoestring (While Wearing Slippers)

2. *Local Experience:* Live like a local in residential neighborhoods.
3. *Comfort:* Often more comfortable and spacious than hotel rooms.
4. *Unique Opportunities:* Can lead to stays in interesting properties in diverse locations.

How House Sitting Works:

1. *Sign Up:* Join a house sitting platform (like TrustedHousesitters or MindMyHouse).
2. *Create a Profile:* Highlight your reliability, experience with pets, and any relevant skills.
3. *Apply for Sits:* Look for house sits that match your travel dates and preferences.
4. *Get Selected:* Homeowners choose you based on your profile and application.
5. *Do the Sit:* Stay in the home, care for any pets, and maintain the property as agreed.

The Lazy Person's Guide to House Sitting:

1. *Build a Great Profile:* Invest time upfront in creating a stellar profile with good photos and references.
2. *Set Up Alerts:* Most platforms allow you to set up email alerts for sits matching your criteria.
3. *Start Local:* Build up references by doing local sits before applying for international ones.
4. *Be Responsive:* Respond quickly to messages from homeowners to increase your chances of being chosen.
5. *Clarify Expectations:* Make sure you understand all responsibilities before agreeing to a sit.

Chapter 10: Travel on a Shoestring (While Wearing Slippers)

Lazy Hacks for Successful House Sitting:

1. *The "Video Chat" Trick:* Offer to video chat with homeowners to build trust and increase your chances of being selected.
2. *The "Off-Platform" Strategy:* Once you've built a relationship with homeowners, they might invite you back directly for future sits.
3. *The "Combine Sits" Approach:* Look for consecutive sits in the same area to minimize travel between sits.
4. *The "Pet Experience" Boost:* Highlight any pet care experience you have, as many sits involve pet sitting.
5. *The "Flexibility" Advantage:* Being flexible with your dates can open up more house sitting opportunities.

What to Consider When House Sitting:

1. *Pet Comfort:* Are you comfortable caring for the types of pets involved?
2. *Location:* Is the house in a location you want to visit and explore?
3. *Duration:* Does the length of the sit work for your travel plans?
4. *Responsibilities:* Are you willing and able to handle all the required tasks?
5. *Timing:* Does the sit align with your preferred travel dates?

What to Watch Out For:

1. *Hidden Costs:* Factor in travel costs to and from the house sit location.
2. *Overly Demanding Homeowners:* Be wary of sits with an excessive list of responsibilities.

Chapter 10: Travel on a Shoestring (While Wearing Slippers)

3. *Unreliable Internet:* If you need to work remotely, ensure the home has reliable internet.

4. *Last-Minute Cancellations:* Have a backup plan in case a sit falls through.

Pro Tip: Create a "Welcome Home" document for homeowners, detailing how you cared for their home and pets. This extra touch can lead to great reviews and repeat sits.

3. Last-Minute Deals: Procrastination Pays Off

For once, putting things off until the last minute can actually work in your favor! Last-minute travel deals can offer significant savings for the flexible traveler.

Why Last-Minute Deals Matter (Even to the Lazy):

1. *Cost Savings:* Hotels and airlines often slash prices to fill empty rooms and seats.

2. *Spontaneity:* Perfect for those who like to travel on a whim.

3. *Upgrades:* Sometimes last-minute bookings can lead to surprise upgrades.

4. *Diverse Options:* Can lead to discovering destinations you might not have considered.

Types of Last-Minute Deals:

1. *Flight Deals:* Airlines trying to fill empty seats.

2. *Hotel Deals:* Properties looking to maximize occupancy.

3. *Vacation Packages:* Combined flight and hotel deals.

4. *Cruise Deals:* Significant discounts on unsold cabins.

The Lazy Person's Guide to Last-Minute Deals:

Chapter 10: Travel on a Shoestring (While Wearing Slippers)

1. *Be Flexible:* The more flexible you are with dates and destinations, the better deals you'll find.
2. *Sign Up for Alerts:* Subscribe to email lists and apps that notify you of last-minute deals.
3. *Check Aggregator Sites:* Use sites like Kayak, Skyscanner, or Hopper to compare prices across multiple providers.
4. *Consider Package Deals:* Sometimes booking flight and hotel together can lead to bigger savings.
5. *Be Ready to Book:* Last-minute deals can disappear quickly, so be prepared to book when you see a good one.

Lazy Hacks for Scoring Last-Minute Deals:

1. *The "Incognito Mode" Trick:* Search for deals in your browser's incognito mode to avoid price hikes based on your search history.
2. *The "Nearby Airports" Strategy:* Check prices from nearby airports - sometimes a short drive can lead to big savings.
3. *The "Hotel Tonight" App:* This app specializes in last-minute hotel deals, often at significant discounts.
4. *The "Repositioning Cruise" Play:* Look for one-way cruises when ships change seasonal routes for amazing deals.
5. *The "Tuesday Booking" Method:* Airlines often release their sales on Monday nights, making Tuesday a good day to book.

Best Resources for Last-Minute Deals:

1. *Skyscanner:* Great for flexible flight searches.
2. *Hopper:* Predicts whether flight prices will rise or fall.

Chapter 10: Travel on a Shoestring (While Wearing Slippers)

3. *Airfarewatchdog:* Sends alerts for low fares to your chosen destinations.
4. *Cruise Critic:* Excellent for last-minute cruise deals.
5. *Travelzoo:* Curates top travel deals, including last-minute options.

What to Watch Out For:

1. *Hidden Fees:* Make sure to factor in all costs, including baggage fees and resort fees.
2. *Inflexible Bookings:* Last-minute deals are often non-refundable, so be sure before you book.
3. *Limited Availability:* Popular destinations might have limited options at the last minute.
4. *Rushed Planning:* Don't forget to check visa requirements and travel advisories in your haste to book.

Pro Tip: Consider traveling during "shoulder season" - the period between peak and off-peak seasons. You can often find great last-minute deals with good weather and fewer crowds.

4. Budget Airlines: No Frills, More Thrills (and Savings)

If you're willing to forgo some comforts, budget airlines can be a fantastic way to save money on travel. Let's explore how to navigate the world of low-cost carriers without losing your mind (or your luggage).

Why Budget Airlines Matter (Even to the Lazy):

1. *Cost Savings:* Often significantly cheaper than traditional airlines.
2. *More Route Options:* Budget airlines sometimes fly to smaller airports closer to your destination.

3. *A La Carte Pricing:* Pay only for what you need.
4. *Newer Fleets:* Many budget airlines have newer, more fuel-efficient planes.

The Basics of Budget Airlines:

- *Bare Bones Service:* The base fare usually only includes a seat on the plane and a small personal item.
- *Additional Fees:* Expect to pay extra for baggage, seat selection, food, and even printing your boarding pass at the airport.
- *Strict Policies:* Budget airlines often have less flexible policies for changes and cancellations.

The Lazy Person's Guide to Budget Airlines:

1. *Pack Light:* Avoid baggage fees by packing only a personal item or carry-on if possible.
2. *Check In Online:* Many budget airlines charge for airport check-in.
3. *Bring Your Own Entertainment:* Don't count on in-flight entertainment systems.
4. *BYO Food:* Pack snacks and an empty water bottle to fill after security.
5. *Be Flexible:* Budget airlines often have limited flight schedules, so be open to different travel dates.

Lazy Hacks for Budget Airline Success:

1. *The "Hidden City" Trick:* Sometimes booking a flight with a layover at your intended destination is cheaper than a direct flight (but be aware of the risks and airline policies).

Chapter 10: Travel on a Shoestring (While Wearing Slippers)

2. *The "Multi-City" Strategy:* Sometimes booking two one-way flights on different airlines is cheaper than a round trip.

3. *The "Price Freeze" Option:* Some booking sites allow you to hold a fare for a small fee while you finalize plans.

4. *The "Membership" Advantage:* Some budget airlines offer membership programs with perks like priority boarding or discounted fees.

5. *The "Comparison Tool" Method:* Use tools like Google Flights or Momondo to compare budget airline prices against traditional carriers.

Popular Budget Airlines Around the World:

- *North America:* Spirit, Frontier, Allegiant
- *Europe:* Ryanair, EasyJet, Wizz Air
- *Asia:* AirAsia, Scoot, Peach
- *Australia/New Zealand:* Jetstar, Tigerair

What to Watch Out For:

1. *Hidden Fees:* Always check the full price including all fees before booking.

2. *Strict Luggage Policies:* Budget airlines often have stricter size and weight limits for luggage.

3. *Limited Customer Service:* Don't expect the same level of service as traditional airlines.

4. *Remote Airports:* Some budget airlines fly to smaller, more distant airports. Factor in transfer costs.

Pro Tip: If you're traveling with a group, consider pooling resources. One person can pay for a checked bag that everyone uses, potentially saving on individual carry-on fees.

Chapter 10: Travel on a Shoestring (While Wearing Slippers)

5. Hostels: Not Just for Backpackers Anymore

Hostels have come a long way from the bare-bones accommodations of yesteryear. Today, many offer comfortable, budget-friendly options for travelers of all ages.

Why Hostels Matter (Even to the Lazy):

1. *Cost Savings:* Generally much cheaper than hotels.
2. *Social Atmosphere:* Easy to meet other travelers.
3. *Central Locations:* Often located in the heart of cities.
4. *Amenities:* Many offer free Wi-Fi, breakfast, and social activities.

Types of Hostel Accommodations:

1. *Dorm Rooms:* Shared rooms with multiple beds (cheapest option).
2. *Private Rooms:* Some hostels offer private rooms, often with en-suite bathrooms.
3. *Female-Only Dorms:* For added comfort and security.
4. *Pod-Style Beds:* Offer more privacy within a shared room.

The Lazy Person's Guide to Hostel Stays:

1. *Book in Advance:* The best hostels fill up quickly, especially in peak season.
2. *Read Reviews:* Check sites like Hostelworld for detailed reviews from other travelers.
3. *Pack Essentials:* Bring earplugs, an eye mask, and a padlock for lockers.
4. *Choose Your Room Type:* Decide whether you're comfortable in a dorm or prefer a private room.

5. *Take Advantage of Amenities:* Use the communal kitchen to save money on meals.

Lazy Hacks for Comfortable Hostel Stays:

1. *The "Bottom Bunk" Trick:* Request a bottom bunk for easier access (some hostels allow this).
2. *The "Shower Flip-Flops" Must-Have:* Always pack flip-flops for communal showers.
3. *The "Sleeping Bag Liner" Strategy:* Bring a sleeping bag liner for added comfort and cleanliness.
4. *The "Power Strip" Charm:* Bring a small power strip to make friends and ensure you always have a place to charge your devices.
5. *The "Quiet Hostel" Search:* Look for "poshtels" or boutique hostels for a quieter, more comfortable experience.

What to Look for in a Hostel:

1. *Location:* Central location can save time and transportation costs.
2. *Security:* Look for hostels with 24-hour reception and secure lockers.
3. *Cleanliness:* Check reviews for comments on cleanliness.
4. *Atmosphere:* Decide if you want a social party hostel or a quieter environment.
5. *Amenities:* Consider what's important to you (Wi-Fi, breakfast, bar, etc.).

What to Watch Out For:

1. *Party Atmosphere:* If you're not into late nights, avoid hostels known for their party scene.

2. *Hidden Costs:* Some hostels charge extra for linens, towels, or luggage storage.

3. *Age Restrictions:* Some hostels have upper age limits, though this is becoming less common.

4. *Lack of Privacy:* Shared rooms mean less privacy. If this is a concern, opt for private rooms.

Pro Tip: If you're a light sleeper, look for smaller dorm rooms (4-6 beds instead of 10-12) or consider spending a bit more for a private room. The extra cost can be worth it for a good night's sleep.

6. Public Transportation: Navigate Like a Local (and Save)

One of the easiest ways to blow your travel budget is on transportation. But with a little know-how, you can navigate like a local and save big.

Why Public Transportation Matters (Even to the Lazy):

1. *Cost Savings:* Usually much cheaper than taxis or rental cars.

2. *Cultural Immersion:* Experience the city like a local.

3. *Eco-Friendly:* Reduce your carbon footprint while traveling.

4. *Avoid Traffic:* In many cities, public transit can be faster than driving.

Types of Public Transportation:

1. *Buses:* Often the most extensive network, but can be slower.

2. *Subways/Metros:* Fast and efficient in many major cities.

3. *Trams/Light Rail:* Common in European cities.

4. *Trains:* Great for intercity travel.
5. *Ferries:* In coastal or island destinations.

The Lazy Person's Guide to Public Transportation:

1. *Research Before You Go:* Learn about the public transit system before you arrive.
2. *Download Transit Apps:* Many cities have apps with real-time transit information.
3. *Get a Transit Pass:* Many cities offer tourist passes for unlimited rides.
4. *Learn Basic Local Terms:* Know how to say "ticket," "bus stop," etc. in the local language.
5. *Travel Off-Peak:* Avoid rush hour for a more comfortable ride.

Lazy Hacks for Mastering Public Transportation:

1. *The "End of the Line" Trick:* Ride to

Chapter 10: Travel on a Shoestring (While Wearing Slippers)

The end of a metro line for a cheap tour of the city.

2. *The "Bus Tour" Hack:* Use regular city buses that pass by major sights as a budget alternative to hop-on-hop-off tours.
3. *The "Offline Map" Strategy:* Download offline maps and transit directions before you go to save on data.
4. *The "Local Help" Approach:* Don't be afraid to ask locals for help - many are happy to assist.
5. *The "Multi-Day Pass" Savings:* Calculate if a multi-day transit pass will save you money, even if you don't use it every day.

What to Consider When Using Public Transportation:

1. *Safety:* Be aware of your surroundings, especially at night.
2. *Schedule:* Check the operating hours, especially for late-night travel.
3. *Accessibility:* If you have mobility issues, check if the system is accessible.
4. *Luggage:* Consider how you'll manage your luggage on crowded trains or buses.
5. *Zones:* Understand the zone system if the city uses one to avoid accidental fare evasion.

What to Watch Out For:

1. *Pickpockets:* Keep your valuables secure, especially in crowded areas.
2. *Ticket Validation:* In some systems, you need to validate your ticket before boarding.
3. *Service Disruptions:* Check for any planned work that might affect your route.

Chapter 10: Travel on a Shoestring (While Wearing Slippers)

4. *Rush Hour:* Be prepared for very crowded conditions during peak times.

Pro Tip: In many European cities, you can get a multi-day transit pass that includes free or discounted entry to major attractions. These can offer great value if you plan to do a lot of sightseeing.

7. Free Walking Tours: Explore on a Shoestring

Free walking tours have become increasingly popular in cities around the world. They're a great way to orient yourself in a new place and learn about its history and culture - all without spending a dime (though tipping is encouraged).

Why Free Walking Tours Matter (Even to the Lazy):

1. *Cost Effective:* No upfront cost, just tip what you think it's worth.
2. *Cultural Insight:* Led by locals who know the city well.
3. *Social Opportunity:* Meet other travelers.
4. *Orientation:* Great way to get your bearings in a new city.

How Free Walking Tours Work:

1. *Find a Tour:* Look online or ask at your accommodation for recommended tours.
2. *Show Up:* Meet at the designated spot at the right time.
3. *Enjoy the Tour:* Follow the guide around the city, listening to stories and facts.
4. *Tip at*

The end: Give what you think the tour was worth and what you can afford.

The Lazy Person's Guide to Free Walking Tours:

1. *Wear Comfortable Shoes:* You'll be on your feet for a few hours.
2. *Bring Water:* Stay hydrated, especially in hot weather.
3. *Charge Your Phone:* You might want to take photos or notes.
4. *Arrive Early:* Popular tours can fill up quickly.
5. *Ask Questions:* Guides are usually happy to give additional info or recommendations.

Lazy Hacks for Making the Most of Free Walking Tours:

1. *The "First Day" Strategy:* Take a tour on your first day to orient yourself and get recommendations for the rest of your trip.
2. *The "Theme Tour" Approach:* Look for specialized tours (food, street art, etc.) that align with your interests.
3. *The "Small Group" Trick:* If multiple guides are available, opt for the one with the smaller group for a more personal experience.
4. *The "Local Insight" Question:* Ask your guide for their favorite local spots not covered in the tour.
5. *The "Photo Op" Plan:* Pay attention to interesting photo spots during the tour that you can return to later.

What to Look for in a Free Walking Tour:

1. *Tour Length:* Most are 2-3 hours. Make sure you're up for the duration.

2. *Starting Location:* Ensure you can easily get to the meeting point.
3. *Language:* Confirm the tour is in a language you understand well.
4. *Group Size:* Smaller groups often mean a better experience.
5. *Tour Focus:* Choose a tour that covers the areas or themes you're most interested in.

What to Watch Out For:

1. *Weather:* Tours usually run rain or shine. Be prepared for the conditions.
2. *Physical Demands:* Some tours involve a lot of walking or stairs. Check if it matches your abilities.
3. *Time Management:* Tours can sometimes run over the stated time.
4. *Overly Commercial Tours:* Some tours might push you to visit certain shops or restaurants.

Pro Tip: If you enjoy your tour, ask the guide if they offer any paid, specialized tours. These can be a great way to dig deeper into a specific aspect of the city with a guide you already know you like.

8. Street Food: Delicious Savings on the Go

One of the joys of travel is trying new foods, but restaurant meals can quickly eat into your budget. Enter street food: delicious, authentic, and easy on the wallet.

Why Street Food Matters (Even to the Lazy):

1. *Cost Savings:* Generally much cheaper than sit-down restaurants.

Chapter 10: Travel on a Shoestring (While Wearing Slippers)

2. *Authentic Flavors:* Often the most genuine local cuisine.
3. *Convenience:* Quick and easy, perfect for on-the-go travelers.
4. *Cultural Experience:* Insight into local food culture and customs.

Types of Street Food:

1. *Food Carts:* Mobile carts selling specific dishes.
2. *Market Stalls:* Found in local markets or dedicated street food markets.
3. *Hole-in-the-Wall Shops:* Tiny restaurants that are essentially permanent street food stalls.
4. *Food Trucks:* Popular in many Western countries.

The Lazy Person's Guide to Street Food:

1. *Follow the Locals:* Long lines of locals usually indicate good food.
2. *Watch the Preparation:* Choose stalls where you can see the food being prepared.
3. *Start Small:* Try a little from different vendors rather than committing to one large meal.
4. *Carry Hand Sanitizer:* Not all stalls have hand-washing facilities.
5. *Learn Basic Food Words:* Know how to say common ingredients in the local language to avoid allergies or dietary restrictions.

Lazy Hacks for Street Food Success:

1. *The "Busy Stall" Rule:* Busy stalls have higher turnover, meaning fresher food.

Chapter 10: Travel on a Shoestring (While Wearing Slippers)

2. *The "Photo Menu" Point:* If there's a language barrier, pointing at pictures can be an easy way to order.

3. *The "Vendor Specialization" Strategy:* Opt for stalls that specialize in one or two dishes rather than those with huge menus.

4. *The "Early Bird" Approach:* Visit popular stalls early before they run out of the best items.

5. *The "Food Tour" Hack:* If you're nervous about trying street food alone, join a guided street food tour for your first experience.

Popular Street Foods Around the World:

- *Thailand:* Pad Thai, Mango Sticky Rice
- *Mexico:* Tacos, Elotes (corn on the cob)
- *Vietnam:* Pho, Banh Mi
- *India:* Samosas, Chai
- *Turkey:* Kebabs, Simit (sesame bread rings)

What to Watch Out For:

1. *Food Safety:* Look for clean preparation areas and vendors using gloves.

2. *Water Source:* Be cautious of dishes made with or washed in untreated water.

3. *Raw Foods:* In some countries, it's safer to avoid raw fruits or vegetables unless you can peel them yourself.

4. *Crowds:* Popular stalls can get very busy. Be prepared to wait or visit during off-peak hours.

Pro Tip: Carry small change and small bills. Street food vendors often have trouble breaking large bills, and in some

Chapter 10: Travel on a Shoestring (While Wearing Slippers)

cultures, it's considered rude to pay with large denominations for small purchases.

9. Couchsurfing: Free Stays with Local Flavor

Couchsurfing takes the concept of staying with locals to a whole new level. It's a platform that connects travelers with hosts who offer free accommodation in their homes.

Why Couchsurfing Matters (Even to the Lazy):

1. *Free Accommodation:* Save money on lodging.
2. *Local Insight:* Get insider tips and potentially a personal guide.
3. *Cultural Exchange:* Truly immerse yourself in local life.
4. *Social Connections:* Meet like-minded travelers and locals.

How Couchsurfing Works:

1. *Create a Profile:* Sign up on the Couchsurfing website or app and create a detailed profile.
2. *Find Hosts:* Search for hosts in your destination and send requests.
3. *Communicate:* Chat with potential hosts to ensure it's a good fit.
4. *Stay:* If accepted, stay with your host for the agreed duration.
5. *Leave a Reference:* After your stay, leave a review for your host.

The Lazy Person's Guide to Couchsurfing:

1. *Complete Your Profile:* A thorough profile increases your chances of being accepted.

2. *Be Clear About Expectations:* Communicate your plans and needs clearly with potential hosts.
3. *Contribute:* Offer to cook a meal or help with chores as a thank you.
4. *Respect Boundaries:* Remember you're a guest in someone's home.
5. *Stay Safe:* Always have a backup plan and trust your instincts.

Lazy Hacks for Couchsurfing Success:

1. *The "Group Event" Strategy:* Attend Couchsurfing meetups in your area to build references before traveling.
2. *The "Host First" Approach:* Host travelers in your own city to build positive references.
3. *The "Last-Minute" Tactic:* Use the "Last-Minute Requests" feature for spontaneous trips.
4. *The "Public Trip" Post:* Create a public trip to let hosts in your destination know you're looking for a place to stay.
5. *The "Shared Interests" Search:* Look for hosts with similar interests for a better connection.

What to Consider When Couchsurfing:

1. *Safety:* Read host references carefully and trust your instincts.
2. *Comfort Level:* Be honest with yourself about what type of accommodation you're comfortable with.
3. *Time Commitment:* Many hosts expect to spend some time with their guests.

Chapter 10: Travel on a Shoestring (While Wearing Slippers)

4. *Cultural Differences:* Be open-minded and respectful of different lifestyles and customs.
5. *Reciprocity:* Consider hosting travelers when you're back home.

What to Watch Out For:

1. *Lack of Privacy:* You're staying in someone's home, often in a shared space.
2. *Potential Cancellations:* Hosts may need to cancel last-minute. Always have a backup plan.
3. *Expectations of Hosts:* Some hosts might expect more interaction than you're comfortable with.
4. *Safety Concerns:* While rare, there can be safety risks. Always prioritize your safety.

Pro Tip: Even if you don't stay with a host, many Couchsurfers offer to meet for coffee or a quick tour. This can be a great way to get local insight without the commitment of staying in someone's home.

10. Work Exchange: Travel Longer on a Tight Budget

For those who want to travel long-term but are short on funds, work exchange programs can be a great solution. These programs allow you to work part-time in exchange for accommodation and sometimes food.

Why Work Exchange Matters (Even to the Lazy):

1. *Extended Travel:* Allows you to travel for longer periods on a limited budget.
2. *Cultural Immersion:* Live and work alongside locals for a deeper travel experience.
3. *Skill Development:* Learn new skills while traveling.

4. *Meaningful Connections:* Build relationships with hosts and other volunteers.

Types of Work Exchange Programs:

1. *WWOOF (World Wide Opportunities on Organic Farms):* Work on organic farms.
2. *Workamping:* Often RV-based work at campgrounds or parks.
3. *HelpX:* Various types of work, from childcare to building projects.
4. *Worldpackers:* Offers a variety of hostel and eco-project placements.
5. *Workaway:* Wide range of opportunities, from teaching to animal care.

The Lazy Person's Guide to Work Exchange:

1. *Choose Wisely:* Pick work that aligns with your interests and abilities.
2. *Read Reviews:* Look for feedback from previous volunteers.
3. *Communicate Clearly:* Ensure you understand the expectations before committing.
4. *Pack Appropriately:* Bring any necessary gear for the type of work you'll be doing.
5. *Be Flexible:* Be open to different tasks and experiences.

Lazy Hacks for Work Exchange Success:

1. *The "Skill Match" Strategy:* Look for opportunities that match skills you already have for an easier transition.

2. *The "Off-Season" Approach:* Some places offer shorter work hours during their off-season.
3. *The "Extend Your Stay" Tactic:* If you're enjoying a placement, ask if you can stay longer for a potentially cushier role.
4. *The "Digital Nomad" Combo:* Look for work exchanges that allow you to also work on your own online projects.
5. *The "Language Learning" Focus:* Choose a placement where you can practice a language you're learning.

What to Consider in a Work Exchange:

1. *Time Commitment:* How many hours are expected? How many days off per week?
2. *Accommodation:* What type of lodging is provided?
3. *Food:* Are meals included or will you need to cook for yourself?
4. *Location:* Is it easily accessible? Are there things to do in the area during your free time?
5. *Length of Stay:* What's the minimum and maximum stay?

What to Watch Out For:

1. *Exploitation:* Ensure the exchange is fair. You shouldn't be working full-time hours for just a bed.
2. *Mismatched Expectations:* Be clear about what's expected from both sides before committing.
3. *Isolation:* Some placements can be in very remote areas. Make sure you're comfortable with the location.

Chapter 10: Travel on a Shoestring (While Wearing Slippers)

4. *Visa Requirements:* Check if you need a special visa for work exchange in your destination country.

5. *Insurance:* Many work exchange programs don't provide insurance. Make sure you're covered.

Pro Tip: Start with a shorter commitment (2-4 weeks) for your first work exchange. This allows you to see if it's a good fit without being locked into a long-term arrangement.

11. Budget Airlines: No Frills, More Thrills (and Savings)

Budget airlines can be a game-changer for the frugal traveler. While they may lack some of the comforts of traditional airlines, the savings can be substantial.

Why Budget Airlines Matter (Even to the Lazy):

1. *Cost Savings:* Often significantly cheaper than traditional airlines.

2. *More Route Options:* Budget airlines sometimes fly to smaller, more convenient airports.

3. *No-Frills Simplicity:* Pay only for what you need.

4. *Newer Fleets:* Many budget airlines have newer, more fuel-efficient planes.

The Lazy Person's Guide to Budget Airlines:

1. *Pack Light:* Most budget airlines charge for checked baggage. Try to fit everything in a carry-on.

2. *Read the Fine Print:* Understand all fees before booking.

3. *Check In Online:* Many budget airlines charge for airport check-in.

4. *Bring Your Own Entertainment:* Don't expect in-flight entertainment systems.

Chapter 10: Travel on a Shoestring (While Wearing Slippers)

5. *BYO Food:* Pack snacks and an empty water bottle to fill after security.

Lazy Hacks for Budget Airline Success:

1. *The "Hidden City" Trick:* Sometimes booking a flight with a layover at your intended destination is cheaper than a direct flight (but be aware of the risks).
2. *The "Fare Alert" Strategy:* Set up fare alerts to catch price drops.
3. *The "Off-Peak" Approach:* Flying on less popular days (like Tuesdays or Wednesdays) can be cheaper.
4. *The "Nearby Airport" Search:* Check prices from nearby airports - a short train ride might save you a lot.
5. *The "Loyalty Program" Play:* Even budget airlines have loyalty programs. Sign up to earn points or perks.

What to Watch Out For:

1. *Hidden Fees:* Budget airlines make money on extras. Be aware of all potential fees.
2. *Strict Luggage Policies:* Oversized or overweight bags can incur hefty fees.
3. *No Refunds:* Many budget airline tickets are non-refundable.
4. *Remote Airports:* Some budget airlines fly to airports far from city centers. Factor in transfer costs.

Pro Tip: If you're traveling with others, consider sharing one checked bag to split the fee, rather than everyone paying for a carry-on.

12. Travel Rewards Credit Cards: Swipe Your Way to Free Travel

Chapter 10: Travel on a Shoestring (While Wearing Slippers)

For the truly lazy traveler, few things beat earning free travel while going about your everyday spending. Travel rewards credit cards can help you do just that.

Why Travel Rewards Cards Matter (Even to the Lazy):

1. *Earn While You Spend:* Get points or miles on purchases you'd make anyway.
2. *Sign-Up Bonuses:* Many cards offer large bonuses just for signing up and meeting a spending requirement.
3. *Travel Perks:* Many cards offer benefits like free checked bags or airport lounge access.
4. *Flexibility:* Some cards allow you to transfer points to multiple airline or hotel partners.

The Lazy Person's Guide to Travel Rewards Cards:

1. *Choose the Right Card:* Pick a card that aligns with your spending habits and travel goals.
2. *Meet the Minimum Spend:* Make sure you can meet the minimum spending requirement to earn the sign-up bonus.
3. *Put Everything on the Card:* Use your card for all possible expenses to maximize point earnings.
4. *Pay in Full:* Always pay your balance in full each month to avoid interest charges.
5. *Set Up Autopay:* Ensure you never miss a payment by setting up automatic payments.

Lazy Hacks for Maximizing Travel Rewards:

1. *The "Category Bonus" Trick:* Use different cards for different spending categories to maximize points.
2. *The "Shopping Portal" Strategy:* Use your card issuer's online shopping portal for extra points on purchases.

Chapter 10: Travel on a Shoestring (While Wearing Slippers)

3. *The "Authorized User" Boost:* Add a trusted family member as an authorized user to earn points on their spending too.
4. *The "Sign-Up Bonus Cycle" Approach:* Apply for a new card every 6-12 months to take advantage of sign-up bonuses (but be mindful of your credit score).
5. *The "Point Pooling" Method:* If allowed, combine points with a spouse or family member for bigger rewards.

Popular Travel Rewards Cards:

1. *Chase Sapphire Preferred:* Flexible points, good sign-up bonus, travel protections.
2. *Capital One Venture:* Easy-to-use miles, good for infrequent travelers.
3. *American Express Platinum:* Luxury travel perks, high annual fee but lots of benefits.
4. *Citi Double Cash:* Simple 2% cash back on everything, can be applied to travel.

What to Watch Out For:

1. *Annual Fees:* Make sure the card's benefits outweigh any annual fee.
2. *High Interest Rates:* If you carry a balance, the high interest rates can quickly negate any rewards.
3. *Temptation to Overspend:* Don't buy things you don't need just to earn points.
4. *Credit Score Impact:* Applying for multiple cards in a short time can temporarily lower your credit score.

Pro Tip: Keep track of your points or miles and their expiration dates. Some programs allow you to keep your points active with small actions like taking a survey or making a small purchase through a shopping portal.

Chapter 10: Travel on a Shoestring (While Wearing Slippers)

13. Off-Season Travel: Embracing the Road Less Traveled

Traveling during the off-season can lead to significant savings and a more authentic experience. Here's how to make the most of it.

Why Off-Season Travel Matters (Even to the Lazy):

1. *Cost Savings:* Flights, accommodation, and activities are often cheaper.
2. *Fewer Crowds:* Enjoy popular attractions without the throngs of tourists.
3. *More Authentic Experience:* Interact with locals when they're not overwhelmed by peak tourist season.
4. *Better Availability:* Easier to book your first-choice hotels and activities.

The Lazy Person's Guide to Off-Season Travel:

1. *Research the Off-Season:* Understand when it is for your destination and why.
2. *Check the Weather:* Know what to expect and pack accordingly.
3. *Look for Deals:* Many hotels and tour operators offer special off-season rates.
4. *Be Flexible:* Some attractions or businesses might have reduced hours or be closed.
5. *Book in Advance:* While not always necessary, it ensures you don't miss out on limited off-season availability.

Lazy Hacks for Off-Season Travel Success:

1. *The "Shoulder Season" Strategy:* Travel just before or after peak season for good weather and fewer crowds.

2. *The "Reverse Seasons" Approach:* Visit typically winter destinations in summer and vice versa.
3. *The "Major Event" Avoidance:* Research local events that might create mini peak seasons and avoid those dates.
4. *The "Weather App" Reliance:* Use weather apps to find pockets of good weather during the off-season.
5. *The "Rainy Day" Plan:* Have a list of indoor activities for destinations with unpredictable off-season weather.

What to Consider for Off-Season Travel:

1. *Reduced Services:* Some restaurants or attractions might be closed or have limited hours.
2. *Weather:* Off-season often means less ideal weather. Be prepared.
3. *Transportation:* Public transport might run less frequently.
4. *Renovations:* Many places do maintenance work during the off-season.
5. *Local Events:* Look for unique off-season festivals or events.

What to Watch Out For:

1. *Extreme Weather:* In some places, off-season means monsoons or very cold temperatures.
2. *Limited Activities:* Some activities might not be available (like beach clubs in winter).
3. *Ghost Towns:* Very small tourist-dependent towns might feel too quiet in the off-season.
4. *Reduced Flight Schedules:* You might have fewer options for flights, especially to smaller destinations.

Chapter 10: Travel on a Shoestring (While Wearing Slippers)

Pro Tip: Use Google's flight search tool and set your dates to "flexible" to easily see how prices vary throughout the year. This can help you identify the sweet spot between good weather and good prices.

14. House Sitting: Live Like a Local for Free

House sitting is a fantastic way to secure free accommodation while traveling. It involves staying in someone's home while they're away, often caring for their pets or plants.

Why House Sitting Matters (Even to the Lazy):

1. *Free Accommodation:* Save money on lodging costs.
2. *Local Experience:* Live in a residential area, not a tourist zone.
3. *Comfort of a Home:* Enjoy amenities like a kitchen and laundry facilities.
4. *Potential for Longer Stays:* House sits can last from a few days to several months.

The Lazy Person's Guide to House Sitting:

1. *Join a Platform:* Sign up for house sitting websites like TrustedHousesitters or MindMyHouse.
2. *Create a Strong Profile:* Include references, police checks, and a friendly photo.
3. *Apply Early:* Popular house sits get many applicants, so be quick.
4. *Start Local:* Build up references by doing local house sits before applying for international ones.
5. *Communicate Clearly:* Make sure you understand all expectations before accepting a sit.

Lazy Hacks for House Sitting Success:

1. *The "Video Chat" Trick:* Offer to video chat with homeowners to build trust and increase your chances of being selected.
2. *The "Off-Platform" Strategy:* Once you've built a relationship with homeowners, they might invite you back directly for future sits.
3. *The "Pet Experience" Boost:* Highlight any pet care experience you have, as many sits involve pet sitting.
4. *The "Combine Sits" Approach:* Look for consecutive sits in the same area to minimize travel between sits.
5. *The "Last-Minute" Availability:* Some homeowners need sitters on short notice. Being available for these can lead to great opportunities.

What to Consider When House Sitting:

1. *Pet Comfort:* Are you comfortable with the pets you'll be caring for?
2. *Location:* Is the house in an area you want to explore?
3. *Duration:* Does the length of the sit work for your travel plans?
4. *Responsibilities:* Are you willing and able to handle all the required tasks?
5. *Internet:* If you need to work remotely, ensure the house has reliable internet.

What to Watch Out For:

1. *Hidden Costs:* Factor in travel costs to and from the house sit location.
2. *Overly Demanding Homeowners:* Be wary of sits with an excessive list of responsibilities.

Chapter 10: Travel on a Shoestring (While Wearing Slippers)

3. *Unreliable Internet:* If you need to work remotely, ensure the home has reliable internet.

4. *Last-Minute Cancellations:* Have a backup plan in case a sit falls through.

Pro Tip: Create a "Welcome Home" document for homeowners, detailing how you cared for their home and pets. This extra touch can lead to great reviews and repeat sits.

15. Travel Hacking: Maximize Rewards, Minimize Costs

Travel hacking is the art of using credit card rewards, loyalty programs, and other strategies to travel for free or at a greatly reduced cost.

Why Travel Hacking Matters (Even to the Lazy):

1. *Free or Cheap Travel:* Fly and stay for little to no cost.

2. *Luxury for Less:* Access premium travel experiences on a budget.

3. *Flexibility:* Accumulate points and miles for future use.

4. *Gamification:* Turn everyday spending into a rewarding game.

The Lazy Person's Guide to Travel Hacking:

1. *Choose the Right Credit Cards:* Focus on cards with big sign-up bonuses and category spending bonuses.

2. *Meet Minimum Spends:* Ensure you can meet the minimum spending requirements to earn sign-up bonuses.

3. *Maximize Category Bonuses:* Use the right card for the right purchases to earn the most points.

4. *Join Loyalty Programs:* Sign up for airline and hotel loyalty programs, even if you don't travel often.

Chapter 10: Travel on a Shoestring (While Wearing Slippers)

   5. *Stack Rewards:* Use online shopping portals, dining programs, and other methods to earn extra points.

Lazy Hacks for Travel Hacking Success:

1. *The "Manufactured Spending" Trick:* Use methods to generate credit card spending without actually spending money (but be careful and ethical).
2. *The "Award Chart Sweet Spot" Strategy:* Learn airline award charts to find the best value redemptions.
3. *The "Status Match" Play:* If you have status with one airline or hotel, ask competitors if they'll match it.
4. *The "Flexible Points" Approach:* Focus on earning flexible points that can be transferred to multiple airlines or hotels.
5. *The "Companion Pass" Goal:* Aim for perks like the Southwest Companion Pass that allow a friend to fly free with you.

What to Consider in Travel Hacking:

1. *Credit Score:* Make sure you have a good credit score and can manage multiple cards responsibly.
2. *Annual Fees:* Calculate whether the benefits of a card outweigh its annual fee.
3. *Redemption Values:* Learn how to calculate the value of your points to ensure you're getting a good deal.
4. *Expiration Dates:* Keep track of when your points or miles might expire.
5. *Travel Goals:* Focus your earning strategy on the type of travel you actually want to do.

What to Watch Out For:

1. *Overspending:* Don't buy things you don't need just to earn points.
2. *Carrying Balances:* Always pay your credit card balances in full to avoid high interest charges.
3. *Analysis Paralysis:* Don't get so caught up in maximizing value that you never actually travel.
4. *Devaluations:* Loyalty programs can change their rules or devalue points, so don't hoard points for too long.

Pro Tip: Use tools like AwardHacker or ExpertFlyer to find the best award flight options, and websites like AwardMapper to find hotel award nights.

Conclusion: Your Lazy Travel Hacking Action Plan

Congratulations, aspiring budget traveler! You've made it through our deep dive into shoestring travel. Let's recap with an action plan to get you started on your journey to savvy, low-cost adventures:

1. *Assess Your Travel Style:*
   - Consider your comfort level with different types of accommodations and transportation
   - Think about your travel goals and priorities
2. *Set Up Your Lazy Travel Foundation:*
   - Sign up for a travel rewards credit card
   - Join airline and hotel loyalty programs
   - Create accounts on house sitting and Couchsurfing websites
3. *Start Earning and Saving:*

- Put your everyday spending on your travel rewards card
- Set up a dedicated savings account for travel
- Look for ways to cut current expenses to funnel more money into travel

4. *Plan Your First Budget Trip:*
    - Choose a destination, considering off-season options
    - Look for budget flight options
    - Explore alternative accommodation like hostels or house sitting
    - Research free walking tours and street food options

5. *Continue Your Travel Education:*
    - Follow travel hacking blogs and forums
    - Stay updated on credit card offers and loyalty program changes
    - Learn from your experiences and refine your strategies

Remember, the key to lazy travel hacking is setting up systems that work for you in the background. Once you've implemented these strategies, you can largely sit back and watch your travel opportunities grow.

Happy travels, and may your adventures be as expansive as your savings!

CONCLUSION: FROM COUCH POTATO TO FINANCIAL HOT POTATO - YOUR LAZY SUCCESS STORY

Congratulations, you financial fledgling! You've made it through our comprehensive guide to lazy money management. Let's take a moment to recap your journey from couch potato to financial hot potato and set you up for continued success.

Your Lazy Financial Journey: A Recap

1. *Couch Change - Finding Money in Your Cushions (and Other Surprising Places)*
   - You learned how to uncover hidden funds in your everyday life.
   - Key takeaway: Small savings add up over time.

2. *Netflix and Bill - Streaming Your Way to Savings*
   - We explored how to optimize your entertainment spending.
   - Key takeaway: Enjoy your screen time without breaking the bank.

3. *Lazy Budgeting - Because Math is Hard, But Being Broke is Harder*
   - You discovered painless ways to track and control your spending.
   - Key takeaway: A little organization goes a long way in managing your money.

4. *Couch Investing - Making Money While Horizontal*
   - We demystified investing and made it accessible for even the laziest among us.

- Key takeaway: Time in the market beats timing the market.

5. *Side Hustles for the Chronically Unmotivated*
   - You learned about easy ways to boost your income without leaving your comfort zone.
   - Key takeaway: There's money to be made in your spare time.

6. *Credit Score Hacking: Boost Your Numbers Without Lifting a Finger*
   - We explored how to improve your creditworthiness with minimal effort.
   - Key takeaway: Good credit opens doors to better financial opportunities.

7. *Taxes for Dummies (and Proud of It)*
   - You discovered how to navigate the tax maze without losing your mind.
   - Key takeaway: A little tax planning can save you big bucks.

8. *Retirement Planning for Those Who'd Rather Not Think About It*
   - We made future planning painless and even a bit exciting.
   - Key takeaway: Starting early, even with small amounts, can lead to a comfortable retirement.

9. *Homeownership: The Ultimate Adulting Move (With Minimal Effort)*

Conclusion: From Couch Potato to Financial Hot Potato - Your Lazy Success Story

- You learned how to navigate the world of real estate without breaking a sweat.
- Key takeaway: Owning a home can be a path to building wealth, if done smartly.

10. *Travel on a Shoestring (While Wearing Slippers)*
    - We explored how to see the world without emptying your wallet.
    - Key takeaway: Amazing experiences don't have to come with a hefty price tag.

Your Lazy Financial Success Toolkit

Throughout this journey, you've acquired a set of tools that will serve you well in your financial life. Let's review some of the key components of your lazy financial success toolkit:

1. *Automation*
   - Set up automatic transfers to savings and investment accounts.
   - Use apps and tools to track spending and investments without constant monitoring.
2. *Simplification*
   - Embrace the "set it and forget it" approach to investing with index funds or robo-advisors.
   - Streamline your accounts and bills for easier management.
3. *Mindful Spending*
   - Focus on value rather than just price.
   - Cut costs on things that don't matter to you to spend on what does.

4. *Strategic Laziness*
   - Use your natural inclination towards inertia to your advantage by setting up good financial habits.
   - Resist the urge to constantly tinker with your investments or budget.
5. *Leverage Technology*
   - Take advantage of apps and online tools to make financial management easier.
   - Use comparison sites to find the best deals on everything from credit cards to travel.
6. *Continuous Learning*
   - Stay informed about personal finance topics through easy-to-digest sources like podcasts or financial blogs.
   - Be open to adjusting your strategies as your life circumstances change.

Your Lazy Financial Action Plan

Now that you're armed with knowledge and tools, it's time to put it all into action. Here's a simple, lazy-friendly action plan to keep you on track:

1. *Assess Your Current Situation*
   - Take stock of your income, expenses, debts, and assets.
   - Check your credit score.
2. *Set Clear, Achievable Goals*
   - Define what financial success looks like for you.

- Break big goals into smaller, manageable steps.

3. *Automate Your Finances*
   - Set up automatic transfers to savings and investment accounts.
   - Use bill pay services to ensure timely payments.

4. *Optimize Your Spending*
   - Review your subscriptions and regular expenses.
   - Look for areas where you can cut costs without sacrificing quality of life.

5. *Start Investing*
   - Open a retirement account if you haven't already.
   - Consider low-cost index funds or robo-advisors for easy, diversified investing.

6. *Protect Your Financial Future*
   - Ensure you have adequate insurance coverage.
   - Start building an emergency fund if you don't have one.

7. *Continually Educate Yourself*
   - Stay informed about personal finance topics.
   - Regularly review and adjust your strategies as needed.

Overcoming Lazy Financial Pitfalls

Conclusion: From Couch Potato to Financial Hot Potato - Your Lazy Success Story

Even with the best lazy financial strategies, there are still some pitfalls to watch out for:

1. *Procrastination*
    - While strategic laziness can be beneficial, don't let it turn into harmful procrastination.
    - Set reminders for important financial tasks.
2. *Lifestyle Inflation*
    - As your income grows, resist the urge to increase your spending proportionally.
    - Continue living below your means to accelerate your financial progress.
3. *Ignoring Your Finances*
    - While automation is great, don't completely tune out from your financial situation.
    - Schedule regular (but infrequent) check-ins to ensure everything is on track.
4. *Failing to Adjust*
    - Life changes, and so should your financial strategies.
    - Be willing to adapt your approach as your circumstances evolve.
5. *Neglecting Self-Care*
    - Remember that your health and wellbeing are also investments.
    - Don't sacrifice your physical or mental health in pursuit of financial goals.

Celebrating Your Lazy Financial Wins

Conclusion: From Couch Potato to Financial Hot Potato - Your Lazy Success Story

As you progress on your lazy financial journey, it's important to acknowledge and celebrate your wins, no matter how small they may seem. Here are some milestones to look out for:

1. *Paying Off a Debt*
    - Whether it's a credit card balance or a student loan, becoming debt-free is a major achievement.
2. *Reaching a Savings Goal*
    - Hit your emergency fund target? That's worth celebrating!
3. *Improving Your Credit Score*
    - Seeing your credit score climb is a testament to your improved financial habits.
4. *Making Your First Investment*
    - Taking that first step into the world of investing is a big deal.
5. *Negotiating a Better Deal*
    - Whether it's a raise at work or a lower rate on a bill, successful negotiation is a valuable skill.
6. *Sticking to Your Budget*
    - Consistently living within your means is an ongoing victory.
7. *Achieving a Financial Goal*
    - Buying a home, taking a debt-free vacation, or reaching a net worth milestone are all causes for celebration.

Remember, every step forward, no matter how small, is progress. Celebrate these wins to stay motivated on your lazy financial journey.

The Power of Community

While this guide has focused on individual strategies for lazy financial success, don't underestimate the power of community in your financial journey. Here are some ways to leverage community for your financial benefit:

1. *Find an Accountability Partner*
    - Team up with a friend who has similar financial goals.
    - Regular check-ins can help keep you both on track.

2. *Join Online Communities*
    - Participate in personal finance forums or social media groups.
    - Learn from others' experiences and share your own insights.

3. *Attend Financial Workshops*
    - Many libraries and community centers offer free financial education workshops.
    - These can be great opportunities to learn and meet like-minded individuals.

4. *Start a Money Club*
    - Form a small group of friends to discuss financial topics and goals.
    - Meet regularly to share progress and challenges.

5. Seek Professional Advice
    - Consider consulting with a financial advisor for personalized guidance.
    - Many offer free initial consultations.

The Road Ahead: Continuing Your Lazy Financial Journey

Congratulations on making it this far! You've laid a solid foundation for your lazy financial success. But remember, personal finance is a lifelong journey. Here are some parting thoughts to keep you motivated and on track:

1. *Stay Curious*
    - The world of finance is always evolving. Keep learning and adapting.
    - Be open to new ideas and strategies that align with your lazy approach.

2. *Be Patient*
    - Financial success doesn't happen overnight. Trust in your lazy, long-term approach.
    - Remember that small, consistent actions compound over time.

3. *Maintain Balance*
    - While financial success is important, don't let it come at the cost of your happiness or relationships.
    - Find a balance between securing your financial future and enjoying the present.

4. *Give Back*
    - As you achieve financial success, consider ways to give back to your community.

- This could be through charitable donations, volunteering, or mentoring others on their financial journeys.

5. *Stay True to Your Lazy Principles*
    - Don't let others pressure you into financial moves that don't align with your lazy approach.
    - Remember that the best financial strategy is one that you can stick to consistently.

Final Thoughts: You've Got This!

As we conclude this guide, remember that you have everything you need to succeed financially. Your natural inclination towards efficiency (some might call it laziness) can be a powerful tool when applied strategically to your finances.

You don't need to become a financial expert or spend hours each day managing your money. By implementing the lazy strategies we've discussed and leveraging the power of automation and compound interest, you can achieve your financial goals while still enjoying life from the comfort of your couch.

So here's to you, savvy couch potato. May your finances flourish, your stress levels stay low, and your favorite spot on the couch remain ever comfortable. You're no longer just a couch potato – you're a financial hot potato, set to sizzle your way to success!

Remember, the journey of a thousand miles begins with a single step... or in your case, maybe just a slight shift on the couch. But that's okay – you're moving in the right direction, and that's what counts.

Conclusion: From Couch Potato to Financial Hot Potato - Your Lazy Success Story

Now, go forth and conquer... or just take a well-deserved nap. After all, you've earned it!

BONUS CHAPTER: THE EMERGENCY FUND - BECAUSE LIFE HAPPENS, EVEN TO LAZY PEOPLE

Welcome back, financial fledglings! You've made it to the bonus chapter, where we'll explore the unsung hero of personal finance: the emergency fund. Don't worry, we'll make building this financial safety net as painless as possible. So settle into your favorite spot on the couch, and let's dive into the world of lazy emergency fund building.

1. Why You Need One (Even If You Think You Don't)

Let's start with the basics: why bother with an emergency fund at all? After all, isn't that what credit cards are for?

Why Emergency Funds Matter (Even to the Lazy):

1. *Peace of Mind:* Sleep easier knowing you can handle financial surprises.
2. *Avoid Debt:* An emergency fund helps you avoid high-interest credit card debt.
3. *Flexibility:* It gives you options when unexpected expenses arise.
4. *Stress Reduction:* Financial emergencies are stressful enough without worrying about how to pay for them.

Types of Emergencies an Emergency Fund Can Cover:

1. *Job Loss:* Covers living expenses while you search for a new job.
2. *Medical Emergencies:* Helps with unexpected health costs not covered by insurance.
3. *Car Repairs:* Keeps you mobile when your vehicle needs fixing.
4. *Home Repairs:* Handles unexpected maintenance issues.

5. *Family Emergencies:* Covers travel costs for family crises.

The Lazy Person's Guide to Understanding Emergency Funds:

1. *Start Small:* Even a small emergency fund is better than none.

2. *Separate Account:* Keep your emergency fund in a separate savings account to avoid temptation.

3. *Easy Access:* Ensure you can access the funds quickly when needed.

4. *Regular Contributions:* Set up automatic transfers to grow your fund over time.

5. *Realistic Goals:* Aim for 3-6 months of living expenses, but don't stress if you're not there yet.

Lazy Hacks for Emergency Fund Motivation:

1. *The "Peace of Mind" Visualization:* Imagine how much better you'll sleep knowing you have a financial cushion.

2. *The "What If" Game:* Play out various emergency scenarios and how much easier they'd be with an emergency fund.

3. *The "Debt Avoidance" Calculation:* Figure out how much interest you'd save by using an emergency fund instead of credit cards.

4. *The "Automate and Forget" Approach:* Set up automatic contributions and pretend that money doesn't exist.

5. *The "Windfall Rule":* Commit to putting a percentage of any unexpected money (tax refunds, gifts, etc.) into your emergency fund.

Bonus Chapter: The Emergency Fund - Because Life Happens, Even to Lazy People

What to Watch Out For:

1. *Temptation to Use for Non-Emergencies:* Define what constitutes an emergency to avoid dipping in unnecessarily.
2. *Neglecting to Replenish:* If you use your fund, make a plan to build it back up.
3. *Keeping Too Much in Cash:* While you want the fund accessible, keeping too much in low-interest savings can mean missing out on growth opportunities.
4. *Forgetting to Adjust:* As your life circumstances change, your emergency fund needs might change too.

Pro Tip: Consider a high-yield savings account for your emergency fund. You'll earn a bit more interest while still keeping the funds easily accessible.

2. Painless Ways to Build Your Safety Net

Now that we understand why emergency funds are crucial, let's explore how to build one without feeling the pinch.

The Lazy Person's Guide to Building an Emergency Fund:

1. *Start with a Goal:* Determine how much you want to save (3-6 months of expenses is a good target).
2. *Automate Savings:* Set up automatic transfers from your checking to your emergency fund.
3. *Use Windfalls Wisely:* Commit to saving a portion of any unexpected money.
4. *Round Up Your Purchases:* Use apps that round up your purchases and save the difference.
5. *Reduce One Expense:* Find one regular expense you can cut and redirect that money to your fund.

Bonus Chapter: The Emergency Fund - Because Life Happens, Even to Lazy People

Lazy Hacks for Effortless Saving:

1. *The "Invisible Money" Trick:* Save your spare change and any $1 bills you receive.

2. *The "Subscription Audit" Strategy:* Cancel unused subscriptions and save that money instead.

3. *The "Bill Negotiation" Approach:* Use apps like Truebill or Trim to lower your bills and save the difference.

4. *The "Cashback Redirect" Play:* Use a cashback credit card and send all the cashback to your emergency fund.

5. *The "No-Spend Challenge":* Try a no-spend week or month and save what you would have spent.

Tools to Help You Save:

1. *Acorns:* Automatically invests your spare change.

2. *Digit:* Analyzes your spending and automatically saves small amounts.

3. *Qapital:* Allows you to set savings rules based on your spending habits.

4. *Chime:* Offers automatic savings features with their checking account.

5. *Your Bank's Savings Tools:* Many banks now offer round-up or automatic savings features.

Creative Ways to Boost Your Emergency Fund:

1. *Sell Unused Items:* Have a lazy yard sale (online, of course) and add the proceeds to your fund.

2. *Take Online Surveys:* Use your couch time to earn a little extra for your fund.

3. *Rent Out Storage Space:* If you have extra space, rent it out on platforms like Neighbor.

4. *Cashback Apps:* Use apps like Ibotta or Rakuten for cashback on purchases you're already making.

5. *Bank Account Bonuses:* Some banks offer sign-up bonuses for new accounts.

What to Watch Out For:

1. *Saving Too Aggressively:* Don't neglect other financial priorities in your rush to build your emergency fund.

2. *Ignoring High-Interest Debt:* If you have high-interest debt, tackle that alongside building your emergency fund.

3. *Keeping Your Fund Too Accessible:* While you want quick access, keeping it in your regular checking account might lead to temptation.

4. *Forgetting to Celebrate Milestones:* Acknowledge your progress to stay motivated.

Pro Tip: Create a visual representation of your emergency fund goal. A simple thermometer chart can be a great motivator as you watch it fill up.

3. Where to Stash Your Cash for Easy Access (But Not Too Easy)

Once you start building your emergency fund, you need to decide where to keep it. The ideal spot balances accessibility with a bit of separation from your everyday spending money.

The Lazy Person's Guide to Choosing an Emergency Fund Account:

Bonus Chapter: The Emergency Fund - Because Life Happens, Even to Lazy People

1. *High-Yield Savings Account:* Offers better interest rates than traditional savings accounts.
2. *Money Market Account:* Similar to a savings account but might offer check-writing privileges.
3. *No-Penalty CD:* Provides higher interest rates with the ability to withdraw without penalties.
4. *Online Savings Account:* Often offers higher rates than brick-and-mortar banks.
5. *Cash Management Account:* Combines features of checking and savings accounts.

Factors to Consider When Choosing an Account:

1. *Interest Rate:* Look for the highest rate you can find.
2. *Accessibility:* Ensure you can access funds quickly in an emergency.
3. *Fees:* Avoid accounts with high fees that could eat into your savings.
4. *Minimum Balance Requirements:* Choose an account with a minimum balance you can comfortably maintain.
5. *FDIC Insurance:* Ensure the account is FDIC insured for protection.

Lazy Hacks for Optimizing Your Emergency Fund Storage:

1. *The "Out of Sight, Out of Mind" Approach:* Choose an account separate from your regular bank to reduce temptation.
2. *The "Ladder" Strategy:* Divide your fund among accounts with different terms for a balance of growth and accessibility.

3. *The "Hybrid" Method:* Keep some funds in a high-yield savings account and some in a no-penalty CD for higher overall returns.

4. *The "Automatic Transfer" Trick:* Set up automatic transfers to your emergency fund account on payday.

5. *The "Interest Rate Alert" System:* Use services like Bankrate to get alerts when better interest rates become available.

Popular Emergency Fund Account Options:

1. *Ally Bank High Yield Savings:* Consistently competitive rates, no minimum balance.

2. *Marcus by Goldman Sachs:* High-yield savings with no fees.

3. *CIT Bank Savings Builder:* Offers higher rates for regular savers.

4. *Discover Bank:* Offers a savings account and cashback checking that can work in tandem.

5. *Betterment Everyday:* Cash management account with competitive rates and FDIC insurance.

What to Watch Out For:

1. *Withdrawal Limits:* Some savings accounts limit the number of withdrawals per month.

2. *Variable Interest Rates:* Rates can change, so keep an eye on your account's performance.

3. *Online-Only Banks:* While often offering better rates, ensure you're comfortable with an online-only experience.

4. *Temptation to Invest:* Resist the urge to invest your emergency fund in the stock market for higher returns.

Pro Tip: Consider keeping a small portion of your emergency fund (like $1,000) in cash at home for immediate needs or in case of bank system outages.

4. How Much is Enough? Calculating Your Ideal Emergency Fund

One of the most common questions about emergency funds is, "How much should I save?" While the standard advice is 3-6 months of expenses, the truth is that the ideal amount can vary based on your personal situation.

The Lazy Person's Guide to Calculating Emergency Fund Size:

1. *Start with Monthly Expenses:* Calculate your essential monthly expenses (rent/mortgage, utilities, food, etc.).
2. *Multiply by Months of Coverage:* Typically 3-6 months, but adjust based on your situation.
3. *Consider Your Job Stability:* Those with less stable income might aim for a larger fund.
4. *Factor in Dependents:* If others rely on your income, you might need a larger cushion.
5. *Adjust for Insurance Coverage:* Good health and disability insurance might allow for a smaller emergency fund.

Factors That Might Increase Your Ideal Fund Size:

1. *Self-Employment:* Irregular income might necessitate a larger fund.
2. *Single Income Household:* With only one income stream, a larger fund provides more security.

3. *Health Issues:* Chronic health conditions might require a bigger financial cushion.
4. *Homeownership:* Homeowners might need more to cover potential repairs.
5. *Older Vehicle:* If your car is prone to breakdowns, a larger fund can help cover repairs.

Factors That Might Decrease Your Ideal Fund Size:

1. *Stable Job:* Those with very secure employment might be comfortable with a smaller fund.
2. *Dual Income Household:* Two incomes provide more stability.
3. *Good Insurance Coverage:* Comprehensive insurance can reduce the need for a large emergency fund.
4. *Low Fixed Expenses:* If your essential expenses are low, you might need less in reserve.
5. *Strong Support Network:* Family or friends who can help in emergencies might allow for a smaller fund.

Lazy Hacks for Emergency Fund Calculation:

1. *The "Bare Bones Budget" Trick:* Calculate the absolute minimum you need to live on and use that for your emergency fund calculation.
2. *The "Tiered Approach" Strategy:* Build your fund in tiers (e.g., $1,000, then one month of expenses, then three months, etc.).
3. *The "Worst Case Scenario" Method:* Estimate costs for your most likely emergency scenarios and use the highest as your target.

4. *The "Percentage of Income" Approach:* Aim to save a percentage of your income (like 20%) until you reach your goal.

5. *The "Emergency Budget" Plan:* Create a stripped-down budget for emergencies to more accurately calculate your needs.

What to Watch Out For:

1. *Overestimating Needs:* While a larger fund provides more security, don't neglect other financial goals.

2. *Underestimating Risks:* Be realistic about potential emergencies and their costs.

3. *Forgetting to Adjust:* As your life circumstances change, so should your emergency fund target.

4. *Ignoring Inflation:* Remember that the cost of living increases over time, so your fund might need periodic boosts.

Pro Tip: Review and recalculate your emergency fund needs annually or after any major life changes (marriage, kids, job change, etc.).

5. When to Use Your Emergency Fund (And When Not To)

Having an emergency fund is great, but knowing when to use it is equally important. Let's explore what constitutes a true financial emergency and what doesn't.

The Lazy Person's Guide to Emergency Fund Usage:

1. *Define "Emergency":* Create a clear definition of what qualifies as an emergency for you.

2. *Use for Unexpected, Necessary Expenses:* Think job loss, medical bills, major home or car repairs.

3. *Avoid Using for Predictable Expenses:* Regular car maintenance or holiday gifts aren't emergencies.
4. *Consider Long-Term Impact:* Will using the fund now prevent a bigger financial disaster later?
5. *Plan to Replenish:* When you do use the fund, create a plan to build it back up.

True Emergencies That Warrant Using Your Fund:

1. Job Loss or Significant Income Reduction
2. Unexpected Medical or Dental Expenses
3. Major Home Repairs (e.g., roof leak, broken furnace)
4. Essential Car Repairs
5. Unplanned Travel for Family Emergencies

Not Emergencies (Even If They Feel Urgent):

1. Planned Expenses (e.g., taxes, insurance premiums)
2. Non-Essential Home or Car Upgrades
3. Vacation Costs
4. Holiday or Birthday Gifts
5. Sales or "Great Deals" on Non-Essential Items

Lazy Hacks for Emergency Fund Decision Making:

1. *The "Sleep On It" Rule:* For non-immediate emergencies, wait 24 hours before deciding to use your fund.
2. *The "Alternative Solutions" Checklist:* Before tapping your fund, list out all other possible solutions.
3. *The "Future Self" Question:* Ask if your future self will thank you or regret this use of the fund.

4. *The "Necessity Scale":* Rate the urgency and importance of the expense on a scale of 1-10.

5. *The "Replenishment Plan" Requirement:* Don't use the fund unless you have a clear plan to rebuild it.

What to Do If You're Unsure:

1. *Consult a Trusted Friend:* Sometimes an outside perspective can clarify if it's a true emergency.

2. *Run the Numbers:* Calculate the long-term cost of not addressing the issue now.

3. *Consider Partial Use:* Maybe you only need to use part of your emergency fund.

4. *Explore Payment Plans:* For medical bills or large repairs, see if you can set up a payment plan instead of depleting your fund.

5. *Seek Professional Advice:* For large financial decisions, consider consulting a financial advisor.

What to Watch Out For:

1. *Emotional Decision Making:* Don't let fear or excitement cloud your judgment.

2. *Lifestyle Inflation:* Be wary of reclassifying luxury items as "necessities."

3. *Frequent Small Withdrawals:* These can deplete your fund over time.

4. *Borrowing from the Fund:* If you "borrow," make sure you have a strict repayment plan.

Pro Tip: Create a "Emergency Fund Usage" document that outlines what qualifies as an emergency for you and your family. Review and update this annually to ensure it still aligns with your financial situation and goals.

6. Rebuilding After Using Your Emergency Fund

Life happens, and there may come a time when you need to dip into your emergency fund. That's okay – it's what it's there for! But once you've used it, it's crucial to have a plan to build it back up.

The Lazy Person's Guide to Rebuilding Your Emergency Fund:

1. *Assess the Damage:* Calculate how much you used and how much you need to replenish.
2. *Set a Realistic Timeline:* Determine how quickly you can reasonably rebuild your fund.
3. *Automate Replenishment:* Set up automatic transfers to refill your fund.
4. *Look for Extra Income:* Consider temporary ways to boost your income to speed up replenishment.
5. *Cut Non-Essential Expenses:* Temporarily reduce discretionary spending to funnel more money into your fund.

Lazy Hacks for Quick Emergency Fund Replenishment:

1. *The "Pause and Redirect" Method:* Pause non-essential subscriptions and redirect that money to your fund.
2. *The "Spare Change Challenge":* Collect all your spare change and small bills for a month and deposit it into your fund.
3. *The "Sell What You Bought" Strategy:* If you have any non-essential items you can part with, sell them to replenish your fund.

4. *The "Temporary Side Hustle" Approach:* Take on a short-term gig (like pet-sitting or online tutoring) specifically to rebuild your fund.
5. *The "Windfall Rule":* Commit to putting any unexpected money (gifts, tax refunds, etc.) directly into your emergency fund until it's replenished.

Tools to Help You Rebuild:

1. *Digit:* This app analyzes your spending and automatically saves small amounts you won't miss.
2. *Qapital:* Set up rules to trigger savings, like rounding up purchases or saving when you visit the gym.
3. *Acorns:* Invest your spare change from everyday purchases.
4. *YNAB (You Need A Budget):* This budgeting app can help you find extra money to redirect to your emergency fund.
5. *Trim:* This service helps you cancel subscriptions and negotiate bills, potentially freeing up money for your fund.

Strategies for Different Replenishment Scenarios:

1. *Small Withdrawal:*
   - Temporarily increase your regular contributions.
   - Skip a few non-essential purchases.
2. *Medium Withdrawal:*
   - Look for areas in your budget to cut back for a few months.
   - Consider a short-term side hustle.
3. *Large Withdrawal:*

- Create a dedicated replenishment budget.
- Look for ways to significantly increase income (ask for overtime, take on freelance work, etc.).
- Consider selling items you no longer need.

4. *Complete Depletion:*
   - Start rebuilding with a small, achievable goal (like $1,000).
   - Review your overall financial plan to see if adjustments are needed.
   - Look for ways to prevent similar emergencies in the future (like improving insurance coverage).

What to Watch Out For:

1. *Neglecting Other Financial Priorities:* While rebuilding is important, don't ignore other crucial areas like retirement savings or high-interest debt.
2. *Burnout:* Don't push yourself too hard in an effort to rebuild quickly. Sustainability is key.
3. *Forgetting the Lesson:* Use this as an opportunity to review what led to using the fund and how you might prevent similar situations in the future.
4. *Scope Creep:* Stick to your original emergency fund goal unless your circumstances have significantly changed.

Pro Tip: Create a visual representation of your replenishment progress. Watching your emergency fund "refill" can be a great motivator to keep going.

7. Emergency Fund Alternatives (For When You're Really in a Pinch)

Bonus Chapter: The Emergency Fund - Because Life Happens, Even to Lazy People

While having a fully-funded emergency fund is ideal, life doesn't always work out perfectly. If you find yourself facing an emergency without adequate savings, here are some alternatives to consider.

The Lazy Person's Guide to Emergency Fund Alternatives:

1. *Understand the Costs:* All alternatives will likely be more expensive than using savings.
2. *Explore Multiple Options:* Don't settle for the first solution you find.
3. *Read the Fine Print:* Understand all terms and conditions before committing.
4. *Have a Repayment Plan:* Know how you'll pay back any borrowed funds.
5. *Consider Long-Term Impact:* Think about how this decision will affect your future finances.

Emergency Fund Alternatives to Consider:

1. *0% APR Credit Card:* If you have good credit, you might qualify for a card with a 0% intro APR.
2. *Personal Loan:* Often have lower interest rates than credit cards.
3. *Home Equity Line of Credit (HELOC):* If you're a homeowner, this can be a low-interest option.
4. *401(k) Loan:* Borrow from yourself, but be aware of the risks.
5. *Family Loan:* Borrowing from family can be interest-free, but can strain relationships.
6. *Peer-to-Peer Lending:* Platforms like Prosper or LendingClub connect borrowers with individual lenders.

7. *Selling Assets:* Consider selling non-essential items of value.

Lazy Hacks for Navigating Emergency Fund Alternatives:

1. *The "Credit Card Surfing" Strategy:* Transfer balances between 0% APR cards to extend your repayment timeline.

2. *The "Secured Personal Loan" Approach:* Offer collateral to get a lower interest rate on a personal loan.

3. *The "Split the Difference" Method:* Use a combination of alternatives to minimize the impact of any one option.

4. *The "Negotiation" Tactic:* Try negotiating with creditors for lower interest rates or extended payment terms.

5. *The "Gig Economy" Solution:* Use platforms like Uber, Lyft, or TaskRabbit for quick cash to cover emergencies.

What to Consider for Each Alternative:

1. *Credit Cards:*
   - Pros: Quick access to funds, potential rewards.
   - Cons: High interest rates after intro period, can damage credit if not managed well.

2. *Personal Loans:*
   - Pros: Fixed repayment terms, potentially lower interest than credit cards.
   - Cons: May require good credit, can take a few days to process.

3. *HELOC:*

- Pros: Low interest rates, tax-deductible interest.
- Cons: Puts your home at risk, can take weeks to set up.

4. *401(k) Loan:*
   - Pros: Borrow from yourself, no credit check.
   - Cons: Reduces retirement savings, must be repaid quickly if you leave your job.

5. *Family Loan:*
   - Pros: Potentially interest-free, flexible terms.
   - Cons: Can strain relationships, may complicate family dynamics.

What to Watch Out For:

1. *High Interest Rates:* Especially with credit cards and some personal loans.
2. *Hidden Fees:* Read all terms carefully to understand the total cost.
3. *Impact on Credit Score:* New loans or high credit utilization can lower your score.
4. *Long-Term Financial Impact:* Consider how the choice will affect your future financial goals.

Pro Tip: If you must use one of these alternatives, make it a priority to build an emergency fund once the crisis has passed to avoid needing these options in the future.

8. Teaching Old Dogs New Tricks: Emergency Funds for Different Life Stages

Your emergency fund needs can change dramatically throughout your life. Let's explore how to adapt your emergency savings strategy for different life stages.

Bonus Chapter: The Emergency Fund - Because Life Happens, Even to Lazy People

The Lazy Person's Guide to Life Stage Emergency Funds:

1. *Assess Your Current Stage:* Consider your age, career status, family situation, and financial goals.
2. *Anticipate Future Changes:* Think about upcoming life transitions that might affect your emergency fund needs.
3. *Adjust Gradually:* Make small, consistent changes rather than dramatic overhauls.
4. *Review Regularly:* Set annual reminders to reassess your emergency fund strategy.
5. *Stay Flexible:* Be prepared to adapt your approach as life throws curveballs.

Emergency Fund Strategies for Different Life Stages:

1. *Young Adult/Recent Graduate:*
    - Focus on building a starter fund ($1,000-$2,000).
    - Prioritize paying off high-interest debt alongside building savings.
    - Consider a slightly larger fund if you have an unstable job or gig work.
2. *Early Career Professional:*
    - Aim for 3-6 months of expenses.
    - Factor in potential career changes or further education.
    - Consider additional savings if you're in a volatile industry.
3. *Married/Partnered without Kids:*

- Decide whether to combine finances and emergency funds.
- Account for both partners' job stability and income levels.
- Consider saving for short-term goals (like a house down payment) separately from your emergency fund.

4. *Parents with Young Children:*
    - Increase fund to account for potential childcare costs or income reduction if a parent needs to stop working.
    - Factor in potential medical expenses for children.
    - Consider life insurance as an additional safety net.

5. *Mid-Career Professional:*
    - Reassess fund size based on increased expenses and potential job market challenges.
    - Consider keeping part of your emergency fund in a more accessible form for quick access.
    - Factor in potential care costs for aging parents.

6. *Near Retirement:*
    - Increase fund size to account for potentially longer job searches if laid off.
    - Consider health care costs more heavily in your calculations.
    - Factor in potential early retirement scenarios.

7. *Retiree:*

- Shift focus from income replacement to covering unexpected expenses.
- Factor in potential long-term care needs.
- Consider keeping a larger portion of your portfolio liquid for emergencies.

Lazy Hacks for Life Stage Emergency Fund Adjustments:

1. *The "Life Event Trigger" System:* Automatically reassess your emergency fund whenever you hit a major life milestone.
2. *The "Percentage of Portfolio" Approach:* As your overall wealth grows, keep a set percentage liquid for emergencies.
3. *The "Sliding Scale" Method:* Adjust your emergency fund size up or down based on your current life stability.
4. *The "Two-Tiered" Strategy:* Keep a smaller amount highly liquid for immediate needs, and a larger amount in slightly less accessible but higher-yielding accounts.
5. *The "Insurance Offset" Tactic:* As you improve your insurance coverage (health, disability, life), you might be able to reduce your emergency fund slightly.

What to Watch Out For:

1. *Lifestyle Inflation:* As your income grows, resist the urge to classify luxuries as necessities in your emergency fund calculations.
2. *Overconfidence:* Don't reduce your emergency fund too much, even if you feel very secure in your job or finances.

3. *Neglecting Other Goals:* Balance emergency fund growth with other important financial objectives like retirement savings.

4. *Forgetting to Adjust:* Life changes can sneak up on you. Set regular reminders to review your emergency fund strategy.

Pro Tip: Create a "financial fire drill" scenario for each life stage. Imagine losing your primary income source and walk through how you'd handle it with your current emergency fund. This can help identify areas where you might need to adjust your strategy.

9. Emergency Fund Psychology: Overcoming Mental Blocks to Saving

Building an emergency fund isn't just about the numbers – it's also about overcoming psychological barriers to saving. Let's explore some common mental blocks and how to overcome them.

The Lazy Person's Guide to Emergency Fund Psychology:

1. *Identify Your Savings Personality:* Are you a natural saver or spender?

2. *Recognize Your Fears:* What worries you about saving (or not saving)?

3. *Visualize Success:* Imagine the peace of mind a fully-funded emergency fund will bring.

4. *Celebrate Small Wins:* Acknowledge every step towards your goal, no matter how small.

5. *Automate to Avoid Decision Fatigue:* Set up automatic transfers to reduce the mental load of saving.

Common Mental Blocks and How to Overcome Them:

Bonus Chapter: The Emergency Fund - Because Life Happens, Even to Lazy People

1. *"I Don't Make Enough to Save"*:
   - Start with saving just 1% of your income and gradually increase.
   - Look for small expenses to cut and redirect to savings.
   - Remember, even small amounts add up over time.

2. *"I'll Start Saving Later"*:
   - Set a specific date to start and put it in your calendar.
   - Start with a very small amount to build the habit.
   - Visualize a future emergency and how you'd feel without savings.

3. *"I'm Too Far Behind, Why Bother?"*:
   - Focus on progress, not perfection.
   - Set small, achievable milestones.
   - Remember that any emergency fund is better than none.

4. *"I Might Miss Out on Fun Experiences"*:
   - Budget for both fun and savings.
   - Find free or low-cost alternatives for expensive activities.
   - Reframe saving as "buying peace of mind."

5. *"I'm Bad with Money"*:
   - Recognize that financial skills can be learned.

    - Start with small, manageable financial tasks to build confidence.
    - Seek out financial education resources.

Lazy Hacks for Positive Savings Psychology:

1. *The "Money Mantra" Technique:* Create a positive phrase about saving and repeat it daily.
2. *The "Visualization Board" Approach:* Create a visual representation of your emergency fund goal and what it represents (security, peace of mind, etc.).
3. *The "Savings Buddy" System:* Partner with a friend to keep each other accountable for emergency fund goals.
4. *The "Future Letter" Strategy:* Write a letter to your future self about why you're saving and read it when you're tempted to spend.
5. *The "Reward Milestone" Method:* Set up small, affordable rewards for hitting emergency fund milestones.

Tools to Support Positive Savings Psychology:

1. *Qapital:* Allows you to set fun savings rules and visualize goals.
2. *Digit:* Saves automatically based on your spending, reducing the psychological burden.
3. *YNAB (You Need A Budget):* Helps you give every dollar a job, including emergency savings.
4. *Mint:* Provides a clear visual of your progress towards savings goals.
5. *Stickk:* Allows you to make a commitment contract and even risk money if you don't meet your goals.

What to Watch Out For:

1. *Comparison Trap:* Don't compare your emergency fund to others'. Everyone's situation is different.//
2. *All-or-Nothing Thinking:* Remember that saving something is always better than saving nothing.
3. *Perfectionism:* Don't let the pursuit of a "perfect" emergency fund prevent you from starting.
4. *Ignoring Emotional Triggers:* Be aware of what triggers unnecessary spending and develop strategies to cope.

Pro Tip: Create a "happiness budget" alongside your emergency fund. Allocate a small amount for things that bring you joy, so you don't feel deprived while saving. This can help maintain motivation for long-term financial goals.

10. Emergency Fund Myths Debunked: Separating Fact from Fiction

There's a lot of advice out there about emergency funds, but not all of it is accurate or applicable to everyone. Let's bust some common myths to help you build a more effective emergency savings strategy.

The Lazy Person's Guide to Emergency Fund Myth Busting:

1. *Question Common Wisdom:* Don't just accept financial advice at face value.
2. *Consider Your Unique Situation:* What works for others may not work for you.
3. *Look for Evidence:* Seek out reputable sources for financial advice.
4. *Be Willing to Adjust:* As you learn more, be open to changing your approach.

Bonus Chapter: The Emergency Fund - Because Life Happens, Even to Lazy People

5. *Trust Your Instincts:* If something doesn't feel right for your situation, it probably isn't.

Common Emergency Fund Myths Debunked:

1. *Myth: You Need 3-6 Months of Expenses, No Exceptions*
    - Reality: The right amount varies based on your individual circumstances.
    - Some may need more (e.g., freelancers, single-income households).
    - Others might be okay with less (e.g., those with very stable jobs and strong safety nets).

2. *Myth: Credit Cards Can Serve as an Emergency Fund*
    - Reality: While credit cards can help in a pinch, they shouldn't be your primary emergency plan.
    - High interest rates can turn a temporary setback into a long-term financial problem.
    - Some emergencies (like job loss) can make it difficult to pay off credit card debt.

3. *Myth: You Should Never Touch Your Emergency Fund*
    - Reality: It's there to be used in true emergencies.
    - The key is to have a plan to replenish it after use.
    - Not using it when you need it can lead to more expensive alternatives (like high-interest loans).

4. *Myth: Your Emergency Fund Should Be in a Regular Savings Account*

- Reality: While it needs to be accessible, there are often better options.
- High-yield savings accounts, money market accounts, or even short-term CDs can offer better returns while maintaining liquidity.

5. *Myth: Once You've Built Your Emergency Fund, You're Done*
    - Reality: Your emergency fund needs change as your life changes.
    - Regularly review and adjust your emergency savings as your income, expenses, and life circumstances evolve.

Lazy Hacks for Myth-Free Emergency Fund Planning:

1. *The "Personal CFO" Approach:* Treat your finances like a business and make decisions based on your specific financial "company."
2. *The "Annual Audit" Method:* Once a year, reassess your emergency fund strategy and adjust as needed.
3. *The "Tiered Liquidity" Strategy:* Keep some funds highly liquid and some in slightly less accessible, higher-yield options.
4. *The "Emergency Categories" System:* Define different levels of emergencies and how much you need for each.
5. *The "Flexibility Fund" Concept:* Think of it as not just for emergencies, but also for opportunities.

Tools for Smarter Emergency Fund Management:

1. *Personal Capital:* Offers a holistic view of your finances to help you make informed decisions.

2. *Bankrate:* Compare rates on savings accounts and CDs to find the best place for your emergency fund.

3. *You Need A Budget (YNAB):* Helps you allocate funds for different purposes, including emergencies.

4. *Mint:* Tracks your spending to help you understand how much you really need in an emergency.

5. *Betterment:* Offers a "two-way sweep" feature that can help optimize your cash management.

What to Watch Out For:

1. *One-Size-Fits-All Advice:* Be wary of emergency fund strategies that don't account for individual circumstances.

2. *Oversimplification:* Building and maintaining an emergency fund is an ongoing process, not a one-time task.

3. *Extremes:* Avoid both over-saving (to the detriment of other financial goals) and under-saving.

4. *Ignoring Opportunity Costs:* Consider what else you could be doing with the money (like investing) if you over-fund your emergency savings.

Pro Tip: Create your own "Emergency Fund Manifesto" that outlines your personal philosophy on emergency savings. Include what constitutes an emergency for you, how much you aim to save, and how you'll use and replenish the fund. Review and update this document annually.

11. The Future of Emergency Funds: Adapting to Changing Financial Landscapes

As the financial world evolves, so too must our approach to emergency funds. Let's explore some trends and innovations that might shape the future of emergency savings.

Bonus Chapter: The Emergency Fund - Because Life Happens, Even to Lazy People

The Lazy Person's Guide to Future-Proofing Your Emergency Fund:

1. *Stay Informed:* Keep an eye on financial news and emerging trends.
2. *Be Open to New Tools:* Explore new financial technologies that can help optimize your emergency savings.
3. *Maintain Flexibility:* Be prepared to adjust your strategy as new options become available.
4. *Balance Innovation with Stability:* Don't abandon tried-and-true methods entirely for new, untested approaches.
5. *Consider Long-Term Trends:* Think about how broader economic and societal changes might affect your emergency fund needs.

Emerging Trends in Emergency Fund Management:

1. *Micro-Savings Apps:*
    - Apps that round up purchases and save the difference.
    - Makes saving feel painless and automatic.
    - Examples: Acorns, Digit, Qapital
2. *AI-Powered Savings:*
    - Artificial intelligence that analyzes your spending and automatically saves optimal amounts.
    - Adapts to your financial habits and patterns.
    - Examples: Digit, Cleo
3. *Hybrid Emergency Funds:*

            - o Combining traditional savings with investment components for potentially higher returns.
            - o Balances liquidity with growth potential.
            - o Examples: Betterment's "two-way sweep," Wealthfront's Cash Account
    4. *Peer-to-Peer Emergency Funds:*
            - o Pooled emergency funds among trusted friends or family members.
            - o Can provide a larger safety net with shared responsibility.
            - o Examples: Informal arrangements, some credit unions exploring this model
    5. *Crypto-Based Emergency Savings:*
            - o Using stablecoins or other cryptocurrencies for emergency funds.
            - o Potential for higher yields, but comes with increased risk and volatility.
            - o Examples: BlockFi, Celsius Network (but be cautious of risks)

Lazy Hacks for Adapting to New Emergency Fund Trends:

1. *The "Pilot Program" Approach:* Try new methods with a small portion of your emergency fund before fully committing.
2. *The "Hybrid Model" Strategy:* Combine traditional and innovative approaches to balance stability and potential benefits.

3. *The "Automatic Upgrade" System:* Set annual reminders to research and consider new emergency fund tools and strategies.

4. *The "Network Effect" Method:* Join online communities or forums to learn from others' experiences with new financial tools.

5. *The "Sandbox" Technique:* Create a small, separate fund to experiment with new financial technologies without risking your main emergency savings.

Potential Future Developments to Watch:

1. *Universal Basic Income (UBI):* Could change how we think about emergency funds if implemented.

2. *Blockchain-Based Insurance:* Might offer new ways to protect against financial emergencies.

3. *Open Banking:* Could lead to more personalized and efficient emergency savings solutions.

4. *Biometric Financial Security:* May change how we access and secure our emergency funds.

5. *Climate Change Considerations:* Might necessitate larger or differently structured emergency funds in some areas.

What to Watch Out For:

1. *Overreliance on Technology:* Ensure you understand and can access your funds even if an app or platform fails.

2. *Privacy Concerns:* Be mindful of the data you're sharing with financial apps and platforms.

3. *Regulatory Changes:* Stay informed about how new financial products are regulated and protected.

4. *Increased Complexity:* Don't let the pursuit of optimization make your emergency fund strategy too complicated to maintain.

Pro Tip: Create a "Financial Innovation" fund separate from your main emergency fund. Use this to explore and experiment with new financial tools and strategies without putting your core emergency savings at risk.

12. Emergency Fund Success Stories: Learning from Real-Life Experiences

Sometimes, the best way to understand the importance of an emergency fund is to hear from those who've benefited from having one. Let's explore some real-life success stories and the lessons we can learn from them.

The Lazy Person's Guide to Learning from Others:

1. *Seek Out Stories:* Look for emergency fund experiences in financial forums or personal finance blogs.
2. *Identify Patterns:* Look for common themes in successful emergency fund strategies.
3. *Adapt, Don't Copy:* Use others' experiences as inspiration, but tailor strategies to your situation.
4. *Share Your Story:* Once you've had success, share your experience to help others.
5. *Learn from Mistakes:* Pay attention to what didn't work as well as what did.

Emergency Fund Success Stories:

1. *The Job Loss Lifesaver*
    - Story: Sarah, a marketing professional, was unexpectedly laid off. Her 6-month emergency

fund allowed her to pay bills and focus on job hunting without panic.

- Lesson: A well-funded emergency fund can provide crucial peace of mind during career transitions.

2. The Medical Emergency Cushion

- Story: The Johnson family faced a $5,000 medical bill not covered by insurance. Their emergency fund prevented them from going into debt.
- Lesson: Health emergencies can happen to anyone, regardless of insurance coverage.

3. The Natural Disaster Recovery

- Story: When a hurricane damaged Tom's home, his emergency fund covered immediate repairs and temporary housing costs while insurance claims were processed.
- Lesson: Emergency funds can bridge the gap when insurance payouts are delayed.

4. The Car Replacement Rescue

- Story: Lisa's car was totaled in an accident. Her emergency fund allowed her to make a down payment on a replacement without resorting to a high-interest loan.
- Lesson: Emergency funds can prevent one financial setback from cascading into larger problems.

5. The Small Business Savior

- - Story: When John's small business faced a cash flow crisis, his personal emergency fund kept the business afloat until revenue improved.
  - Lesson: Emergency funds can be crucial for entrepreneurs facing business uncertainties.

Lazy Hacks Inspired by Success Stories:

1. *The "Sinking Fund" Strategy:* Create multiple small funds for specific potential emergencies (car repairs, medical, etc.).
2. *The "Windfall Allocation" Rule:* Commit to putting a percentage of any unexpected income into your emergency fund.
3. *The "Visualization" Technique:* Create a vision board or written statement about how your emergency fund will help in specific scenarios.
4. *The "Emergency Drill" Practice:* Periodically walk through how you'd handle different emergency scenarios with your current fund.
5. *The "Gratitude Journal" Approach:* Regularly write down how your emergency fund has provided peace of mind or helped avoid stress.

Common Themes in Emergency Fund Success:

1. *Consistency:* Regular contributions, even small ones, build substantial funds over time.
2. *Automation:* Many success stories involve automatic transfers to emergency savings.
3. *Emotional Benefits:* The peace of mind from having an emergency fund is often as valuable as the financial security.

4. *Flexibility:* Successful savers often adjust their emergency fund strategy as their life circumstances change.

5. *Resistance to Temptation:* Keeping emergency funds separate from regular savings helps avoid dipping into them unnecessarily.

What to Watch Out For:

1. *Survivorship Bias:* Remember that you're more likely to hear success stories than failures.

2. *Comparing Your Chapter 1 to Someone Else's Chapter 20:* Everyone's financial journey is different.

3. *Overlooking the Sacrifices:* Building an emergency fund often requires trade-offs that may not be mentioned in success stories.

4. *Ignoring Context:* Economic conditions, location, and personal circumstances all play a role in emergency fund success.

Pro Tip: Start your own "Emergency Fund Success Journal." Document your progress, challenges, and wins. Include how your emergency fund has helped you, even in small ways. This can serve as motivation and a valuable resource to look back on and learn from.

Conclusion: Your Lazy Emergency Fund Action Plan

Congratulations, financial fledgling! You've made it through our deep dive into the world of emergency funds. Let's wrap up with a simple, lazy-friendly action plan to get your emergency savings on track.

1. *Assess Your Current Situation:*
    - Calculate your monthly essential expenses.

Bonus Chapter: The Emergency Fund - Because Life Happens, Even to Lazy People

- Determine how much you currently have saved for emergencies.
- Identify potential emergencies you might face.

2. *Set Your Emergency Fund Goal:*
    - Aim for 3-6 months of expenses, adjusting based on your personal circumstances.
    - Break this goal down into smaller, achievable milestones.

3. *Choose Your Savings Vehicle:*
    - Open a separate high-yield savings account for your emergency fund.
    - Consider a mix of savings accounts and no-penalty CDs for better returns.

4. *Automate Your Savings:*
    - Set up automatic transfers from your checking account to your emergency fund.
    - Start with a small amount if necessary and increase over time.

5. *Find Extra Money to Save:*
    - Review your budget for potential cuts.
    - Consider using cashback apps or taking on a side hustle for additional savings.

6. *Protect and Grow Your Fund:*
    - Regularly review your emergency fund's interest rate.

- Consider laddering CDs or using a high-yield savings account to maximize returns while maintaining liquidity.

7. *Regularly Review and Adjust:*
    - Set a calendar reminder to review your emergency fund every 6 months.
    - Adjust your savings goal and strategy as your life circumstances change.

8. *Prepare for Usage:*
    - Define what constitutes an emergency for you.
    - Create a plan for how you'll replenish your fund if you need to use it.

9. *Stay Motivated:*
    - Track your progress and celebrate milestones.
    - Remind yourself of the peace of mind an emergency fund provides.

10. *Educate Yourself:*
    - Stay informed about personal finance trends and emergency fund strategies.
    - Learn from others' experiences and adapt strategies to your situation.

Remember, building an emergency fund is a journey, not a destination. It's okay to start small and build up over time. The most important thing is to start and to stay consistent.

As you embark on your emergency fund journey, keep in mind that this financial cushion is more than just money in the bank – it's peace of mind, freedom, and the power to face life's unexpected challenges with confidence.

Bonus Chapter: The Emergency Fund - Because Life Happens, Even to Lazy People

So here's to you, savvy saver. May your emergency fund grow steadily, your financial stress decrease dramatically, and your peace of mind increase exponentially. You've taken the first step towards financial resilience, and that's something to be proud of.

Now, go forth and save... or just take a well-deserved nap. After all, you're on your way to mastering the art of lazy emergency fund building!

APPENDIX A: GLOSSARY OF FINANCIAL TERMS FOR THE PERPETUALLY CONFUSED

Welcome to the appendix that will (hopefully) demystify the world of finance for you. Don't worry if you've been nodding along to financial advice while secretly having no clue what's being said - we've got you covered. Let's break down some common financial terms into language that even the most financially confused can understand.

A

Annual Percentage Rate (APR): The yearly cost of borrowing money, including fees. It's like the price tag on a loan.

Asset: Anything you own that has value. Think of it as your financial toy box.

Amortization: Paying off a loan over time with regular payments. It's like slowly eating a giant sandwich - bite by bite, it eventually disappears.

B

Budget: A plan for how you'll spend your money. It's like a diet, but for your wallet.

Bond: A loan you make to a company or government. They promise to pay you back with interest. It's like being the bank, but with less paperwork.

Bear Market: When the stock market is feeling grumpy and prices are falling.

Bull Market: When the stock market is in a good mood and prices are rising.

C

Capital Gain: The profit you make when you sell something for more than you paid for it. It's like finding money in your pocket, but you put it there.

Appendix A: Glossary of Financial Terms for the Perpetually Confused

Credit Score: A number that tells lenders how good you are with money. It's like your financial report card.

Compound Interest: When you earn interest on your interest. It's like a snowball rolling downhill, getting bigger as it goes.

D

Diversification: Not putting all your eggs in one basket. It's financial speak for "don't gamble everything on that hot new cryptocurrency your cousin told you about."

Dividend: Money a company pays to its shareholders. It's like getting a bonus for being a part-owner.

Debt-to-Income Ratio: How much you owe compared to how much you earn. It's like seeing if your appetite is bigger than your wallet.

E

Emergency Fund: Money set aside for unexpected expenses. It's your financial umbrella for rainy days.

Equity: The value of something you own minus what you owe on it. For your house, it's what would be left if you sold it and paid off the mortgage.

Exchange-Traded Fund (ETF): A basket of investments that trades like a stock. It's like buying a pre-made financial smoothie instead of choosing all the ingredients yourself.

F

FICO Score: A specific type of credit score. It's like your financial GPA.

Fixed Income: Investments that pay a set amount of interest, like bonds. It's the plain vanilla ice cream of the investment world.

Appendix A: Glossary of Financial Terms for the Perpetually Confused

Foreclosure: When the bank takes back a house because the owner couldn't pay the mortgage. It's like the repo man, but for houses.

G

Gross Income: Your total income before taxes and deductions. It's the number that makes you feel rich until you see your actual paycheck.

Growth Stock: A stock expected to grow faster than the market average. It's like betting on the up-and-coming sports team.

H

Hedge: An investment to reduce the risk of adverse price movements. It's like buying insurance for your investments.

High-Yield Savings Account: A savings account that pays higher interest than a regular one. It's like a regular savings account, but with a better attitude.

I

Index Fund: A fund that tracks a market index, like the S&P 500. It's like buying a slice of the entire stock market pie.

Inflation: When prices go up and the value of money goes down. It's why your grandparents keep talking about how a soda used to cost a nickel.

IRA (Individual Retirement Account): A personal retirement savings account with tax benefits. It's like a piggy bank for grown-ups.

J

Junk Bond: A high-risk, high-yield bond. It's the bad boy of the bond world.

K

Appendix A: Glossary of Financial Terms for the Perpetually Confused

Keogh Plan: A retirement plan for self-employed individuals. It's like a 401(k) for people who are their own boss.

L

Liability: Something you owe. It's the "you owe me" part of your finances.

Liquidity: How easily you can turn an asset into cash. It's like how quickly you can turn your stuff into pizza money.

M

Margin: Borrowing money to invest. It's like using the bank's money to gamble in the stock market casino.

Mutual Fund: A professionally managed investment fund. It's like hiring a financial chef to cook up your investment meal.

N

Net Worth: The value of everything you own minus everything you owe. It's your financial report card.

NASDAQ: A stock exchange known for tech companies. It's like the cool kids' table of the stock market.

O

Options: Contracts that give you the right to buy or sell an asset at a specific price. It's like putting a down payment on maybe buying something later.

Opportunity Cost: What you give up when you choose one option over another. It's why you can't have your cake and eat it too.

P

Portfolio: A collection of investments. It's your financial wardrobe.

Appendix A: Glossary of Financial Terms for the Perpetually Confused

Price-to-Earnings Ratio (P/E Ratio): A company's stock price divided by its earnings per share. It's like figuring out if a stock is on sale or overpriced.

Q

Qualified Dividend: A dividend that's taxed at a lower rate. It's like getting a tax discount on your investment allowance.

R

Recession: A period of economic decline. It's when the economy catches a cold.

Roth IRA: A retirement account where you pay taxes on money going in, but not coming out. It's like pre-paying for your retirement party.

S

Stock: A piece of ownership in a company. It's like buying a tiny slice of a business pie.

Sinking Fund: Money set aside for a specific future expense. It's like having a separate piggy bank for each financial goal.

T

Tax Deduction: An expense you can subtract from your taxable income. It's like a coupon for your taxes.

Treasury Bill: A short-term government debt security. It's like lending money to Uncle Sam.

U

Underwriting: The process of evaluating the risk of insuring a person or asset. It's like when the cool kids decide if you can sit at their table.

V

Appendix A: Glossary of Financial Terms for the Perpetually Confused

Volatility: How much and how quickly an investment's price changes. It's the mood swings of the financial world.

W

W-2: The form that reports your annual wages and the amount of taxes withheld. It's your annual "here's how much you made" report card.

401(k): An employer-sponsored retirement savings plan. It's like a workplace piggy bank with tax benefits.

X

XYZ: Stock symbols you see when examples are given, Xs are used for any unknown or unspecified symbol. Think of it as "blah blah blah" in finance speak.

Y

Yield: The income return on an investment. It's like the allowance your investments give you.

Z

Zero-Coupon Bond: A bond that doesn't pay interest but is sold at a discount. It's like buying a gift card for less than its value, but you have to wait to use it.

Remember, understanding these terms is the first step to financial literacy. Don't be afraid to ask questions or look up terms you don't understand. After all, everyone starts somewhere, and there's no shame in being a financial newbie. Keep this glossary handy, and soon you'll be throwing around financial jargon like a pro (or at least understanding what the pros are saying).

APPENDIX B: RESOURCES FOR THE MARGINALLY MOTIVATED

Welcome to the appendix that's here to help you help yourself... with minimal effort, of course. We've compiled a list of resources that can aid your financial journey, even if you're only marginally motivated. These tools, apps, websites, and books are designed to make managing your money as painless as possible.

1. Money Management Apps

For those who'd rather tap a screen than balance a checkbook:

Mint:

- What it does: Tracks spending, creates budgets, monitors bills
- Why it's great for the lazy: Automatically categorizes your spending
- Effort level: Low (just link your accounts and let it do its thing)

You Need A Budget (YNAB):

- What it does: Helps you create and stick to a budget
- Why it's great for the lazy: Teaches you to give every dollar a job
- Effort level: Medium (requires some initial setup, but then it's smooth sailing)

Personal Capital:

- What it does: Tracks investments, net worth, and spending
- Why it's great for the lazy: Gives you a complete financial picture in one place

- Effort level: Low (link accounts and get insights)

Acorns:

- What it does: Invests your spare change
- Why it's great for the lazy: Invest without thinking about it
- Effort level: Very Low (set it and forget it)

2. Websites for Financial Education

For when you're ready to learn... from the comfort of your couch:

Investopedia:

- What it offers: Comprehensive financial dictionary and educational articles
- Why it's great for the lazy: Easy to understand explanations of complex topics
- Effort level: Medium (reading required, but at your own pace)

NerdWallet:

- What it offers: Comparisons of financial products, educational content
- Why it's great for the lazy: Does the research for you
- Effort level: Low (just search for what you need)

Khan Academy - Personal Finance:

- What it offers: Free courses on various financial topics
- Why it's great for the lazy: Video lessons you can watch in your pajamas
- Effort level: Medium (learning requires some effort, but the format is easy)

Reddit - r/personalfinance:

- What it offers: Community-driven financial advice and discussions
- Why it's great for the lazy: Get answers to your specific questions
- Effort level: Low (browse or post questions at your leisure)

3. YouTube Channels

For visual learners who prefer watching to reading:

Two Cents:

- Content: Short, entertaining videos on personal finance topics
- Why it's great for the lazy: Makes learning about money fun
- Effort level: Very Low (just hit play)

Graham Stephan:

- Content: Personal finance and investing advice with a dose of humor
- Why it's great for the lazy: Entertaining and informative
- Effort level: Low (easy to binge-watch)

The Financial Diet:

- Content: Practical money advice, especially for younger adults
- Why it's great for the lazy: Relatable content in digestible formats
- Effort level: Low (short videos on various topics)

4. Podcasts

Appendix B: Resources for the Marginally Motivated

For multitaskers who want to learn while doing other things:

Planet Money:

- Content: Makes economics and finance interesting and accessible
- Why it's great for the lazy: Learn while you do other tasks
- Effort level: Very Low (just listen)

So Money with Farnoosh Torabi:

- Content: Interviews with financial experts and successful individuals
- Why it's great for the lazy: Get advice from the pros without any effort
- Effort level: Very Low (listen during your commute or while doing chores)

ChooseFI:

- Content: Focuses on financial independence and early retirement
- Why it's great for the lazy: Inspires you to make your money work harder than you do
- Effort level: Low (listen and dream about early retirement)

5. Books

For those rare moments when you're motivated to read:

"The Simple Path to Wealth" by JL Collins:

- Content: Straightforward advice on investing and financial independence
- Why it's great for the lazy: Simplifies complex topics

Appendix B: Resources for the Marginally Motivated

- Effort level: Medium (it's a book, but an easy read)

"The Psychology of Money" by Morgan Housel:

- Content: Explores the weird ways people think about money
- Why it's great for the lazy: Short chapters and engaging stories
- Effort level: Medium (readable, but makes you think)

"I Will Teach You to Be Rich" by Ramit Sethi:

- Content: A six-week program to whip your finances into shape
- Why it's great for the lazy: Provides specific actions to take
- Effort level: Medium-High (requires some work, but holds your hand through it)

6. Investing Tools

For when you're ready to grow your money with minimal effort:

Robinhood:

- What it does: Commission-free stock and ETF trading
- Why it's great for the lazy: Easy to use app for beginner investors
- Effort level: Low (but be careful not to get caught up in day trading)

Betterment:

- What it does: Robo-advisor for automated investing
- Why it's great for the lazy: Set your goals and let algorithms do the work

- Effort level: Low (answer some questions and let it invest for you)

M1 Finance:

- What it does: Automated investing with more customization
- Why it's great for the lazy: Allows for some control without too much effort
- Effort level: Medium (requires some initial setup, then it's automated)

7. Credit Score Tools

For keeping an eye on your financial reputation without much work:

Credit Karma:

- What it does: Provides free credit scores and monitoring
- Why it's great for the lazy: Alerts you to changes in your credit report
- Effort level: Very Low (set up an account and get regular updates)

CreditWise from Capital One:

- What it does: Offers free credit score and simulator
- Why it's great for the lazy: See how actions might impact your credit score
- Effort level: Low (play around with the simulator to learn)

8. Savings Tools

For squirreling away money without feeling the pinch:

Appendix B: Resources for the Marginally Motivated

Digit:

- What it does: Analyzes your spending and automatically saves small amounts
- Why it's great for the lazy: Save without thinking about it
- Effort level: Very Low (set it up and let it save for you)

Qapital:

- What it does: Allows you to set savings rules based on your spending
- Why it's great for the lazy: Makes saving feel like a game
- Effort level: Low (set up your rules and watch your savings grow)

Remember, the key to using these resources effectively is to find the ones that resonate with you. You don't need to use all of them – pick a few that seem interesting and give them a try. Even small steps towards better financial management can make a big difference over time.

And hey, if you've made it this far in the book, you're already more motivated than you think! Keep up the good work, and remember: managing your money doesn't have to be hard. With these tools at your disposal, you can make significant progress without breaking a sweat.

APPENDIX C: WORKSHEETS (THAT YOU'LL PROBABLY NEVER FILL OUT, BUT HEY, THEY'RE HERE)

Welcome to the section of the book that you'll likely flip through, nod approvingly at, and then promptly forget about. But just in case you're feeling particularly motivated (or guilty), we've prepared some worksheets to help you on your financial journey. Don't worry, we've designed them with the lazy in mind – minimal writing required!

1. The "Where's My Money Going?" Tracker

Instructions: For one week, jot down everything you spend money on. Yes, even that 2 AM snack run.

Day	Item	Cost	Was It Worth It? (Y/N)
Mon			
Tue			
Wed			
Thu			
Fri			
Sat			
Sun			

Total Spent: $_____

Number of "Not Worth It" purchases: _____

Lazy Analysis: If more than half your purchases weren't worth it, maybe rethink your spending habits. Or don't. We're not your mom.

2. The "Bare Minimum" Budget

Instructions: Fill in your absolute essential expenses. Be honest – Netflix is not essential (probably).

Appendix C: Worksheets (That You'll Probably Never Fill Out, But Hey, They're Here)

Expense Category	Monthly Amount
Rent/Mortgage	
Utilities	
Groceries	
Transportation	
Insurance	
Minimum Debt Payments	
Other Essential Expenses	

Total Essential Expenses: $_____

Lazy Tip: If this number is higher than your income, you might have a problem. Consider downgrading your lifestyle or upgrading your income.

3. The "Dream a Little Dream" Goal Setting Worksheet

Instructions: Write down your financial goals. Don't worry, no one's going to hold you to them.

Short-Term Goals (1 year or less):

1. _____ Cost: $_____
2. _____ Cost: $_____
3. _____ Cost: $_____

Medium-Term Goals (1-5 years):

1. _____ Cost: $_____
2. _____ Cost: $_____
3. _____ Cost: $_____

Long-Term Goals (5+ years):

1. _____ Cost: $_____
2. _____ Cost: $_____
3. _____ Cost: $_____

Appendix C: Worksheets (That You'll Probably Never Fill Out, But Hey, They're Here)

Lazy Action Plan: Pick the goal that seems the least daunting and maybe think about taking a step towards it. Eventually.

4. The "Debt Be Gone" Tracker

Instructions: List your debts from smallest to largest. Cross them off as you pay them off (if you ever do).

Debt	Total Amount	Interest Rate	Minimum Payment
1.			
2.			
3.			
4.			
5.			

Lazy Debt Payoff Strategy: Pay the minimum on all debts. Throw any extra money at the smallest debt. Repeat until debt-free or until you get bored and give up.

5. The "Where's My Money?" Net Worth Calculator

Instructions: List your assets (what you own) and liabilities (what you owe). Subtract liabilities from assets to get your net worth.

Assets:

Cash and Savings: $_____

Investments: $_____

Property Value: $_____

Other Assets: $_____

Total Assets: $_____

Liabilities:

Appendix C: Worksheets (That You'll Probably Never Fill Out, But Hey, They're Here)

Credit Card Debt: $_____

Student Loans: $_____

Mortgage: $_____

Other Debts: $_____

Total Liabilities: $_____

Net Worth (Assets - Liabilities): $_____

Lazy Analysis: If this number is positive, congratulations! If it's negative, well, at least you're not alone.

6. The "Retirement? That's Future Me's Problem" Calculator

Instructions: Use this to figure out how much you might need for retirement. Or don't, and just hope for the best.

Current Age: _____

Desired Retirement Age: _____

Current Annual Income: $_____

Expected Annual Expenses in Retirement: $_____

Current Retirement Savings: $_____

Monthly Savings Towards Retirement: $_____

Lazy Retirement Strategy: Take your current age, subtract it from 100, and put that percentage of your income into low-cost index funds. Adjust as needed if you start to panic about the future.

7. The "Savings Challenge" Tracker

Instructions: Choose a savings challenge and track your progress. Or don't. We're not here to judge.

Challenge: ☐ 52-Week Savings Challenge ☐ $5 Bill Challenge ☐ No-Spend Month

Appendix C: Worksheets (That You'll Probably Never Fill Out, But Hey, They're Here)

Week/Day	Amount Saved	Total Saved
1		
2		
3		
4		

Lazy Hack: Set up automatic transfers to your savings account and pretend that money doesn't exist.

8. The "Emergency Fund" Progress Tracker

Instructions: Track your progress towards your emergency fund goal. Try not to think about all the emergencies that could happen.

Emergency Fund Goal: $_____ (3-6 months of expenses, remember?)

Month	Amount Saved	Total Saved	% of Goal Reached
1			
2			
3			
4			
5			
6			

Lazy Emergency Fund Strategy: Set up automatic transfers to a high-yield savings account. Forget about it until you need it.

9. The "Side Hustle" Ideas Brainstorm

Instructions: List potential side hustles based on your skills and interests. Don't worry, thinking about them is often more fun than actually doing them.

Appendix C: Worksheets (That You'll Probably Never Fill Out, But Hey, They're Here)

Skills/Interests	Potential Side Hustle	Effort Required (1-10)
1.		
2.		
3.		
4.		
5.		

Lazy Side Hustle Tip: Look for passive income opportunities. The less effort, the better.

10. The "Financial Freedom" Visualization Board

Instructions: Use this space to draw or write about what financial freedom looks like to you. Stick figures are perfectly acceptable.

[Large Empty Box for Drawing/Writing]

Lazy Visualization Technique: Close your eyes and imagine not having to work. That's it. That's the technique.

Remember, the mere act of looking at these worksheets is a step in the right direction. If you actually fill them out, well, you might not be as lazy as you think! But don't worry, your secret is safe with us. Now go forth and conquer your finances... or take a nap. Both are valid choices.

www.ingramcontent.com/pod-product-compliance
Lightning Source LLC
Chambersburg PA
CBHW031607210526
45464CB00004B/1463